System Reliability and Security

Because of the growing reliance on software, concerns are growing as to how reliable a system is before it is commissioned for use, how high the level of reliability is in the system, and how many vulnerabilities exist in the system before its operationalization. Equally pressing issues include how to secure the system from internal and external security threats that may exist in the face of resident vulnerabilities. The two problems are considered increasingly important because they necessitate the development of tools and techniques capable of analyzing dependability and security aspects of a system. These concerns become more pronounced in the cases of safety-critical and mission-critical systems.

System Reliability and Security: Techniques and Methodologies focuses on the use of soft computing techniques and analytical techniques in the modeling and analysis of dependable and secure systems. It examines systems and applications having complex distributed or networked architectures in such fields as:

- Nuclear energy
- Ground transportation systems
- Air traffic control
- Healthcare and medicine
- Communications

System reliability engineering is a multidisciplinary field that uses computational methods for estimating or predicting the reliability aspects of a system and analyzing failure data obtained from real-world projects. System security is a related field that ensures that even a reliable system is secure against accidental or deliberate intrusions and is free of vulnerabilities. This book covers the tools and techniques, cutting-edge research topics, and methodologies in the areas of system reliability and security. It examines prediction models and methods as well as how to secure a system as it is being developed.

Javaid Iqbal is Associate Professor in the Post Graduate Department of Computer Science, University of Kashmir, Srinagar Jammu and Kashmir, India. He obtained his PhD in Computer Science from the University of Kashmir in 2014.

Faheem Syeed Masoodi is Assistant Professor in the Department of Computer Science, University of Kashmir. Earlier, he served as Assistant Professor at the College of Computer Science, University of Jizan, Saudi Arabia.

Ishfaq Ahmad Malik completed his PhD degree in 2019 from Department of Mathematics, National Institute of Technology, Srinagar, Jammu and Kashmir, India.

Shozab Khurshid completed her PhD degree in 2019 from the Post-Graduate Department of Computer Science, University of Kashmir, India.

Iqra Saraf completed her PhD degree in 2019 from the Post-Graduate Department of Computer Science, University of Kashmir, India. Her research interests include software reliability, software optimization, and software security.

Alwi M. Bamhdi is an associate professor in the Department of Computer Sciences, Umm Al-Qura University, Saudi Arabia. He received his MSc and PhD in computer science in 2014 from Heriot-Watt University, UK.

System Reliability and Security

Security

Techniques and Methodologies

Edited by
Javaid Iqbal, Faheem Syeed Masoodi,
Ishfaq Ahmad Malik, Shozab Khurshid,
Iqra Saraf, and Alwi M. Bamhdi

CRC Press
Taylor & Francis Group

AN AUERBACH BOOK

First edition published 2024
by CRC Press
6000 Broken Sound Parkway NW, Suite 300, Boca Raton, FL 33487-2742

and by CRC Press
4 Park Square, Milton Park, Abingdon, Oxon, OX14 4RN

CRC Press is an imprint of Taylor & Francis Group, LLC

© 2024 Taylor & Francis Group, LLC

ISBN: 9781032386928 (hbk)
ISBN: 9781032386911 (pbk)
ISBN: 9781032624983 (ebk)

DOI: 10.1201/9781032624983

Typeset in Garamond
by Newgen Publishing UK

Contents

Contributors

Binnaser Aziz Abdullah
Department of Computer Science, Sir Sayyed College of Arts, Commerce & Science, Aurangabad, (MS) India

Imtiaz Ahmed
National Institute of Technology, Srinagar, India

Vahida Akhter
Department of Higher Education, J&K, India

Alwi M. Bamhdi
College of Computing in Al-Qunfudah, Umm Al-Qura University, Kingdom of Saudi Arabia

Mohammad Idrees Bhat
School of Computer Science, MIT–World Peace University, Pune, India

Shubhanita Dasgupta Charkrabarty
Department of Geography, Lovely Professional University, Phagwara, Punjab, India

Sudharson D.
Department of AI&DS, Kumaraguru College of Technology, Coimbatore, Tamil Nadu, India

Aafaq Mohi Ud Din
Department of CSE, National Institute of Technology, Srinagar, India Srinagar, India

Tadashi Dohi
Graduate School of Advanced Science and Engineering, Hiroshima University, Higashi-Hiroshima, Japan

Refath Farooq
Department of Computer Science, University of Kashmir, Srinagar India

Asutosh Goswami
Department of Earth Sciences and Remote Sensing, JIS University, Agarpara, Kolkata, India

Gousia Habib
Department of CSE, National Institute of Technology, Srinagar, India

Mohammad Imran
NTT Data Information Processing Services Private Limited, Bangalore, India

Javaid Iqbal
Department of Computer Science, University of Kashmir, India

Chathuri L. Jayasinghe
Department of Statistics, Faculty of Applied Sciences, University of Sri Jayewardenepura, Sri Lanka

Siqiao Li
Graduate School of Advanced Science and Engineering, Hiroshima University, Higashi-Hiroshima, Japan

Priyanka Majumder
Department of Earth Sciences and Remote Sensing, JIS University, Agarpara, Kolkata, India

Nyla Manzoor
Department of Computer Science, University of Kashmir, Srinagar, India

Faheem Syeed Masoodi
Department of Computer Science, University of Kashmir, Srinagar, India

Hiroyuki Okamura
Graduate School of Advanced Science and Engineering, Hiroshima University, Higashi-Hiroshima, Japan

Suhail Qadir
Information Systems Department, King Khalid University, Abha, Kingdom of Saudi Arabia

Shaima Qureshi
Department of CSE, National Institute of Technology, Srinagar, India

Kailas P. S.
Department of AI&DS, Kumaraguru College of Technology, Coimbatore, Tamil Nadu, India

Suhel Sen
Department of Geography, Lovely Professional University, Phagwara, Punjab, India

Senthilnathan T.
CHRIST (Deemed to be University), Bangalore, India

Tawseef Ahmed Teli
Department of Higher Education, J&K, India

Poornima V.
Department of AI&DS, Kumaraguru College of Technology, Coimbatore, Tamil Nadu, India

K. Vignesh
Thiagarajar School of Management, Madurai, Tamil Nadu, India

Shreya Vijay
Department of AI&DS, Kumaraguru College of Technology, Coimbatore, Tamil Nadu, India

Pramod Kumar Yadav
National Institute of Technology, Srinagar, India

Syed Irfan Yaqoob
School of Computer Science, MIT–World Peace University, Pune, India

Chapter 1

GNN Approach for Software Reliability

Aafaq Mohi Ud Din,[1] Shaima Qureshi,[1]
and Javaid Iqbal[2]

[1]Department of CSE, National Institute of Technology, Srinagar, India

[2]Department of Computer Science, University of Kashmir, India

Acronyms with Definitions

AST	abstract syntax tree
CNN	convolution neural network
DBN	deep belief network
DFG	data flow graph
DL	deep learning
FCG	function call graph
GNN	graph neural network
KMM	kernel mean matching
LRC	logistic regression classifier
LSTM	long short-term memory network
RNN	recurrent neural network
SDP	software defect prediction
SE	software engineering
SQA	software quality assurance

DOI: 10.1201/9781032624983-1

1.1 Introduction

In the domain of software Engineering, SDP is one of the frontier research areas, which is crucial to software quality assurance (SQA) [1]. It is now more challenging to produce high-quality, low-cost, and maintainable software, and the likelihood of producing software faults has increased as a result of software's growing complexity and dependency. SDP has developed into one of the frontier research areas in software engineering, which assists developers and testers in identifying software flaws in good time [2. Defect predictors can assist software engineers to more effectively use their limited testing and maintenance resources by identifying fault-prone modules (instances) before testing. This lowers costs and improves software quality [1, 3–6].

Software module classification using SDP models is based on the qualities that are used to identify them. In the past, the modules qualitative or quantitative descriptions or the processes of their development are used to manually design the features. But these factors ignore the clear syntax and semantics that define a programming language used to create software and that provide additional information about the software modules. Because human feature creation and models using these features have reached their performance limit, there is a demand for those models that extract features automatically from the source code of the software module [7]. These models were created using deep learning techniques, which give them the ability to automatically recognize sophisticated underlying patterns from high-dimensional data, like the ASTs [8]. Programs' unique syntactic structures and the wealth of semantic data they contain are concealed in ASTs, which aid in more precise analysis and defect location.

The extraction of features from ASTs to identify problematic source code has been proposed in a number of deep learning-based models in recent years. For this purpose, the DBN [9], CNN [10, 11, 12], LSTM [13], RNN [14], E-D model [15], and GNNs [16, 17] are currently being considered.

Although the proposed defect prediction methods collect features for software modules from the ASTs of the modules source code, the vast majority of them see ASTs as linear sequences of nodes and use NLP models to produce embedding vectors of these sequences. By doing this, they ignore the ASTs structure and prevent the use of additional source-code-related data that could be used to build features that are more expressive than those produced by linear AST node sequences. In fact, recent studies have shown that extracting characteristics from a representation of source code in a graph or tree, as opposed to a list of AST nodes, produces better results for a number of problems like [18], including code categorization [19, 20], code clone detection [19, 21, 22], plagiarism detection [23], variable naming [24], etc. These tasks are performed using T-based methods, although none of these methods are focused on the problem of foreseeing software defects.

By relying on the capacity of graph neural networks (GNNs) to employ somewhat unstructured data types, such as ASTs, input data enables GNNS to learn to recognize flawed software modules. The whole source code of the module can be kept when using the graph representation of ASTs as input data; however, when ASTs must first be translated into the form suitable for the feature extraction and/ or classification mode, this is not always achievable. To put it another way, we can handle the data in its native shape without running the risk of losing important information if we choose a model that is appropriate for the data. The GNN model explicitly uses ASTs as graphs produced from the software modules source code. ASTs are converted into two matrices, the connection (adjacency) matrix and the characteristic matrix, to construct the representations [25]. While the feature matrix identifies the AST nodes, the connection matrix elements demonstrate whether or not two network nodes are adjacent. In order to discover faulty software modules in a subsequent project version, the GNN is fed with these matrices.

1.2   Software Defect Prediction Approaches

The study of SDP is crucial to the area of SE. The creation of models for estimating defect rates, identifying defect patterns, and categorizing software module defect proneness typically into defective and non-defective has received a lot of attention in this area [26, 27]. We initially give a quick overview of the conventional software fault prediction process in this section. Then, with an emphasis on techniques utilizing AST, we explore various deep-learning methodologies suggested in the literature.

1.2.1 Traditional SDP Techniques

The basis of conventional defect prediction models is the use of artificially constructed metrics for filtering fault data and creating effective classifiers. Nagappan et al. [28] suggested churn metrics and merged them with software constraints in order to anticipate faults. Moser et al. [29] conducted a thorough assessment of the efficacy of change measurements and static code characteristics for flaw prediction. Additionally, Arar et al. [30] choose the relevant characteristics by using Naïve Bayes technique to eliminate repeated ones. The class imbalance issue in software failure prediction was addressed by Mousavi et al. in their paper [31] using the concept of ensemble learning. Additionally, Jing et al. [32] created a dictionary learning technique based on evaluating misclassification costs for software prediction.

Many studies focus on removing components or events from the source project that have no bearing on the destination project. To eliminate instances of the source project whose attributes are too distinct to those of the destination project, Turhan et al. [33] proposed a neighbor filter technique. Additionally, to choose features that have a strong link with the destination project, Yu et al. [34] used feature selection based on correlation. Ma et al. [35] proposed a technique known as transfer Naïve

Bayes, which builds a Naïve Bayes classifier utilizing training instances with their weights adjusted using a data gravity approach [36].

Recent research has shown that if we can fully utilize the target projects little amount of labeled data, the prediction performance may increase. By using the data gravity approach to first set the weights of the source projects data, Chen et al. [37] then changed them using a little amount of labeled data from the destination project by developing a prediction model called TrAdaboost [38]. With the KMM approach, Qiu et al. [39] created a unique multiple-component weights learning model. The weights of the source instances in each component are adjusted using KMM after the source project data is divided into numerous parts. Then, using a portion of the labeled data from the target project as well as the source instances with weights in each component, it develops prediction models. In order to create a more accurate ensemble classifier, it then initializes and optimizes the source component weights.

1.2.2 Deep Learning in SDP

Researchers have recently benefited from deep learning methods since they can immediately learn features from the data without the requirement for manual feature construction. These methods are typically used in existing studies to derive pertinent characteristics from software source code that is represented as an AST, CFG, or DFG [14, 40].

Most prior research has used DL techniques to derive characteristics from sequential AST node sequences, which represent the components of the software's source code. In order to bridge the gap between the semantics of programs and defect prediction characteristics, Wang et al. [9] employed DL approaches to automatically discover the semantic representation of programs from their source code. To acquire the token vectors, they first extracted the abstract syntax trees of the programs. Then they employed a DBN to automatically learn semantic features based on the token vectors. Additionally, to create a hybrid model, Lie et al. [10] merged artificial measurements with features learned by convolutional neural networks that are based on deep learning. Pan et al. [11] presented a comparable but more intricate CNN design, and they claim that in some assessment metrics, their model beats current methods. In addition, Fan et al. [13] suggested an approach that first embeds the AST token sequence in a module. The bidirectional LSTM network with an attention mechanism receives the embedding after that in order to capture key properties, which are subsequently provided as input to a classifier. Zhang et al.'s [15] proposal is another intricate deep model. To utilize the structural information as well the node feature information associated with the AST, a much lower number of models are present in literature.

Comparably, Zhao et al. [17] developed an unsupervised technique using graph attention networks and hierarchical dependency structures for understanding the contextual semantics of source code. From a software modules source code, the method extracts features to express it in AST and CFG. LRCs are trained for three tasks, including flaw prediction, using the characteristics and the related defect label. On every task considered, their strategy outperformed open-source project baseline methodologies.

1.2.3 Summary

We can make the following observations by contrasting and analyzing the aforementioned machine-learning/deep-learning-based defect prediction approaches: (1) In order to accommodate various prediction scenarios, defect prediction systems typically directly use or adapt well-known machine learning algorithms. (2) The majority of defect prediction algorithms use supervised learning strategies to create classification models. Prediction performance, particularly classification accuracy, may generally be improved using supervised defect prediction approaches. (3) Deep learning approaches learn features automatically, which is better than learning on manually created features. (4) GNN models optimize the downstream task of defect prediction by utilizing the graph structure of a program (AST/CFG/DFG) and incorporating both node as well neighborhood information.

1.3 Understanding the Structure of a Software Program as Graph

1.3.1 Abstract Syntax Tree

An AST is a model of source code that only captures information that is structural and content-related, not all the information that appears in the code. It depicts a program at the level of abstract syntax. A method declaration, if statement, variable access, etc. are just a few examples of the constructs that each node in an AST denotes from the source code [41].

1.3.2 Function Call Graph

Information about control flow in source code is described using FCG [42]. In a function call graph, each node stands for a different function, and the edges show how different functions call one another. As it is crucial for comprehending the hierarchical structure of the program, defining the function–calling connection is an essential part of program analysis.

1.3.3 Data Flow Graph

A DFG is a type of graph model used to represent the potential for concurrent execution of software components in computers [43]. Variable declarations, operands, operators, structures, etc. are represented by DFG nodes, and their edges display the data links that connect these entities. In addition to studying the programs dynamic runtime data flow information, DFG can be used to define the data logic and program functions in the source code. From the viewpoint of data transmission, DFG defines the transfer and modification of data streams from input to output. As a result of its ability to explain the logic that the program must adhere to, it has become one of the most popular tools for program analysis.

AST, FCG, and DFG features are combined to create the full AST, which incorporates both static syntactic information and dynamic runtime information.

Shown in Figure 1.1 is a combined program analysis graph with complete AST that includes the properties of AST, FCG, and DFG and that corresponds to the source code of Figure 1.1. The dashed curve arrow in Figure 1.1 indicates the data stream, whereas the solid arrow indicates the function call. This combination speeds

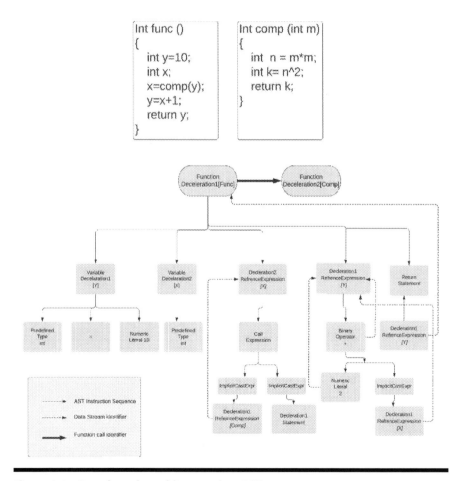

Figure 1.1   Sample code and its complete AST.

the distribution of data in GNN and improves the efficacy of training the model by significantly boosting the information in the program-graph.

1.4 GNN Approach for Defect Rate Prediction Using Graph Structure of a Program

GNNs recently emerged as a powerful approach for representation learning on graphs. GNNs usage of a type of neural message passing, in which vector messages are passed between nodes and updated by neural networks, makes it unique [44]. A hidden embedding $h_v^{(k)}$ for each node $v \in V$ is updated throughout each message-passing iteration in accordance with data collected from v's graph neighborhood $N(v)$. It all begins with a graph represented by $G = (V, E, X)$, where V represents the vertex set, E stands for the edge set, and X stands for the feature matrix; each node then gathers additional feature vectors from its immediate neighbors. The node then combines the information collected from its neighbors with its own information to create a new vector. These new vectors are combined to form the embedding matrix H. The adjacency matrix A, feature matrix X, and weight matrix W of the general GNN framework comprise a single message-passing layer. The collection of these new vectors produces an embedding matrix H. A single message-passing layer is represented by the general GNN frameworks adjacency matrix A, feature matrix X, and weight matrix W.

$$H = A^{-T} X W^T$$

1.4.1 GNN Architecture

This section provides a description of the GNNs overall architecture [45–47]. Figure 1.2 illustrates its three main parts: an input layer, GNN layers, and a task-based prediction layer [48].

1.4.1.1 Input Layer

The computational representation of a graph is computed by the input layer and then transferred to the GNN layer. There are numerous ways to express a graph in a computer-readable format, and all of them use matrices [48]. Before giving the feature matrix (node/edge) to the GNN layer, each feature x_i for each node i is embedded to a d-dimensional representation $h_i^{(k=0)}$ using a linear transformation.

$$h_i^0 = B^0 x_i + b^0$$

where B^0, b^0 are biases.

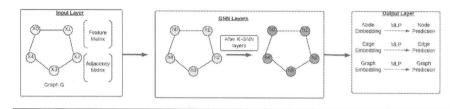

Figure 1.2   Steps in a typical experimental procedure for GNNs: embedding the network node or edge characteristics, calculating convolution using several GNN layers, etc. by employing a task-specific MLP layer to forecast.

1.4.1.2 GNN Layers

Recursive neighborhood diffusion, also known as message passing, is a method used by each GNN layer to compute d-dimensional representations for the graphs nodes and edges. Each graph node in this technique gathers information from surrounding nodes to characterize the local graph structure. Building node representations from each nodes L-hop neighborhood is made possible by stacking L-GNN layers.

Let $h_i^{(k)}$ denote the feature vector at layer k associated with node i. The core feature vector $h_i^{(k)}$ and the feature vectors $h_j^{(k)}$ for all nodes j in the vicinity of node i are subjected to nonlinear transformations to produce the updated characteristics $h_i^{(k+1)}$ at the following layer $k+1$ (defined by the graph structure). As a result, the most general representation of the feature vector $h_i^{(k+1)}$ at vertex i in the subsequent layer of the GNN is

$$h_i^{k+1} = f\left(h_i^k, \left\{ h_j^k : j \to i \right\}\right)$$

where $[j \to i]$ denotes the collection of neighboring nodes j pointed to node i, which can be replaced by $j \in N_i$, the set of neighbors of node i, if the graph is undirected. To put it another way, a GNN is defined by a mapping f that accepts as input a vector $h_i^{(k)}$ (the feature vector of the center vertex) and an unordered set of vectors $h_j^{(k)}$ (the feature vectors of all neighboring vertices). A class of GNNs is instantiated by the arbitrary selection of the mapping function f.

1.4.1.3 Output Layer

Each networks last element is a prediction layer, which computes task-dependent outputs and provides them with a loss function for end-to-end training of the networks parameters. The output of the last message-passing GCN layer for each graph node serves as the input of the prediction layer (or uses features from all intermediate layers).

1.4.2 Applying GNN to AST

The general approach for software defect prediction with the GNN pipeline involves the following steps (see the flowchart in Figure 1.3).

Step 1: Adjacency matrix A, the AST's node feature matrix V and the matching labels make up a GNN models input. The adjacency matrix A, commonly known as a propagation matrix, depicts the information propagation rules from node i to node j. Information is transmitted from node i to node j under the control of the propagation matrix. The numbers "0" and "1" indicate no propagation and full propagation, respectively.

Step 2: The GNN model has an incremental k -step of node state information propagation procedure as the initial feature information of node i is initialized to $x_i^{(0)}$. During the k th step, each target node i captures all neighbor node features to get the updated node embedding vector $h_i^{(k)} \in R^d$ as depicted in the following equation:

$$h_i^{(k)} = \Sigma_{j \in N_i} A_{ij} \cdot h_j^{(k-1)}$$

where N_i is neighborhood set of node i .

Step 3: Once the final graph node-embedding vector expression $h_i^{(k)}$ for each node is obtained, the graph embedding vector h_G of the entire AST is calculated. A simple way to obtain a graph-embedding h_G is to use the mean, sum, or max of every node-embedding h_i .

$$\underline{Mean:} \ h_G = \frac{1}{N}\Sigma_{i=0}^N h_i \qquad Sum: h_G = \Sigma_{i=0}^N h_i \qquad Max: h_G = \max_{i=0}^N \left(h_i\right)$$

Figure 1.3   Flowchart of defect prediction using GNN.

Recent techniques suggest that for each layer, embedding nodes are summed, and the result is concatenated.

$$h_G = \sum_{i=0}^{N} h_i^0 \; \| \cdots \| \sum_{i=0}^{N} h_i^k$$

Step 4: Finally, the h_G obtained in Step 3 is given an input to the classifier (multi-layer perceptron) to generate the label l_G.

$$l_G = \text{softmax}\left(h_G\right).$$

1.5 Conclusion

Software reliability has emerged as a key metric for assessing the quality of modern software as its scope and complexity continue to grow. With the continuous development of larger and more complicated software systems, there is a greater need for accurate and speedy techniques for identifying potential faults in source code. For this objective, a variety of models have been proposed, but DL models that analyze ASTs from source code so far have emerged as the best solution. But many of these models either do not work with tree-structured data, like ASTs, or they only use a small portion of the available data.

The main idea of this approach is to use an AST that is a graph description of a source code. Usage of the abstract syntax tree has several advantages such as programming language independence and gives a correct description of the source code. The next advantage is the fact that a correctly constructed abstract syntax tree will automatically ignore unnecessary information present in the source code, such as gaps.

By adding node feature information and k-hop neighborhood information around each node, graph neural networks, which are specialized neural network designs that operate on graph data (ASTs), can be used to optimize downstream tasks like node classification or graph classification.

References

[1] Z. Li, X.-Y. Jing, X. Zhu, Progress on approaches to software defect prediction, *IET Software* 12 (3) (2018) 161–175.

[2] L. L. Minku, E. Mendes, B. Turhan, Data mining for software engineering and humans in the loop, *Progress in Artificial Intelligence* 5 (4) (2016) 307–314.

[3] J. Iqbal, S. Quadri, N. Ahmad, An imperfect-debugging model with a learning-factor based fault-detection rate, in: 2014 International Conference on Computing for Sustainable Global Development (INDIACom), IEEE, 2014, pp. 383–387.

[4]   S. Khurshid, J. Iqbal, I. A. Malik, B. Yousuf, Modelling of NHPP based software reliability growth model from the perspective of testing coverage, error propagation, and fault withdrawal efficiency, *International Journal of Reliability, Quality, and Safety Engineering* (2022) 2250013.

[5]   I. Saraf, A. K. Shrivastava, J. Iqbal, Effort-based fault detection and correlation modelling for multi release of software, *International Journal of Information and Computer Security* 14 (3–4) (2021) 354–379.

[6]   J. Iqbal, Software reliability growth models: A comparison of linear and exponential fault content functions for the study of imperfect debugging situations, *Cogent Engineering* 4 (1) (2017) 1286739.

[7]   T. Menzies, Z. Milton, B. Turhan, B. Cukic, Y. Jiang, and A. Bener, Defect prediction from static code features: current results, limitations, and new approaches, *Automated Software Engineering* 17 (4) (2010) 375–407.

[8]   Y. LeCun, Y. Bengio, G. Hinton, et al., Deep Learning, *Nature*, 521 (7553), 436–444, Google Scholar Google Scholar Cross Ref Cross Ref (2015).

[9]   S. Wang, T. Liu, J. Nam, and L. Tan, Deep semantic feature learning for software defect prediction, IEEE Transactions on Software Engineering 46 (12) (2018) 1267–1293.

[10] J. Li, P. He, J. Zhu, and M. R. Lyu, Software defect prediction via convolutional neural network, in: 2017 IEEE international conference on software quality, reliability, and security (QRS), IEEE, 2017, pp. 318–328.

[11] C. Pan, M. Lu, B. Xu, H. Gao, An improved CNN model for within-project software defect prediction, *Applied Sciences* 9 (10) (2019) 2138

[12] S. Meilong, P. He, H. Xiao, H. Li, C. Zeng, An approach to semantic and structural feature learning for software defect prediction, *Mathematical Problems in Engineering* 2020 (2020).

[13] H. Liang, Y. Yu, L. Jiang, and Z. Xie, Seml: A semantic LSTM model for software defect prediction, *IEEE Access* 7 (2019) 83812–83824.

[14] G. Fan, X. Diao, H. Yu, K. Yang, and L. Chen, Software defect prediction via attention-based recurrent neural networks, *Scientific Programming* 2019 (2019).

[15] Q. Zhang, B. Wu, Software defect prediction via transformer, in: 2020 IEEE 4th Information Technology, Networking, Electronic, and Automation Control Conference (ITNEC), Vol. 1, IEEE, 2020, pp. 874–879.

[16] J. Xu, F. Wang, and J. Ai, Defect prediction with semantics and context features of codes based on graph representation learning, *IEEE Transactions on Reliability* 70 (2) (2020), 613–625.

[17] Z. Zhao, B. Yang, G. Li, H. Liu, and Z. Jin, Precise learning of source code contextual semantics via hierarchical dependence structure and graph attention networks, *Journal of Systems and Software*, 184 (2022), 111108.

[18] L. Silic, A. S. Kurdija, K. Vladimir, and M. Silic, Graph neural network for source code defect prediction, *IEEE Access* 10 (2022) 10402–10415. doi:10.1109/ACCESS.2022.3144598.

[19] J. Zhang, X. Wang, H. Zhang, H. Sun, K. Wang, X. Liu, A novel neural source code representation based on abstract syntax tree, in: 2019 IEEE/ACM 41st International Conference on Software Engineering (ICSE), IEEE, 2019, pp. 783–794.

[20] L. Mou, G. Li, L. Zhang, T. Wang, Z. Jin, Convolutional neural networks over tree structures for programming language processing, in: Thirtieth AAAI conference on artificial intelligence, 2016.

[21] M. White, M. Tufano, C. Vendome, and D. Poshyvanyk, Deep learning code fragments for code clone detection, in: 2016 31st IEEE/ACM International Conference on Automated Software Engineering (ASE), IEEE, 2016, pp. 87–98.

[22] W. Wang, G. Li, B. Ma, X. Xia, and Z. Jin, Detecting code clones with graph neural networks and flow-augmented abstract syntax trees, in: 2020 IEEE 27th International Conference on Software Analysis, Evolution, and Reengineering (SANER), IEEE, 2020, pp. 261–271.

[23] J. Zhao, K. Xia, Y. Fu, and B. Cui, An AST-based code plagiarism detection algorithm, in: 2015 10th International Conference on Broadband and Wireless Computing, Communication, and Applications (BWCCA), IEEE, 2015, pp. 178–182.

[24] M. Allamanis, M. Brockschmidt, and M. Khademi, Learning to represent programs with graphs, arXiv preprint arXiv:1711.00740 (2017).

[25] L. Silic, A. S. Kurdija, K. Vladimir, and M. Silic, Graph neural network for source code defect prediction, *IEEE Access* 10 (2022) 10402–10415.

[26] Q. Song, Z. Jia, M. Shepperd, S. Ying, and J. Liu, A general software defect proneness prediction framework, *IEEE Transactions on Software Engineering* 37 (3) (2010) 356–370.

[27] J. Iqbal, T. Firdous, A. K. Shrivastava, and I. Saraf, Modeling and predicting software vulnerabilities using a sigmoid function, *International Journal of Information Technology*, 14 (2) (2022), 649–655.

[28] N. Nagappan, T. Ball, Using software dependencies and churn metrics to predict field failures: An empirical case study, in: First International Symposium on Empirical Software Engineering and Measurement (ESEM 2007), IEEE, 2007, pp. 364–373.

[29] R. Moser, W. Pedrycz, G. Succi, A comparative analysis of the efficiency of change metrics and static code attributes for defect prediction, in: Proceedings of the 30th International Conference on Software Engineering, 2008, pp. 181–190.

[30] O. F. Arar, K. Ayan, A feature dependent naive Bayes approach and its application to the software defect prediction problem, *Applied Soft Computing* 59 (2017) 197–209.

[31] R. Mousavi, M. Eftekhari, and F. Rahdari, Omni-ensemble learning (oel): utilizing over-bagging, static, and dynamic ensemble selection approaches for software defect prediction, *International Journal on Artificial Intelligence Tools*, 27 (06) (2018), 1850024.

[32] X.-Y. Jing, S. Ying, Z.-W. Zhang, S.-S. Wu, and J. Liu, Dictionary learning based software defect prediction, in: Proceedings of the 36th International Conference on Software Engineering, 2014, pp. 414–423.

[33] B. Turhan, T. Menzies, A. B. Bener, J. Di Stefano, On the relative value of cross-company and within-company data for defect prediction, *Empirical Software Engineering*, 14 (5) (2009), 540–578.

[34] Q. Yu, S. Jiang, and J. Qian, Which is more important for cross-project defect prediction: instance or feature?, in: 2016 International Conference on Software Analysis, Testing, and Evolution (SATE), IEEE, 2016, pp. 90–95.

[35] Y. Ma, G. Luo, X. Zeng, and A. Chen, Transfer learning for cross-company software defect prediction, *Information and Software Technology* 54 (3) (2012), 248–256.

[36] L. Peng, B. Yang, Y. Chen, and A. Abraham, Data gravitation based classification, *Information Sciences* 179 (6) (2009) 809–819.

[37] L. Chen, B. Fang, Z. Shang, and Y. Tang, Negative sample reduction in cross company software defect prediction, *Information and Software Technology* 62 (2015) 67–77.

[38] Y. Yao, G. Doretto, Boosting for transfer learning with multiple sources, in: 2010 IEEE Computer Society Conference on Computer Vision and Pattern Recognition, IEEE, 2010, pp. 1855–1862.

[39] S. Qiu, L. Lu, and S. Jiang, Multiple-component weights model for cross project software defect prediction, *IET Software* 12 (4) (2018) 345–355.

[40] J. Wu, J. Xu, and X. Meng, Reliable compilation optimization selection based on gate graph neural networks, in: SEKE, 2020, pp. 270–275.

[41] V. R. Shen, Novel code plagiarism detection based on abstract syntax trees and fuzzy petri nets, *International Journal of Engineering Education*, 1 (1) (2019), 46–56.

[42] M. Hassen, P. K. Chan, Scalable function call graph-based malware classification, in: Proceedings of the Seventh ACM Conference on Data and Application Security and Privacy, 2017, pp. 239–248.

[43] C. Weyerhaeuser, T. Mindnich, D. Baeumges, and G. S. Kazmaier, Augmented query optimization by a data flow graph model optimizer, US Patent 10,241,961 (Mar. 26, 2019).

[44] J. Gilmer, S. S. Schoenholz, P. F. Riley, O. Vinyl's, and G. E. Dahl, Neural message passing for quantum chemistry, in: International conference on machine learning, PMLR, 2017, pp. 1263–1272.

[45] T. N. Kipf, M. Welling, Semi-supervised classification with graph convolutional networks, arXiv preprint arXiv:1609.02907 (2016).

[46] P. Vellkovic, G. Cucurull, A. Casanova, A. Romero, P. Lio, and Y. Bengio, Graph Attention Networks, International Conference on Learning Representations (2018).

[47] W. L. Hamilton, R. Ying, and J. Leskovec, Inductive representation learning on large graphs, in: Proceedings of the 31st International Conference on Neural Information Processing Systems, 2017, pp. 1025–1035.

[48] A. Mohi ud Din, S. Qureshi, A review of challenges and solutions in the design and implementation of deep graph neural networks, *International Journal of Computers and Applications* (2022), 1–10.e

Chapter 2

Software Reliability Prediction Using Neural Networks
A Non-parametric Approach

Aafaq Mohi Ud Din,[1] Javaid Iqbal,[2]
and Shaima Qureshi[1]

[1]Department of CSE, National Institute of Technology, Srinagar, India
[2]Department of Computer Science, University of Kashmir, India

Acronyms with Definitions

ANN	artificial neural network
FFNN	feed forward neural network
LM	Levenberg–Marquadt
MAE	mean absolute error
MSE	mean square error
MTBF	mean time between failures
MTTF	mean time to failure
MTTR	mean time to repair
NARX NN	nonlinear auto-regressive neural network
NHPP	non-homogeneous Poisson process
PDF	probability density function

DOI: 10.1201/9781032624983-2

RNN   recurrent neural network
SDP   software defect prediction
SE   software engineering
SQA   software quality assurance
SRGM software reliability growth model
SSE   sum of squared errors
WNN   wavelet neural network

2.1 Introduction

In modern real-time systems, software is becoming more and more important. As a result, the quality of software products has come under increasing scrutiny from the perspectives of users and software developers, with reliability taking the lead. Furthermore, the size and complexity of software products have increased rapidly, which has prompted researchers to pay more attention to quality evaluation by quantitatively estimating the length of the software testing period to avoid any uninvited and unpredicted circumstances during the operational phase. This study presents the application of neural network models for improved software reliability prediction in real situations and empirically studies an assessment method of software reliability growth using ANN.

To evaluate the relation between software reliability and time and other parameters, a large number of SRGMs have been developed in the literature. Models that use parameters and models that do not use parameters make up the two primary divisions. Based on assumptions regarding the nature of software failures, the stochastic behavior of the software failure process, and the development settings, parametric models estimate the model parameters. Non–homogeneous Poisson process (NHPP) models, which have been effectively applied in real-world reliability engineering, are the most widely used parametric models [1–6]. However, it has been shown that no single such model can obtain accurate predictions for all cases [7–9].However, non-parametric models, such as neural networks and support vector machines (SVM), are more adaptable because they do not make the same assumptions as parametric models and may forecast dependability measures only based on fault history. Artificial neural networks, also called "neural networks," behave in a manner like the human brain. The brain is extremely complex and nonlinear, and it operates similarly to a parallel computer. Thus a neural network is made up of both large parallel distributed processors and basic processing units. It naturally has the capacity to store experimental data and make it accessible for utilization. Artificial neural networks fall short of the brains complexity. In two aspects, it is like the brain: (1) The network uses a learning process to help its users absorb information from their surroundings. (2) The synaptic weights, which are the interneuron connection strengths, are where learned information is kept. Learning algorithm refers to the process utilized to carry out learning. To accomplish a goal, a learning algorithm systematically modifies the synaptic weights of network

2.2 Approaches for Software Reliability Modeling

The study of SDP is crucial to the field of software engineering. The creation of models for estimating defect rates, identifying defect patterns, and categorizing software module defect proneness typically into defective and non–defective has received a lot of attention in this area [10].We initially give a quick overview of the conventional software fault prediction process in this section. Then, with an emphasis on techniques utilizing Neural networks, we explore various deep learning methodologies suggested in the literature.

2.2.1 Parametric Software Reliability Growth Models

Based on assumptions about the characteristics of software faults, the behavior of the software failure process, and development settings, parametric models estimate the model parameters. NHPP models are the most often used parametric models [1–3, 11–22] that have been effectively applied in real-world software engineering. There are several well-liked models in this category.

2.2.1.1 Yamada Delayed S-shaped Model

The model is NHPP-based, but it makes use of a different mean value function to account for the delay in failure reporting. Its S-shaped mean value function [4] is described as follows:

$$m(t) = a(1 - (1 + bt)e^{-bt})$$

2.2.1.2 Goel–Okumoto Model

This model was developed by Goel–Okumoto and describes failure detection as NHPP with an exponentially decreasing rate function. This is how the mean value function looks [4]:

$$m(t) = a(1 - e^{-bt})$$

2.2.1.3 Generalized Goel NHPP Mode

The exponential distribution used in this model presupposes a pattern of declining defect rates or failure instances, where the failure rate first increases and then drops. With the addition of the parameter c, Goel presented a generalization of the Goel–Okumoto model [4]. This is how its mean value function looks:

$$m(t) = a\left(1 - e^{-bt^c}\right)$$

2.2.1.4 Logistic Growth Curve Model

The logistic growth model has an S-shaped curve [23]. Its mean value function is:

$$m(t) = \frac{a}{1 + ke^{-bt}}$$

2.2.1.5 MO Model

This model predicts that early failures are more common than late failures and that subsequent repair attempts often lead to a greater decline in failure rates. The model has taken this trait into consideration [23]. Its mean value function looks like this:

$$m(t) = a\ln(1 + bt)$$

2.2.1.6 Pham–Nordmann–Zhang (PNZ) Model

The PNZ model [24] accounts for the imperfect debugging phenomenon by considering that flaws may be created during the debugging phase. With an inflection S-shaped model, the fault detection rate function is non-decreasing time-dependent, and the model assumes that the introduction rate is a linear function with time-dependent total fault content. Its mean value function looks like this:

$$m(t) = \frac{a\left(1 - e^{-bt}\right)\left(1 - \dfrac{\alpha}{b}\right) + \alpha at}{1 + \beta e^{-bt}}$$

2.2.1.7 Pham–Zhang (P-Z) Model

The P-Z model [5] presupposes that the constant introduction rate is an exponential function of testing time and that the error detection function is non-decreasing with an inflection S-shaped model. This is how its mean value function looks:

$$m(t) = \frac{1}{\left(1+\beta e^{-bt}\right)}\left((c+a)\left(1-e^{-bt}\right) - \frac{ab}{b-\alpha}\left(e^{-\alpha t} - e^{-bt}\right)\right)$$

2.2.1.8 Yamada Imperfect Debugging Model 1

This model [6] is based on a fixed fault detection rate and an exponential fault content function. The following is the mean value function:

$$m(t) = \frac{ab\left(e^{\alpha t} - e^{-bt}\right)}{a+b}$$

2.2.1.9 Yamada Imperfect Debugging Model 2

The fault introduction and detection rates are assumed to be constant in this model [6]. This is how its mean value function looks:

$$m(t) = a\left(1-e^{-bt}\right)\left(1-\frac{\alpha}{b}\right) + \alpha at$$

It has been demonstrated, nonetheless, that these models are rigid and that no single model can produce precise forecasts in every circumstance.

2.2.2 Non-parametric Reliability Growth Models

Researchers have recently benefited from deep learning methods because they can learn features from data without the need for manual feature construction and are flexible. Non-parametric models, such as neural networks, are more adaptable and can predict reliability metrics without making any assumptions [25]. Non-parametric models are built using failure statistics. A powerful method for forecasting software reliability is a neural network.

In order to find the sources of forecast uncertainty in a recent gas market model, Werbos [26] suggested back-propagation learning as an alternative to regression techniques. Thus it is possible to draw the conclusion that neural network models are very helpful for regression forecasting techniques in the face of data uncertainty.

Shadmehr et al. [27] determined model parameters of the pharma kinetics system using a FFNN and expected noise in the observed data sample. The performance was better than the best maximum likelihood estimator, according to the authors comparison of the results to those of the best Bayesian estimator [28].

ANN tools and feed-forward networks with backpropagation algorithms are used to predict reliability and software quality[7–9]. The failure dataset served as the input, while reliability served as the output, in the connectionist model. These publications discuss data representation techniques, network architecture, and some irrational assumptions in software reliability models. Software reliability was predicted by Karunanithi et al. [29] using a feed-forward network and a recurrent network. The scientists came to the conclusion that neural networks beat analytical models in terms of predictive accuracy at end-point predictions after comparing the results to 14 different literature-representative datasets. Sitte [30] studied parametric recalibration models and neural networks as two techniques for software reliability prediction. These methods separate parametric recalibration models from neural networks in the context of software reliability prediction, and they concluded that neural networks are considerably easier to use and are more accurate predictors.

RNNs were utilized by Tian et al. [31] to forecast software reliability. The network is trained using Bayesian regularization. The authors claim that, compared to well-known prediction methodologies, their suggested strategy achieved a lower average relative prediction error.

RajKiran et al. [32] used WNN to predict the reliability of software. The following two wavelet types were employed by the authors as transfer functions in this study: Morlet wavelet and Gaussian wavelet.

An ANN-based model for forecasting software reliability was developed by Lo [33]. With no irrational presumptions, this approach evaluates numerous conventional software reliability and growth models.

2.3 Software Reliability

The possibility that software will carry out a required function under specific circumstances for a specific amount of time is referred to as "software reliability." Evaluation of software reliability is a vital component in quantifying the quality of any software product throughout the testing phase [34–36].

2.3.1 Software Reliability Measures

■ Failure Rate: This is how frequently failures happen. It also shows how many failures occurred within a specific time frame.

■ MTBF: This stands for the typical interval between failures. The MTBF is the period of time required before a failure happens. It is inversely proportional to the failure rate.

■ Reliability: The possibility that a product will carry out a required function without error under predetermined circumstances for a predetermined amount of time is known as "reliability."

■ Availability: Availability is the likelihood that a particular item is in a usable state at any given time. It accounts for maintenance work and downtime.

Table 2.1   Prediction Criteria

Prediction criteria	Formula*
Relative error (RE)	$RE_i = \left(\left\| (F_i - D_i)/D_i \right\| \right) * 100$
Average error (AE)	$AE = 1/n \sum\limits_{1}^{n} RE_i$
Root mean square error (RMSE)	$RMSE = \left[\sqrt{\sum\limits_{1}^{n} (F_i - D_i)^2} \right] / n$
Normalized root mean square error (NRMSE)	$NRMSE = \left[\sqrt{\sum\limits_{1}^{n} (F_i - D_i)^2} \right] / \sum\limits_{1}^{n} F_i^2$
Mean absolute error (MAE)	$MAE = \left[\sum\limits_{1}^{n} \left\| (F_i - D_i) \right\| \right] / n$

Table 2.2   Statistics of the Failure Datasets

Properties \ dataset	Project name	Code size lines/inst.	#Failures	Reference
Data1	CCP	1000	27	[37]
Data2	RTCC	21700	136	[38]
Data3	DE	40000	46	[39]
Data4	DB	1317000	328	[39]
Data5	AS	240000	3207	[40]
Data6	RCA	870000	535	[41]

2.3.2 Parameter Estimation Techniques

Different methods can be employed to evaluate and contrast the performance of particular models (as shown in Table 2.1).

2.3.3 Failure Data Sets

We carefully craft the prediction challenge and data split for each dataset so that meeting high prediction performance on the task would directly affect the relevant application. See Table 2.2.

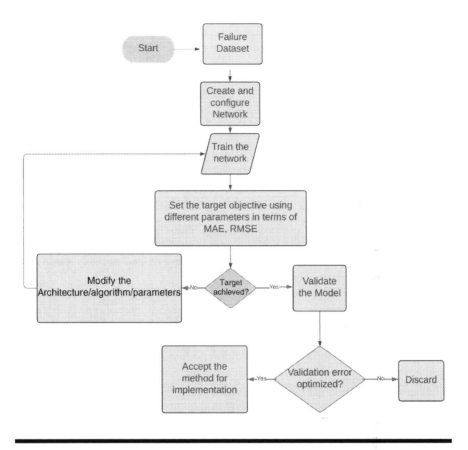

Figure 2.1   Flowchart for predicting software reliability using neural network architecture with failure history as input.

2.4 ANN Approach for Reliability

Recently, neural networks have become a potent method for forecasting reliability. In order to increase the precision and consistency of software reliability prediction, reliability is essential. The general stages for using an ANN pipeline to anticipate software faults are as follows (refer to the flowchart in Figure 2.1):

Step 1—Collect failure data: The software's history of failures is documented in the failure dataset (a sample failure dataset is shown in Table 2.3).

After 25 minutes of the test, the first failure happened. The second failure happened 55 minutes into the test, while the sixth failure happened 119 minutes into the test. Before being fed into the neural network as depicted in the picture, the failure dataset is preprocessed as shown in Figure 2.2.

Table 2.3   Failure Dataset Sample

Failure record	Actual time of failure (minutes)	Time between failures
1	25	25
2	55	30
3	70	15
4	95	15
5	112	17
6	119	7

Figure 2.2   Flowchart of data preprocessing.

Step 2—Network creation and configuration: .In the approach for the feed-forward neural network, the basic FFNN architecture consists of two steps:

1. Feed-forward step
2. Back-propagation

The input vector X is fed to the input layer and is propagated through a weight layer V as:

$$\text{net}_j(t) = \sum_{i}^{n}\left(v_{ji}\right)x_i(t) + \theta_i$$
$$y_j(t) = f\left(\text{net}_j\right)(t)$$

where n is the number of input nodes, θ is the bias, and f is an activation function. The networks output is calculated using state and weight W connected to an output layer.

$$y_k(t) = g\left(\text{net}_k(t)\right)$$
$$g\left(\text{net}_k(t)\right) = \sum Y_j(t)\omega_{kj} + \theta_k$$

where m is the number of states or hidden nodes, θ is bias, and g is an activation function.

Step 3—Approach for nonlinear auto-regressive neural network: The basic NARX neural network architecture consists of two steps:

1. Feed-forward step
2. Back-propagation with recurrent

The input vector X is propagated with a layer associated with weight V and combined with the previous state activation associated with a recurrent weight U.

$$\eta_{etj}(t) = \sum_{i}^{n}(v_j)(x_i(t)) + \sum_{n}^{m}(U_{jh})(y_h(t-1) + \theta_j$$
$$y_j(t) = f(\text{net}_j)(t)$$

where n is the number of input nodes, θ is a bias, m is the number of states or hidden node, and f is an activation function.

The output of the network is calculated by state and weight w associated with that output layer.

$$y_k(t) = g(net_k(t))$$
$$g(net_k(t)) = \sum_{j}^{m} y_j(t)\omega_{kj} + \theta_k$$

where g is an activation function

Step 4—Training algorithm: The issue of minimizing a nonlinear function has a numerical answer thanks to the training process. The Levenberg–Marquardt algorithm, steepest descent method, and Gauss–Newton algorithm are three common training algorithms. Following are the steps in the general training procedure (as depicted in pseudo-code in Figure 2.3).

1. Using the initial weights, calculate the overall error (SSE).
2. Update weights and make adjustments.
3. Calculate the overall error using the updated weights.
4. If the update causes the current total error to grow, retract the step (such as returning the weight vector to its initial value) and raise the combination coefficient μ by a factor of 10 or by other amounts. Then return to step 2 and attempt another update.
5. If the update reduces the current total error, accept the step (for example, keep the new weight vector as it is now) and reduce the combination coefficient μ by a factor of 10 or by the same factor as step 4.
6. As soon as the current total error is less than the necessary amount, proceed to step ii using the revised weights.

```
For all patterns
% Forward computation
    For all layers
        For all neurons in the layer
            Calculate net;
            Calculate output;
            Calculate slope;
        end;
      end;
% Backward Computation
    Initial delta as slope;
      For all outputs
        Calculate error;
        For all layers
          For all neurons in the previous layer
            For all neurons in the current layer
              Multiply delta through weights
              Sum the back propagated delta at proper nodes
            end;
            Multiply delta by slope;
          end;
        end
    end
```

Figure 2.3   Levenberg–Marquardt algorithm implementation.

2.5 Conclusion

As the scope and complexity of modern software continue to grow, software reliability has emerged as a key metric for assessing its quality. More precise and quick methods for finding potential source code faults are required as larger and more complex software systems continue to be developed. Utilizing the source codes failure history is the methods fundamental tenet. The findings suggest that neural network models outperform existing analytical models in terms of prediction error, making them a better choice for software reliability testing. Neural network models perform better on larger datasets than on smaller datasets.

References

[1]   J. Iqbal, S. Quadri, N. Ahmad, An imperfect-debugging model with learning-factor based fault-detection rate, in: 2014 International Conference on Computing for Sustainable Global Development (INDIACom), IEEE, 2014, pp. 383–387.

[2]   J. Iqbal, N. Ahmad, S. Quadri, A software reliability growth model with two types of learning and a negligence factor, in: 2013 IEEE Second International Conference on Image Information Processing (ICIIP-2013), IEEE, 2013, pp. 678–683.

[3]   J. Iqbal, Software reliability growth models: A comparison of linear and exponential fault content functions for study of imperfect debugging situations, *Cogent Engineering* 4 (1) (2017) 1286739.

[4]   C.-Y. Huang, M. R. Lyu, S.-Y. Kuo, A unified scheme of some nonhomogeneous Poisson process models for software reliability estimation, *IEEE Transactions on Software Engineering* 29 (3) (2003) 261–269.

[5]   H. Pham, X. Zhang, An NHPP software reliability model and its comparison, *International Journal of Reliability, Quality and Safety Engineering* 4 (03) (1997) 269–282.

[6]   S. Yamada, K. Tokuno, S. Osaki, Imperfect debugging models with fault introduction rate for software reliability assessment, *International Journal of Systems Science* 23 (12) (1992) 2241–2252.

[7]   T. M. Khoshgoftaar, D. L. Lanning, A. S. Pandya, A comparative study of pattern recognition techniques for quality evaluation of telecommunications software, *IEEE Journal on Selected Areas in Communications* 12 (2) (1994) 279–291.

[8]   Y. Singh, P. Kumar, Prediction of software reliability using feed forward neural networks, in: 2010 International Conference on Computational Intelligence and Software Engineering, IEEE, 2010, pp. 1–5.

[9]   M. K. Bhuyan, D. P. Mohapatra, S. Sethi, A survey of computational intelligence approaches for software reliability prediction, *ACM SIGSOFT Software Engineering Notes* 39 (2) (2014) 1–10.

[10]   Q. Song, Z. Jia, M. Shepperd, S. Ying, J. Liu, A general software defect–proneness prediction framework, *IEEE Transactions on Software Engineering* 37 (3) (2010) 356–370.

[11]   S. Li, Q. Yin, P. Guo, M. R. Lyu, A hierarchical mixture model for software reliability prediction, *Applied Mathematics and Computation* 185 (2) (2007) 1120–1130.

[12]   J. D. Musa, *Software Reliability Engineering: More Reliable Software, Faster and Cheaper*, Tata McGraw-Hill Education, 2004.

[13]   Y. K. Malaiya, M. N. Li, J. M. Bieman, R. Karcich, Software reliability growth with test coverage, *IEEE Transactions on Reliability* 51 (4) (2002) 420–426.

[14]   S. Khurshid, A. K. Shrivastava, J. Iqbal, Fault prediction modelling in open source software under imperfect debugging and change-point, *International Journal of Open Source Software and Processes (IJOSSP)* 9 (2) (2018) 1–17.

[15]   I. Saraf, J. Iqbal, Generalized software fault detection and correction modeling framework through imperfect debugging, error generation and change point, *International Journal of Information Technology* 11 (4) (2019) 751–757.

[16]   I. Saraf, A. Shrivastava, J. Iqbal, Generalised fault detection and correction modelling framework for multi-release of software, *International Journal of Industrial and Systems Engineering* 34 (4) (2020) 464–493.

[17]   S. Khurshid, A. K. Shrivastava, J. Iqbal, Generalized multi-release framework for fault prediction in open source software, *International Journal of Software Innovation (IJSI)* 7 (4) (2019) 86–107.

[18] S. Khurshid, A. Shrivastava, J. Iqbal, Effort based software reliability model with fault reduction factor, change point and imperfect debugging, *International Journal of Information Technology* 13 (1) (2021) 331–340.

[19] I. Saraf, J. Iqbal, A. K. Shrivastava, S. Khurshid, Modelling reliability growth for multi-version open source software considering varied testing and debugging factors, *Quality and Reliability Engineering International* 38 (4) (2022) 1814–1825.

[20] S. Khurshid, A. K. Shrivastava, J. Iqbal, Generalised multi release framework for fault determination with fault reduction factor, *International Journal of Information and Computer Security* 17 (1–2) (2022) 164–178.

[21] S. Khurshid, J. Iqbal, I. A. Malik, B. Yousuf, Modelling of NHPP based software reliability growth model from the perspective of testing coverage, error propagation and fault withdrawal efficiency, *International Journal of Reliability, Quality and Safety Engineering* (2022) 2250013.

[22] J. Iqbal, T. Firdous, A. K. Shrivastava, I. Saraf, Modelling and predicting software vulnerabilities using a sigmoid function, *International Journal of Information Technology* 14 (2) (2022) 649–655.

[23] G. Aggarwal, V. Gupta, Software reliability growth model, *International Journal of Advanced Research in Computer Science and Software Engineering* 4 (1) (2014) 475–479.

[24] H. Pham, L. Nordmann, Z. Zhang, A general imperfect-software-debugging model with s-shaped fault-detection rate, *IEEE Transactions on Reliability* 48 (2) (1999) 169–175.

[25] A. Mohi ud din, S. Qureshi, A review of challenges and solutions in the design and implementation of deep graph neural networks, *International Journal of Computers and Applications* (2022) 1–10.

[26] P. J. Werbos, Generalization of backpropagation with application to a recurrent gas market model, *Neural Networks* 1 (4) (1988) 339–356.

[27] R. Shadmehr, D. D'Argenio, A comparison of a neural network based estimator and two statistical estimators in a sparse and noisy data environment, in: Proc. IJCNN, Washington DC, 1990, pp. 289–292.

[28] N. Karunanithi, Y. K. Malaiya, L. D. Whitley, Prediction of software reliability using neural networks, in: ISSRE, 1991, pp. 124–130.

[29] N. Karunanithi, D. Whitley, Prediction of software reliability using feedforward and recurrent neural nets, in: [Proceedings 1992] IJCNN International Joint Conference on Neural Networks, Vol. 1, IEEE, 1992, pp. 800–805.

[30] R. Sitte, Comparison of software-reliability-growth predictions: neural networks vs parametric-recalibration, *IEEE transactions on Reliability* 48 (3) (1999) 285–291.

[31] L. Tian, A. Noore, Software reliability prediction using recurrent neural network with Bayesian regularization, *International Journal of Neural Systems* 14 (03) (2004) 165–174.

[32] N. R. Kiran, V. Ravi, Software reliability prediction using wavelet neural networks, in: International Conference on Computational Intelligence and Multimedia Applications (ICCIMA 2007), Vol. 1, IEEE, 2007, pp. 195–199.

[33] J.-H. Lo, The implementation of artificial neural networks applying to software reliability modeling, in: 2009 Chinese control and decision conference, IEEE, 2009, pp. 4349–4354.

[34] J. D. Musa, *Software Reliability Data*. Data Analysis Center for Software (1980). www.thedacs.com/databases/sled/swrel.php

[35] R. K. Iyer, I. Lee, Measurement-based analysis of software reliability, *Handbook of Software Reliability Engineering* (1996) 303–358.

[36] J. D. Musa, K. Okumoto, A logarithmic Poisson execution time model for software reliability measurement, in: Proceedings of the 7th international conference on Software engineering, Citeseer, 1984, pp. 230–238.

[37] K.-i. Matsumoto, K. Inoue, T. Kikuno, K. Torii, Experimental evaluation of software reliability growth models, in: 1988 The Eighteenth International Symposium on Fault-Tolerant Computing. Digest of Papers, IEEE Computer Society, 1988, pp. 148–149.

[38] J. D. Musa, A. Iannino, K. Okumoto, *Software Reliability: Measurement, Prediction, Application*, McGraw-Hill, Inc., 1987.

[39] M. Ohba, Software reliability analysis models, *IBM Journal of Research and Development* 28 (4) (1984) 428–443.

[40] M. L. Shooman, Probabilistic models for software reliability prediction, in: *Statistical Computer Performance Evaluation*, Elsevier, 1972, pp. 485–502.

[41] Y. Tohma, H. Yamano, M. Ohba, R. Jacoby, Parameter estimation of the hypergeometric distribution model for real test/debug data, in: Proceedings. 1991 International Symposium on Software Reliability Engineering, IEEE Computer Society, 1991, pp. 28–29.

Chapter 3

Analysis and Modeling of Software Reliability Using Deep Learning Methods

Gousia Habib and Shaima Qureshi

Department of CSE, National Institute of Technology, Srinagar, India

3.1 Introduction

To increase software reliability, developers use software defect prediction to discover probable flaws and to prioritize their testing resources. The conventional approach for predicting defects involves handcrafted features incorporated into machine learning classifiers. As a result, these handcrafted features frequently failed to grab the program semantics and structural information. A better understanding of program functionality can be gained by modeling the data, which can help predict defects more accurately.

In the current era, machine learning (ML) is becoming increasingly important as a research tool due to its numerous frameworks and approaches to learning. Software defect prediction aims to help developers identify probable defects and to prioritize testing resources as the volume of software increases. Most traditional software defect prediction methods use static code measurements to train machine learning classifiers to predict software defects. It is common for academics to use statistical

DOI: 10.1201/9781032624983-3

methods to classify software modules, determine whether they are defect prone, and then train their models using ML techniques. Models that are designed correctly are crucial to obtaining the best results from deep neural networks (DNN) and convolutional neural networks (CNNs). DNNs and CNNs require appropriate design decisions to perform well as classifiers. This importance is especially apparent when predicting the likelihood of software modules failing. It might be possible to reduce test costs by concentrating on modules with high error rates when recognized correctly. An NCNN (neural network correlation network) model is presented in this chapter for predicting software flaws. Python with Keras and TensorFlow as a framework is used for coding purpose.

3.2 Related Work

Information retrieval when combined with machine learning can increase performance in locating bug reports. This was argued by Lam et al. [1]. Huo et al. [2] used CNN to illustrate that software corpora have a "naturalness" quality; that is, source code created by real developer people have a wealth of statistical properties. Through the use of *n*-grams, a statistical language model for software languages, they completed a code completion challenge. As a result of its tremendous potential for feature generations, deep learning techniques have recently been employed in software engineering [3–6] enhancing information-retrieval-based tasks.

Integrating features from source code in programs and natural language in bug reports as unified features can improve bug localization. A recurrent neural network (RNN) was used in Raychev et al.'s [7] code completion method, and a decision-tree-based method was used in their forthcoming paper [8]. A study by White et al. [9] advocated using deep learning to represent sequential software languages and to detect code clones using their models. According to Mou et al. [10], a tree-based CNN is a better model of source code while maintaining structural information.

The RNN encoder-decoder paradigm was used by Gu et al. [11] to solve the challenge of returning API call sequences based on the user's natural language queries. Furthermore, based on deep learning approaches, program synthesis [12], [13], [14] is becoming an important study topic. Deep learning is also used to predict defects. Yang et al. [15] used DBN to build new features for change-level defect prediction using 14 existing change-level features. DBN was also used by Wang et al. [13] to anticipate file-level defects using token vectors taken from program ASTs.

In contrast to the previous work, we use DNN to construct features directly from raw source code rather than using preexisting features. Farid et al. [16] presented CBIL, a unique hybrid model, in 2021. CBIL is capable of anticipating the portions of source code that are incorrect. As vectors, tokens from the abstract syntax tree (AST) were extracted from the source code. Integer vectors were transformed into dense vectors using mapping and word embedding.

Cong et al. [17] adopted an ML-based CPDP technique in 2021 that employs existing training data from a single project with a sufficient number of flaws and defect labels. KTSVMs were utilized to apply DA for matching the training data to tackle this difficulty in numerous applications. Furthermore, the CPDP model in this study used KTSVMs with DA functions, also known as DA-KTSVM. The results show that the provided approach can achieve superior prediction performance and efficiency over existing CPDP schemes whenever the training sample data is appropriate.

Wang et al. [18] used a deep belief network (DBN) model to predict or uncover software defects based on program abstract syntax trees (ASTs). Modeling fault detection and correction procedures with recurrent neural networks were used by Hu et al. [19]. In addition, they used a genetic algorithm to optimize network configuration to improve failure prediction. In addition to nonparametric methodologies, other non-parametric methods were used to predict software failures. For example, Wang et al. [18] used a deep belief network to learn semantic features from source code to predict defects. The results suggest that the proposed model captures fault features better than previous approaches. Based on a genetic algorithm, Tian and Noore [20] proposed an evolutionary neural network model to predict cumulative software failure times. More details of the software reliability and detection techniques and deep learning strategies can be found in [21–28].

3.2.1 Novel Deep Learning Solutions for Software Defect Detection and Reliability

Several software reliability models have been developed over the past four decades to analyze software dependability. These models include parameterized and nonparametric models. There is a limit to the accuracy with which each model can predict software fault numbers in some testing scenarios, although these models are reliable in assessing the dependability of software in some scenarios.

Modern software, in particular, comes in various sizes and purposes, making software reliability assessment a tough undertaking. The deep neural network (NN) model, a recently created deep learning model, provides adequate prediction performance. This deep learning model can adjust to capture the training characteristics and deepen the layer levels. RNN encoder-decoder neural network is also a good solution to the software detection problem.

Due to the short-term memory of RNN, we cannot process long sequences of software programs, so it is not much of a feasible solution. The sequence of the program in the software can vary; therefore, long-term memory is needed for better prediction. LSTM is the best solution, but it also processes sequence-to-sequence samples. Also, by multiplying and adding, LSTMs make minor alterations to the data. Cell states are a technique used by LSTMs to transmit information. Thus significant and less important information can be selectively remembered or forgotten by LSTMs.

When sentences are excessively long, LSTMs still perform poorly, which is the same issue that often affects RNNs. The likelihood of retaining context from a world far removed from the one currently being processed diminishes exponentially with distance, which explains why. Consequently, the model frequently needs to remember the content of far-off positions in the sequence when phrases are lengthy. Since sentences must be processed word by word, another issue with RNNs and LSTMs is that it is challenging to parallelize the job. Researchers developed a method for focusing on particular words to address some of these issues. By concentrating on a portion of a subset of the information they are given, neural networks can exhibit this similar behavior.

3.2.2 Transformers as a Novel Proposed Solution

Transformers are more powerful parallel processing models that are the most suitable and powerful solutions for better software reliability and can be very helpful in defect detection with higher-end performance. The proposed architecture is given in Figure 3.1. The proposed methods consist of three major components: the batch of source code files or set of code documents, the word2vec algorithm for tokenization, and a powerful deep learning model transformer. The next sections unravel each component of the proposed model one by one.

3.2.2.1 Introduction to Word Embedding and word2vec

Word embedding is one of the most common ways to define document vocabulary. It can identify a word's position within a document, its semantic and syntactic similarity, and its relationship to other words. Using shallow neural networks, Word2Vec is one of the most popular methods for learning word embeddings. An embedding

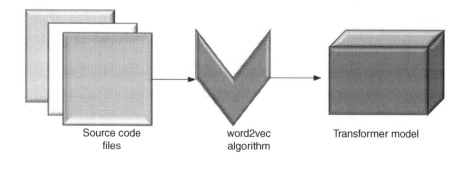

Source code   word2vec   Transformer model
files   algorithm

Figure 3.1   Novel proposed architecture.

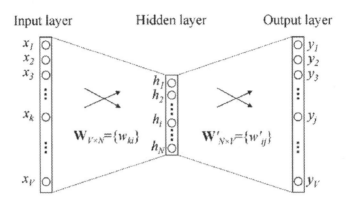

Figure 3.2   Simple CBOW model with one-word context.

of this type can be created using word2vec. Obtaining it requires neural networks in two ways: Common Bag of Words (CBOW) and Skip Gram.

CBOW model: A context-based approach predicts the word corresponding to the context by analyzing each word's context. The neural network should be given the word "excellent" as input. In this example, we use only the word "wonderful" as a context input for predicting the target word ("day"). Using the one-hot encoding of the input word ("day"), we quantify the output error compared to the one-hot encoding of the target word. Learning the vector representation of the target word is the first step toward forecasting it. CBOW is best illustrated by Figure 3.2.

An encoded vector of size V is used as the input or context word. N neurons in the hidden layer produce a vector as its output that has a V-length and contains the softmax values The weight matrix Win (V*N dimensional matrix) transfers the input x to the hidden layer, while W'nv (N*V dimensional matrix) sends hidden layer output to the final output layer. Alternatively, we can use the Skip gram CBOW represented in Figure 3.3 model as discussed next.

This is just the multi-context flipped CBOW model, which outputs probabilistic distributions upon being given words as inputs. CBOW is very fast and has better performance in representing frequent words. Word2vec internally uses a supervised classification model to obtain these embeddings from the corpus, even though word2vec is an unsupervised model that allows you to provide a corpus without any label information and build dense word embeddings.

3.2.2.2 Transformer Deep Learning Model

A sequence-to-sequence (seq2seq) model represents the Transformer. This indicates that it is appropriate for any issue where the output is a sequence and the data has some degree of ordering. Speech recognition, abstractive summarization, and

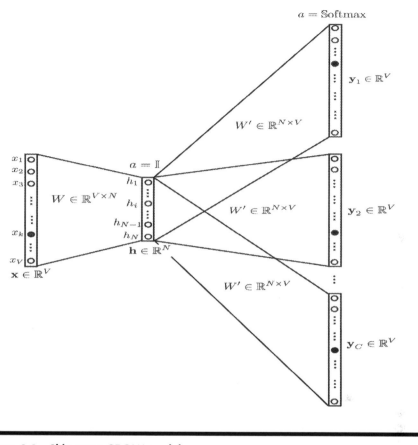

Figure 3.3 Skip-gram CBOW model.

machine translation are a few examples of uses. Even state-of-the-art computer vision has recently been improved with Vision Transformers (Vit). The high-level visualization of the Transformer is given in Figure 3.4.

The encoders are all exact replicas of one another. In a similar vein, every decoder is the same. The finer details of the encoder and decoder are given in Figure 3.5

The crucial self-attention layer, which calculates the relationships between the words in the sequence, is present in the encoder along with a feed-forward layer. The self-attention layer, feed-forward layer, and a second encoder-decoder attention layer are all included in the decoder. There is a unique set of weights for each encoder and decoder. All Transformer architectures are defined by a reusable module called the Encoder. Along with the two levels just mentioned, it also features two layer-norm layers and residual skip connections all around both layers, as given in Figure 3.6.

Artificial intelligence (AI) research has found that ideas like residual connections and (batch) normalization enhance performance, shorten training

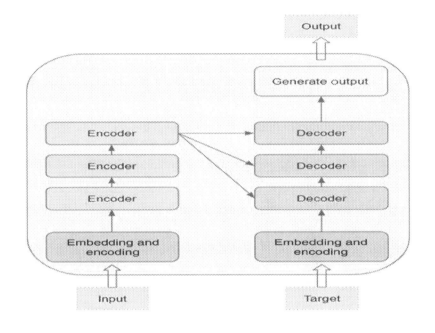

Figure 3.4   High-level representation of the Transformer.

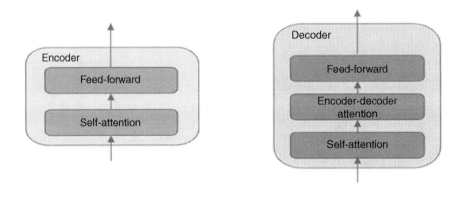

Figure 3.5   Finer level representation of the Transformer.

times, and enable the formation of deeper networks. As a result, the Transformer has after-each attention layer and after-each feed-forward layer residual connections and normalization. For enhanced generalization, dropout is additionally introduced to each layer. A residual connection is when the output of a network's previous layer (or sublayer) is added to the output of the current

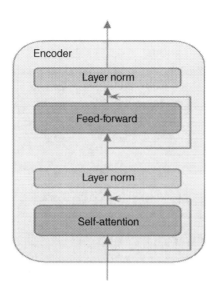

Figure 3.6   Encoder with a layer-norm layer and FFN.

layer. Because the network can essentially "skip" some layers, this enables the creation of incredibly deep networks. A feed-forward network is layered on top of each attention layer. This comprises two completely interconnected layers with a dropout for the inner layer and text-ReLU-ReLU activation (text-ReLU(x) = max $(0, x)$ ReLu(x) = max $(0, x)$. For the input layer's standard dimensions, the transformer paper uses the text model = 512d model = 512 and d ff = 2048d ff =2048 for the inner layer.

A multiheaded attention layer (MHSA) and a fully connected feed-forward network (FFN) comprise a single encoder layer. We also consider layer normalization and residual connections, as already explained.

After the decoding layer comes to a masked multihead attention layer that includes memory, the encoder's output is memory. The final step is a feed-forward network. Again, layer normalization and residual connections are included in these elements.

Batch normalization is a common characteristic of contemporary deep-learning-based computer vision models. This kind of normalization, however, requires a substantial batch size and does not naturally lend itself to recurrence. Layer normalization is used in the conventional Transformer architecture. Layer normalization is consistent even with tiny batch sizes (text batch size 8).

The model lacks knowledge of the relative positions of the embedded tokens in a sequence, in contrast to recurrent and convolutional networks. As a result, we must add encoding to the input embeddings for the encoder and decoder to inject

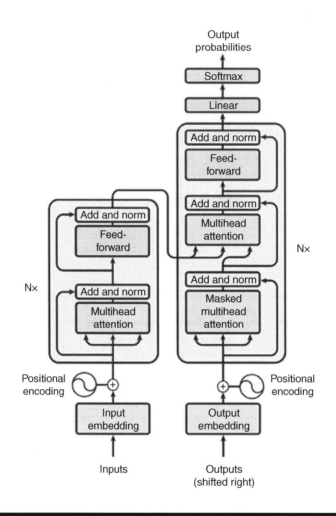

Figure 3.7   Overall architecture of the proposed method.

this information. This information may be static or acquired and may be added in various ways. The Transformer applies sine and cosine transforms for each position (text, position, position). For even dimensions (2 $i2$) sine is employed, while for odd dimensions (2 i + 12 i + 1), cosine.

The decoder's vector output must then be translated into a final output. This is a probability distribution over the entire vocabulary for each position for sequence-to-sequence challenges like language translation. The output of the decoder is converted into a matrix of logits with the dimension of the target language by one completely connected layer. Finally, the overall visualization of the proposed model is given in Figure 3.7.

3.3 Conclusion

This chapter briefly introduced software defect detection methods and various solutions. The chapter also discussed their applications and limitations. Based on the research of previous methods, a novel and powerful parallel processing and deep learning model, i.e., the Transformer, is proposed to combat all these problems. Also, the model has greater performance and is a computationally fast solution.

References

[1] A. N. Lam, A. T. Nguyen, H. A. Nguyen, and T. N. Nguyen, "Combining deep learning with information retrieval to localize buggy files for bug reports (n)," in ASE'15: Proc. of the International Conference on Automated Software Engineering, 2015.

[2] X. Huo, M. Li, and Z.-H. Zhou, "Learning unified features from natural and programming languages for locating buggy source code," in Proceedings of IJCAI'2016.

[3] A. Hindle, E. T. Barr, Z. Su, M. Gabel, and P. Devanbu, "On the naturalness of software," in ICSE'12: Proc. of the International Conference on Software Engineering, 2012.

[4] O. Abdel-Hamid, A.-r. Mohamed, H. Jiang, and G. Penn, "Applying convolutional neural networks concepts to hybrid NN-HMM model for speech recognition," in ICASSP'12: Proc. of the International Conference on Acoustics, Speech and Signal Processing, 2012.

[5] A. Krizhevsky, I. Sutskever, and G. E. Hinton, "ImageNet classification with deep convolutional neural networks," in NIPS'12: Proc. of the Advances in Neural Information Processing Systems, 2012.

[6] X. Zhang, J. Zhao, and Y. LeCun, "Character-level convolutional networks for text classification," in NIPS'15: Proc. of the Advances in Neural Information Processing Systems, 2015.

[7] V. Raychev, M. Vechev, and E. Yahav, "Code completion with statistical language models," in *ACM SIGPLAN Notices*, 49 (6) (ACM 2014), 419–428.

[8] V. Raychev, P. Bielik, and M. Vechev, "Probabilistic model for code with decision trees," in OOPSLA'16: Proc. of the International Conference on Object-Oriented Programming, Systems, Languages, and Applications, 2016.

[9] M. White, M. Tufano, C. Vendome, and D. Poshyvanyk, "Deep learning code fragments for code clone detection," in ASE'16: Proc. of the International Conference on Automated Software Engineering, 2016.

[10] L. Mou, G. Li, L. Zhang, T. Wang, and Z. Jin, "Convolutional neural networks over tree structures for programming language processing," arXiv preprint arXiv:1409.5718, 2014.

[11] C. Liu, X. Chen, E. C. Shin, M. Chen, and D. Song, "Latent attention for if-then program synthesis," in NIPS'16: Proc. of the Advances in Neural Information Processing Systems, 2016.

[12] S. Reed and N. De Freitas, "Neural programmer-interpreters," arXiv preprint arXiv:1511.06279, 2015.

[13] M. Balog, A. L. Gaunt, M. Brockschmidt, S. Nowozin, and D. Tarlow, "Deepcoder: Learning to write programs," arXiv preprint arXiv:1611.01989, 2016.

[14] C. Shu and H. Zhang, "Neural programming by example," in AAAI'17: Proc. of the AAAI Conference on Artificial Intelligence, 2017.

[15] X. Yang, D. Lo, X. Xia, Y. Zhang, and J. Sun, "Deep learning for just-in-time defect prediction," in QRS'15: Proc. of the International Conference on Software Quality, Reliability and Security, 2015.

[16] A. B. Farid, E. M. Fathy, A. S. Eldin, and, L. A. Abd-Elmegid. Software defect prediction using hybrid model (CBIL) of convolutional neural network (CNN) and bidirectional long short-term memory (Bi-LSTM). *PeerJ Computer Science*, 7 (2021), e739.

[17] C. Jin. Cross-project software defect prediction based on domain adaptation learning and optimization. *Expert Systems with Applications*, 171 (2021), 114637.

[18] S. Wang, T. Liu, L. Tan, Automatically learning semantic features for defect prediction. In: International conference on software engineering. IEEE; 2017. p. 297–308.

[19] Q. P. Hu, M. Xie, S.H. Ng, et al. Robust recurrent neural network modelling for software fault detection and correction prediction. *Reliability Engineering & System Safety*, 92 (3) (2007), 332–340

[20] L. Tian, A. Noore. Evolutionary neural network modelling for software cumulative failure time prediction. *Reliability Engineering & System Safety*, 87(1) (2005), 45–51.

[21] J. Iqbal. Software reliability growth models: A comparison of linear and exponential fault content functions for study of imperfect debugging situations. *Cogent Engineering*, 4 (1) (2017), 1286739.

[22] I. Saraf, & J. Iqbal. Generalized multi-release modelling of software reliability growth models from the perspective of two types of imperfect debugging and change point. *Quality and Reliability Engineering International*, 35(7) (2019), 2358–2370.

[23] I. Saraf, & J. Iqbal. Generalized software fault detection and correction modeling framework through imperfect debugging, error generation and change point. *International Journal of Information Technology*, 11(4) (2019), 751–757.

[24] S. Khurshid, J. Iqbal, I. A. Malik, & B. Yousuf. (2022). Modelling of NHPP Based Software Reliability Growth Model from the Perspective of Testing Coverage, Error Propagation and Fault Withdrawal Efficiency. *International Journal of Reliability, Quality and Safety Engineering*, 2250013.

[25] Habib, G., & Qureshi, S. Optimization and acceleration of convolutional neural networks: A survey. *Journal of King Saud University-Computer and Information Sciences,* 34(7) (2022), 4244–4268.

[26] G. Habib, & S. Qureshi. Biomedical Image Classification using CNN by Exploiting Deep Domain Transfer Learning. *International Journal of Computing and Digital Systems*, 10 (2020), 2–11.

[27] Habib, G., & Qureshi, S. (2021). Comparative Analysis of LBP Variants with the Introduction of New Radial and Circumferential Derivatives. *International Journal of Computing and Digital System*.

[28] Habib, G., & Qureshi, S. GAPCNN with HyPar: Global Average Pooling convolutional neural network with novel NNLU activation function and HYBRID parallelism. *Frontiers in Computational Neuroscience*, 16(2022), 1004988.

Chapter 4

Fixed-Design Local Polynomial Approach for Estimation and Hypothesis Testing of Reliability Measures

Chathuri L. Jayasinghe
Department of Statistics, Faculty of Applied Sciences,
University of Sri Jayewardenepura, Sri Lanka

This chapter presents two classes of non-parametric estimators, empirical and smooth non-parametric estimators, for three popular and important component reliability measures. The smooth estimators that were proposed by Jayasinghe utilizing a fixed-design local polynomial approach are presented, along with their practical and asymptotic properties and those of their empirical estimators based on simulation experiments. The chapter also discusses hypothesis testing procedures based on fixed-design local polynomial regression for comparing MRL and EIT functions of two populations. Cramer–von Mises- (CM-) and Kolmogorov–Smirnov- (KS-) type test statistics are presented. Decision rule constructions are demonstrated based on the critical values derived using the asymptotic distributions of the test statistics and bootstrapping approach.

DOI: 10.1201/9781032624983-4

4.1 Introduction

To avoid economic and human catastrophes and as a safety measure, systematic analyses are conducted by reliability practitioners to continuously monitor the current working status and verify the reliability of their engineered products and machines. This process involves estimation of reliability measures and their statistical comparison among different products, conditions, environments, etc. Thus it is crucial to use reliable estimators for estimating reliability measures and to employ efficient hypothesis tests in the process.

The standard method used in the estimation of reliability encompass a parametric procedure that entails assuming appropriate probability distributions for the lifetimes concerned. This approach provides reasonably accurate inferences if valid parametric distributions are incorporated. However, unreliable inferences mislead conclusions, and decisions will be reached when the models assumed are invalid. As observed by Jayasinghe (2013), the identification and suggestion of appropriate distributions for non–monotone reliability functions are cumbersome tasks. They can be seen as another disadvantage of the parametric method given the fact that non-monotone behaviors are more prominent than monotone models in real-life scenarios. Among non-monotone behaviors, the bathtub-shaped failure rate (BFR) and upside-down bathtub–shaped mean residual life (UBMRL) behaviors are observed as most common. It is viewed that various mixtures of parametric distributions are suitable to model such behaviors. Inferencing using the parametric approach particularly in such situations is time-consuming and cumbersome.

In these circumstances, reliability inferencing by adopting a non-parametric perspective offers a promising alternative. Empirical approach and the standard kernel density estimation are mainly utilized as the basis in most existing non-parametric estimators, which are both evaluated as less efficient. The empirical estimators, by design, tend to provide highly undersmoothed estimates. On the other hand, estimators produced based on conventional kernel density estimators have the effect of boundary bias and, in consequence, the quality of the estimation is hampered. However, construction of estimators utilizing the fixed-design local polynomial regression (LPR) model as proposed in Jayasinghe (2013) seems to produce a more efficient class of estimators since LPR automatically alleviates the boundary bias problem. Fixed-design LPR further enhances efficiency by incorporating information collected at a set of equally spaced design points. This technique was adopted by Jayasinghe (2013) in the construction of non-parametric hypothesis testing procedures. Consequently, these testing procedures, which compare a function throughout the whole support of the random variable, were utilized to compare two expected inactivity time (EIT) functions and two mean residual life (MRL) functions. This chapter presents an encapsulation of fixed-design LPR approach for estimation and hypothesis testing of reliability measures (Jayasinghe, 2013; Jayasinghe and Zeephongsekul, 2011, 2013a,b, 2017).

4.2 Popular Component Reliability Measures

To access the reliability of a component in a system, component reliability measures are utilized. Here we present three such measures: the reversed hazard rate (RHR) function, mean residual life (MRL) function, and expected inactivity time (EIT) function. Suppose that the probability density function (pdf) and the cumulative distribution function (cdf) of the failure time random variable T are denoted by $f(t)$ and $F(t)$, respectively. Then for any $t > a$, where $a = \inf\{t : F(t) > 0\}$, the RHR function, denoted by $r(t)$, is defined by the following equation:

$$r(t) = \frac{f(t)}{F(t)} \tag{4.1}$$

Then $r(t)dt$ is the conditional probability of a failure of the component in the interval $(t - dt, \ t)$ given that the failure had occurred in $[a,t]$ and assuming that $F(t)$ is absolutely continuous. Keilson and Sumita (1982) refer to the RHR function as the *dual failure function* since it is related to the hazard rate (HR) function $h(t)$ (also known as the failure rate function) defined by $h(t) = \frac{f(t)}{S(t)}$, where $S(t) = 1 - F(t)$ is the survival function. This is because, if $Y = -T$ has a hazard rate $h(-t)$ on $(-t_2, -t_1)$, then T has the RHR on the interval of support $(t_1, t_2) : -\infty < t_1 \le t_2 < \infty$ (cf. Block et al., 1998). In the context of reliability, however, this duality is of no relevance since in reliability the lifetime random variable T is a non-negative random variable. Hence, the properties and consequently estimation of the RHR function of a non-negative random variable with an infinite support cannot be obtained from the corresponding HR function by applying the notion of duality. Analysis of the RHR function also facilitates the revealing of unique information regarding left-censored observations, making it an important measure in reliability and related areas.

Apart from reliability, the RHR function is also prominent in forensic and actuarial sciences to get an indication regarding the time of occurrence of a death of an individual for left-censored observations. RHR has been applied in finance; e.g., see Eeckhoudt and Gollier (1995), Block et al. (1998), Kijima and Ohnishi (1999), Li and Xu (2008). Shaked and Shanthikumar (2007) discuss orderings based on RHR of a k-out-of-n system and its connection to parallel systems.

The properties of the RHR function has been discussed in depth by Block et al. (1998), Chandra and Roy (2001); Finkelstein (2002), Nanda et al. (2003), Jayasinghe and Zeephongsekul (2012), Jayasinghe (2013). One important property is that an increasing RHR (IRHR) is not possible with a non–negative random variable and hence will be the case in all RHRs in reliability (refer to Block et al., 1998 for a proof). Further classifications of RHR function can be given as follows. A non–negative random variable said to have a decreasing reversed hazard rate (DRHR) if its RHR function is decreasing in $t > a$ and is said to possess a decreasing reversed hazard rate on average (DRHA) if $\frac{1}{t}\int_a^t r(u)\,du$ is decreasing in $t > a$. Further classifications include increasing reversed mean residual Life (IRMR), increasing reversed variance residual life (IRVR) (cf. Nanda et al. , 2003). Further from Eq. (3.1), it is apparent that $r(t)$ converges to $f(t)$ as $t \to \infty$.

Another measure that has grabbed the attention of reliability practitioners in recent times is the expected inactivity time (EIT) function, defined as

$$e(t) = E(t - T \mid T < t) = \begin{cases} \int_a^t \dfrac{F(u)}{F(t)}\,du & \text{if } F(t) > 0, \\ 0, & \text{otherwise.} \end{cases} \tag{4.2}$$

The EIT function gives the expected value or the mean of the elapsed time since the failure or occurrence of the event of interest of a certain component/system given that it has already failed by time t. RHR measure, discussed previously, is closely related to EIT. It is observed that, if the failure time random variable has a DRHR, then $e(t)$ is increasing in $t \in (a,b)$; where $-\infty < a < b < \infty$. Furthermore, the following relationship between RHR and EIT is evident if $e(t)$ is differentiable (Kundu et al., 2010):

$$r(t) = \frac{1 - e'(t)}{e(t)} \tag{4.3}$$

Note that as explained earlier, $r(t)$ provides information regarding event occurrence at a instantaneous time before local point t, whereas EIT function considers the full conditional expected inactivity time prior to t. Thus, EIT is seen as a more descriptive measure of the aging process than RHR is.

Recent applications of EIT are discussed by Li and Xu (2006), Badia and Berrade (2008), Ortega (2009), while Badia and Berrade (2008) also review its properties with mixtures of distributions. In analyses of different maintenance policies in reliability, EIT has been found to be useful (see, e.g., Finkelstein, 2002). EIT properties relevant to components in a parallel system and their orderings have been investigated by Kundu and Nanda (2010). Further, stochastic-comparisons-based EIT can be found in Kayid and Ahmad (2004), Ahmad and Kayid (2005), Li and Xu (2006). How the measure can be used in a discrete lifetime context to determine reliability of a system is provided by Goliforushani and Asadi (2008). Estimation of incubation times of diseases using EIT has been demonstrated by, e.g., Keiding and Gill (1990), Keiding (1991), Andersen et al.(1993), Jayasinghe and Zeephongsekul (2013b). To estimate times of occurrences of events such as time of death in forensic science and life insurance, EIT function has been applied (e.g., Gupta and Nanda, 2001). Applications of this reliability measure in risk theory and econometrics are given, e.g., by Eeckhoudt and Gollier (1995) and Kijima and Ohnishi (1999). EIT ordering is further discussed by Li and Xu (2006) and, in particular, Ortega (2009), which obtain the RHR order characterisations based on the EIT order.

Properties of the EIT function have been discussed thoroughly by Asadi and Berred (2011) and Goliforushani and Asadi (2008). Assuming that $a = 0$, by Eq. (4.2), note that

$$e(t) = t - \int_0^t \frac{uf(u)}{F(t)} du \qquad (4.4)$$

It is then apparent that $0 < e(t) < t$. Also, if μ is the mean, then $e(b) = b - \frac{\mu}{F(b)}$, and further $t - e(t)$ is non-decreasing in t.

The third component reliability measure we intend to discuss is the popular mean residual life (MRL) function. Given that the component has survived up to age t or the event has not occurred by time t, the average or the expected value of its residual life or remaining time to event, i.e., $T - t$ is:

$$m(t) = E(T - t | T \rangle t) = \begin{cases} \dfrac{\int_t^\infty \bar{F}(y) dy}{\bar{F}(t)} & \text{if } \bar{F}(t) > 0 \\ 0 & \text{otherwise} \end{cases} \qquad (4.5)$$

provided that $E(T) < \infty$.

MRL function is associated with the well-known hazard rate function $h(t)$ (cf. Finkelstein, 2002):

$$h(t) = \frac{1 + m'(t)}{m(t)} \qquad (4.6)$$

However, $h(t)$ is only an instantaneous rate concentrated at a local point t, whereas the MRL function accounts for the full conditional expected survival time after t. Thus MRL provides more descriptive information related to the aging process than $h(t)$. The MRL function is a popularly used reliability measure in studies conducted in the contexts of non-repairable and repairable technical systems

(Reinertsen, 1996, Siddiqui, 1994). Estimation of burn-in time of a component or a system using MRL has been discussed in Block and Savits (1997), Park (1985), Watson (1964). In proposing and implementing warranty servicing strategies involving minimal and imperfect repairs, Yun et al. (2008) involved MRL function. When analyzing and testing tensile strength of engineered materials, Guess et al. (2005) demonstrated how MRL function can be utilized.

Rajarshia and Rajarshib (1988) point out that non-monotone MRL models are more realistic than monotone models. As previously pointed out, it is not easy to obtain non–monotone (e.g., bathtub–shaped) MRL models from mixtures of standard lifetime distributions such as exponential, Weibull, or gamma (Wondmagegnehu et al., 2005), and it has been observed that some parametric models do not behave as predicted in real life [e.g., see Block and Joe (1997), Klutke et al. (2003), Wondmagegnehu et al. (2005)].

The first non-parametric estimator for MRL function, a simple empirical estimator, was introduced by Yang (1978). It was widely applied and studied in the literature due to its simplicity. Next, several kernel-density-based estimators were then proposed; for a review, see Guillamon et al. (1998). The estimator introduced by Abdous and Berred (2005) uses an integrated weighted local linear smoothing technique to smooth the empirical estimator introduced by Yang (1978). These estimators, particularly the one proposed by Abdous and Berred (2005) perform exceptionally well in estimating monotonically decreasing mean residual life (DMRL) functions but was observed to be poor in non-DMRL scenarios.

Due to the unique importance of RHR and EIT functions and the limitation imposed by the parametric approach, Jayasinghe (2013) proposed several non-parametric-approach-based estimators which included an empirical estimator and a smooth estimator for each of these measures. Further, to efficiently model non-DMRL functions, Jayasinghe (2013) introduced another empirical estimator and a smooth estimator. In the following sections, we present these empirical estimators and smooth estimators, respectively.

4.2.1 Empirical Estimators

Let $T_1, \ldots, T_N$ be a random sample of size N from a distribution with pdf as $f(t)$ of the life random variable T. Let b_i, $i = 1, 2, \ldots, n$ be bins in an equally spaced mesh over $[a, b]$ with $a = \inf\{t : F(t) > 0\}$ and $b = \sup\{t : F(t) < 1\}$ with bin centers, t_i. An empirical estimator for RHR function at t_i, as defined by Jayasinghe (2013), is given by

$$r_N(t_i) = \frac{f_i}{\Delta \sum_{j=1}^{i} f_j} \qquad (4.7)$$

where f_i is the frequency of the bin b_i and $\Delta = \dfrac{b-a}{n}$ refers to the bin width.

Here, $\Delta \equiv \Delta_n$ is a function of n and $\Delta \to 0$ as $n \to \infty$. It was observed that the performance of this estimator is highly influenced by the choice of the bin width, and Jayasinghe and Zeephongsekul (2011) provide a good review of the methods that can effectively determine an appropriate Δ. Further, it is reasonable to assume that the number of bins $n \equiv n(N)$ and $n \to \infty$ as $N \to \infty$.

Suppose that $T_{(1)}, T_{(2)}, \ldots, T_{(N)}$ denote order statistics of the sample $T_1, T_2, \ldots, T_N$. Then, when no ties are evident, the empirical estimator for cdf is given by

$$
F_N(t) = \begin{cases} 0 & \text{for } t < T_{(1)}, \\ \dfrac{j}{N} & \text{for } T_{(j)} \le t < T_{(j+1)} \text{ and } j = 1, \ldots, N-1 \\ 1 & \text{for } t \ge T_{(N)}. \end{cases} \tag{4.8}
$$

Then, for any $t \ge T_{(1)}$, an empirical estimator for EIT can be derived by substituting $F_N(t)$ for $F(t)$ in Eq. (4.2) (cf. Jayasinghe (2013)):

$$
e_N(t) = \sum_{j=1}^{N} \left\{ t - \bar{T}_j \right\} \mathbf{I}_{\left[T_{(j)}, T_{(j+1)} \right)}(t) \tag{4.9}
$$

where $\bar{T}_j = \dfrac{1}{j} \sum_{k=1}^{j} T_{(k)}$ for $j = 1, \ldots, N$ and $T_{(N+1)} = \sup\{t : F(t) < 1\} = b$.

When ties are present, the empirical estimator will be modified as follows. Suppose that $\tilde{T}_{(1)} < \tilde{T}_{(2)} < \tilde{T}_{(3)} \ldots$ are the distinct ordered times of failure in the sample, and let a_i = number of tied observations at time $\tilde{T}_{(i)}$ and

$$
b_i = \sum_{j=1}^{i} a_j \text{ for } i = 1, \ldots, l < N
$$

Then the empirical estimator for EIT, adjusted for ties, is given by

$$
\tilde{e}_l(t) = \sum_{j=1}^{l} \left\{ t - \frac{1}{b_j} \sum_{i=1}^{j} a_i \tilde{T}_{(i)} \right\} \mathbf{I}_{\left[\tilde{T}_{(j)}, \tilde{T}_{(j+1)} \right)}(t) \tag{4.10}
$$

Note that, when there are no ties, i.e., when $N = l$, $a_i = 1$, and $b_i = \sum_{j=1}^{i} a_j = i$,

then $\tilde{e}_l(t)$ becomes analogous to $e_N(t)$ as would be expected.

Finally, the empirical estimator for MRL function at t_i proposed by Jayasinghe (2013):

$$m_N\left(t_i\right) = \frac{\Delta \sum_{j=i}^{n}\left(N+1-F_j\right)}{\left(N+1-F_i\right)} \qquad (4.11)$$

In Eq. (4.11), $F_i = \sum_{j=1}^{i} f_j$ where f_i is the frequency of the bin b_i and Δ is the binwidth. In both numerator and the denominator, the term $N+1$ is presented instead of N to avoid $m_N\left(t_n\right) = 0$ in the numerator and to avoid $m_N\left(t_n\right)$ becoming undefined in the denominator.

It can be shown using asymptotic theory that the empirical estimators proposed here for the RHR, EIT, and MRL functions hold the following properties: each empirical estimator is asymptotically unbiased, variance of each empirical estimator converges to zero asymptotically, and the covariance of each empirical estimator converges to zero asymptotically. For a detailed discussion on asymptotics and proofs, the reader is referred to, in general, Jayasinghe (2013)); RHR context: Jayasinghe and Zeephongsekul (2011); EIT context: Jayasinghe and Zeephongsekul (2013b); and MRL context: Jayasinghe and Zeephongsekul (2013a).

4.2.2 Fixed-Design Local Polynomial Estimators

In this section, we introduce fixed-design local polynomial estimators for any reliability function $g(t)$, at *any* point $t \in [a,b)$ where $a = \inf\left\{t : F(t) > 0\right\}$ and $b = \sup\left\{t : F(t) < 1\right\}$ using the fixed-design non-parametric regression concepts discussed in Chapter 2 of Jayasinghe (2013). The local polynomial estimator of order p for any reliability function $g(t)$ [here $g(t)$ can be any one of $r(t)$, $e(t)$, or $m(t)$ functions], denoted by $\hat{g}(t; p)$, is given by

$$\hat{g}(t; p) = \mathbf{e}_1^T (\mathbf{T}_p^T \mathbf{W}_n \mathbf{T}_p)^{-1} \mathbf{T}_p^T \mathbf{W}_n \mathbf{Y}_n \qquad 4.(12)$$

where $\mathbf{e}_1^T = (1,0,0,\ldots,0)_{(p+1)\times1}$,

$$\mathbf{W}_n = diag\{K_h(t_i - t)\}_{1\leq i\leq n},$$

$$\mathbf{Y}_n = (y_1 \quad y_2 \quad \cdots \quad y_n)^T,$$

and

$$
\mathbf{T}_p =
\begin{pmatrix}
1 & (t_1 - t) & \cdots & (t_1 - t)^p \\
1 & (t_2 - t) & \cdots & (t_2 - t)^p \\
\vdots & \vdots & & \vdots \\
1 & (t_n - t) & \cdots & (t_n - t)^p
\end{pmatrix}
$$

Here, $Y_n^T = g_N(t)^T = \left(g_N(t_1), g_N(t_2), \ldots, g_N(t_n)\right)_{n\times1}$, where $g_N(t_i)$ is the empirical estimate of $g(.)$ at t_i. Furthermore, the local polynomial estimator for the jth derivative of the function $g(t)$, $\hat{g}^{(j)}(t;p)$, can also be obtained from the fitted fixeddesign LPR model. The reader is referred to Jayasinghe (2013) for a detailed discussion.

The choice of value of p, the order of the local polynomial, is directly associated with the presumed shape of the reliability function $g(t)$ under consideration with special reference given to the behavior of the lifetime random variable when presuming. It is reasonable that we opt for $p = 0,1$ when the presumed shape of the function is a flat or a non–sloped function, whereas for a sloped function, $p = 1$ is recommendable. Higher orders, i.e., $p = 2,\ 3\ldots$, on the other hand, should typically be used if the function consists of peaks or valleys, as also mentioned by Fan and Gijbels (1995). In the current context, the reliability functions we are concerned with consist of functions of various behaviors. Hence local linear (LL), local quadratic (LQ), and local cubic (LC) estimators for the function $g(t)$ were obtained by letting $p = 1,\ 2$ and 3 in Eq. (4.12), respectively. In addition to estimation of the reliability measures, indirect estimators for RHR and hazard rate can be derived noting their relationships with EIT and MRL, respectively, as given by Eqs. (4.3) and (4.6) by getting the corresponding first derivative estimates of EIT or MRL. For example, an indirect estimate of hazard rate at time t can be obtained through

$$\hat{h}(t) = \frac{\hat{m}'(t,p)+1}{\hat{m}(t,p)} \tag{4.13}$$

where $\hat{m}(t,p)$ and $\hat{m}(t,p)$ are the local polynomial estimate of $m(t)$ and the local polynomial estimate of $m'(t)$, respectively. It is a must to mention here that the estimator given in Eq. (4.13) for the hazard rate function is not analogous to the local linear estimator for the hazard rate function introduced by Bagkavos and Patil (2008).

4.2.2.1 Fixed-Design Local Polynomial Estimators: Asymptotic Properties

Under certain assumptions it can be shown that the local polynomial estimators presented in Section 4.2.2 are asymptotically unbiased and consistent. It has been observed that bias of the fixed-design LPR estimator is dependent on the order of the local polynomial; e.g., see Jayasinghe (2013). The following assumptions are required in the derivations of the asymptotic properties:

A1 As $N \to \infty$, the bandwidth, $h \to 0$ and $\Delta = o(h)$.

A2 The kernel function $K(\cdot)$ is a bounded, symmetric, real-valued measurable function. Additionally, it possesses the following properties: $\int K(u)du = 1$, $K''(u)$ is continuous and absolutely integrable, $\int u^i K(u)du = 0$ for all i odd and $\int u^i K(u)du = \mu_i < \infty$ for all i even.

A3 The reliability function $g(t)$ is bounded, continuously differentiable up to order $p+2$, where p is the order of the local polynomial. $g'(\cdot)$ is bounded.

A4 As $N \to \infty$, $\Delta N \to \infty$.

A5 As $N \to \infty$, $Nh \to \infty$.

A6 $F(\cdot)$ is continuous, and the first derivative exists and is bounded.

A7 $F^N(t) = 0(N^{-1})$, $\bar{F}^N(t) = 0(\bar{F}N^{-1})$, $F^N(t) = 0(\bar{F}N^{-1})$, and $\bar{F}^N(t) = 0(\Delta N^{-1})$ as $N \to \infty$.

A8 As $N \to \infty$, $Nh^2 \to 0$.

The following asymptotic results can be derived for these fixed-design LPR estimators:

■ Under assumptions **A1–A8**, it can be shown that $\hat{g}(t;p)$ is an asymptotically unbiased and consistent estimator of the reliability function $g(t)$, i.e., $E(\hat{g}(t;p)) \to g(t)$ and $\text{plim}_{N\to\infty} \hat{g}(t;p) = g(t)$, respectively.

■ Under the same assumptions, the standardized $\hat{g}(t;p)$, i.e. $\dfrac{\hat{g}(t;p) - E\left(\hat{g}(t;p)\right)}{\sqrt{Var\left(\hat{g}(t;p)\right)}}$,

converges in distribution to the normal $N(0,1)$ random variable.

The reader is referred to Chapters 3–5 of Jayasinghe (2013) for specific proofs related to RHR, EIT, and MRL local polynomial estimators, respectively.

4.2.2.2 Dealing with a Randomly Censored Dataset

Let $X_1, X_2, \ldots, X_N$ be the i.i.d. random variables representing lifetime random variables of N components, and let $C_1, C_2, \ldots, C_N$ denote their random censoring times, which are also i.i.d. Here, we will also assume that X and C are independent. Let us then denote their observed randomly right-censored data by T_i's and note that they are actually $T_i = min(X_i, C_i)$ with indicator $\delta_i = \mathbf{I}_{\{X \le C\}}$ indicating whether the ith observation has or has not been censored. Then the observed survival data (T_i, δ_i) for $i = 1, 2, \ldots, N$ are a random sample from (T, δ). Furthermore, let $\bar{F}(\cdot)$ and $f(\cdot)$ denote the survival function and pdf of lifetime random variable X and $\bar{Z}(\cdot)$ and let $z(\cdot)$ denote the survival function and pdf of the censoring random variable C, respectively. Then the RHR and EIT functions in the presence of right-censoring are defined by

$$r_c(x) = \frac{f(x)\bar{Z}(x)}{1 - \bar{F}(x)\bar{Z}(x)} \qquad (4.14)$$

and

$$e_c(x) = \int_0^x \frac{1 - \bar{F}(u)\bar{Z}(u)}{1 - \bar{F}(x)\bar{Z}(x)} du \qquad (4.15)$$

respectively, where it is assumed $\bar{F}(x)\bar{Z}(x) < 1$. In the context of MRL function, which accounts for right-censoring, the function can be redefined as

$$M_c(x) = \int_x^\infty \frac{\bar{F}(u)\bar{Z}(u)}{\bar{F}(x)\bar{Z}(x)} du \qquad (4.16)$$

provided $\bar{F}(x)\bar{Z}(x) < 1$. To estimate $r_c(x)$, $e_c(x)$, and $M_c(x)$, the local polynomial estimators adjusted for censoring introduced by Fan et al. (1996) can be used.

Another approach is to introduce an empirical estimator which can accommodate right-censoring based on, for example, the Kaplan–Meier estimator for survival function and then use it to estimate the function under consideration at bin centers and consequently solve it as a fixed-design non-parametric regression problem and proceed as suggested for a complete data case. For example, in the context of MRL function, an empirical estimator for $M_c(x)$ can be constructed based on Kaplan–Meier estimator:

$$M_{c,N}(t_i) = \Delta \sum_{j=i}^{n} \frac{\prod_{k \le j} \left(\dfrac{N - F_k}{N + 1 - F_k} \right)^{\delta_k}}{\prod_{l \le i} \left(\dfrac{N - F_l}{N + 1 - F_l} \right)^{\delta_l}} \tag{4.17}$$

to approximate $M_c(t_i)$, for $i = 1, \dots n$. Then, based on bivariate data $\left(t_i, M_{c,N}(t_i) \right)$, $i = 1, \dots, n$, the estimation of MRL function at a given point $t \in (a,b)$ can be formulated as a fixed design non-parametric regression problem in the presence of a censored data set.

4.2.2.3 *Optimal Bin Width and Bandwidth Selection*

As demonstrated theoretically, both bin width and bandwidth are important counterparts in determining the performance of the proposed local polynomial estimators of the reliability measures. While estimation of reliability function through its empirical estimator at bin centers requires a bin width, the bandwidth improves the accuracy of the local polynomial estimate of the reliability function at *any point t*.

For effective determination of the optimal bin width required for computation of an empirical estimator at bin centers, we need to employ methods that effectively select the bin width considering the properties and characteristics of the empirical distribution of the data. It is recommended that the optimal bin width should consider both mathematical and practical performance as well as simplicity and consequently lead to a visualization of the essential characteristics of the data but without giving too much importance to the data itself to avoid overfitting. It has been observed that most bin width selection methods provide an optimal number of bins, $\hat{n} \propto N^{1/3}$. For a detailed discussion on methods available, the reader is referred to Jayasinghe and Zeephongsekul (2011).

To address the problem of optimal bandwidth selection, we present two methods: a "plug-in" method and the Akaike information criterion correction (AICC) method. The plug-in method produces an optimal global bandwidth that minimizes the AMISE of the LPR estimator. These methods were determined by Jayasinghe (2013) and Jayasinghe and Zeephongsekul (2011, 2013a,b) as highly efficient in estimating the RHR, EIT, and MRL functions through extensive simulation studies. The mean integrated squared error of $\hat{g}(t;p)$ is given by

$$MISE\left(\widehat{M}(t;p)\right) = \int;\left\{Bias^2\left(\hat{g}(t;p)\right) + Var\left(\hat{g}(t;p)\right)\right\}\, w(t)\, dt$$

where $w(x)$ denotes an appropriately chosen weight function. Then MISE is approximated by AMISE by assuming that, as $N \to \infty$, $\dfrac{\Delta}{h} \to 0$, and $h \to 0$. As noted in Section 4.2.2.1 the bias of the fixed design local polynomial estimator of the reliability fucntion $\hat{g}(t;p)$ depends on the odd- or evenness of p, the order of the local polynomial. Therefore, the minimum value of AMISE of $\hat{g}(t;p)$ can be expressed as

$$\hat{h}_{AMISE} = \begin{cases} (Q(p+1)\,\Theta)^{1/(2p+3)}, & \text{for odd } p \\ (Q(p+2)\,\Theta)^{1/(2p+5)}, & \text{for even } p \end{cases} \tag{4.18}$$

where $Q(a) = [(a)!]^2/((2a)[\int u^a\, K_0^*(u)\,du]^2 \int [g^{(a)}(t)]^2\, w(t)\,dt)$ and

$$\Theta = \Delta \int [K_0^*(u)]^2\, du \int \sigma^2(t)w(t)dt$$

$$w(t) = \sum_{i=1}^{n} \delta_{t_i}(t) \tag{4.19}$$

where δ_x is the *Dirac* measure defined for any bounded set A by

$$\delta_x(A) = \begin{cases} 1, & \text{if } x \in A \\ 0, & \text{otherwise} \end{cases} \tag{4.20}$$

and $t_i, i = 1,2\ldots,n$ are the bin centers. With this choice as the weight function, $\int \sigma^2(t)w(t)\,dt$ can be approximated as a sum of $\sigma^2(t_i), i = 1,2\ldots,n$. A further simplification of the substitution for the preceding integral would be to assume that variance is homogeneous; then approximate the sum by $n\,\sigma^2 \simeq n\,s^2\left(g_N(t_i)\right)$, where $s^2\left(g_N\left(t_i\right)\right)$ is the sample variance of $g_N\left(t_i\right)$'s where $g_N\left(t_i\right)$ is the empirical estimate of the reliability function $g(.)$ at t_i.

The extension of Akaike's information criterion in the context of bandwidth selection in non-parametric regression was introduced by Hurvich et al. (1998). This improved version of the criterion, Akaike's information criterion corrected (AICC), has been demonstrated as capable of avoiding the large variability and tendency to undersmooth as observed with classical bandwidth selectors such as the cross-validation variants. In the current context of our local polynomial estimators, the following function is minimized with respect to h

$$AICC = \log\left(\hat{\epsilon}^2\right) + \frac{2\left\{tr\left(\tilde{H}\right)+1\right\}}{n - tr\left(\tilde{H}\right) - 2} + 1 \tag{4.21}$$

to find the optimal bandwidth, where $\hat{\epsilon}^2 = \dfrac{g_n(t)^T(I-\tilde{H})^T\left(I-\tilde{H}\right)g_n(t)}{n}$ and $\tilde{H} = T_p(T_p^T W_n T_p)^{-1}T_p^T W_n$, i.e., the hat matrix of the fixed design regression model.

4.2.3 *Performance of Proposed Estimators*

The practical performance of the demonstrated RHR, EIT, and MRL fixed-design LPR estimators has been evaluated as highly efficient in estimating RHR, EIT, and MRL functions through extensive simulation studies and real-life examples. In the simulation studies, various lifetime distributions with different parameters were considered to facilitate evaluation of the performance for functions with varying behaviors.

In the context of RHR LPR estimator evaluation, simulated samples with varying sizes from Weibull, exponential, gamma, lognormal, normal distributions were chosen to depict DRHRs with varying decreasing patterns. The average mean squared error (AMSE) criterion was employed to compare the estimated values with the true values. The results as given in Jayasinghe and Zeephongsekul (2011) indicate that AMISE-based bandwidth selection method, together with proposed local polynomial estimators, generally provide good estimates for $r(t)$. Results of all the distributions except normal distribution suggest that higher-order polynomial estimators (LQ and LC) provide significantly better estimates of the RHR function, especially when the sample size is small.

Simulation study related to EIT estimators was performed by Jayasinghe and Zeephongsekul (2013b) using samples from uniform, exponential, normal, Weibull, gamma, lognormal, and beta distributions, and the results indicated that these non-parametric estimators perform very favorably when compared to the empirical estimator. The results also indicate that in some instances it is worth considering higher-order local polynomial estimators, especially when the sample size is small.

The simulation study and real-life example results related to MRL estimators also indicated that the proposed estimators perform significantly better in estimating MRL functions, particularly MRL models with constant, bathtub-shaped, upside-down bathtub-shaped MRL functions compared to the empirical estimator by Yang (1978) and the kernel estimator by Guillamon et al. (1998).

4.3 Non-parametric Hypothesis Tests for Comparing Reliability Functions

In reliability we are often required to conduct comparisons between reliability measures of two (or more) aging processes. Use of a statistical hypothesis test to conduct such a comparison will allow a valid and a reliable conclusion. The hypothesis we are attempting to test in this scenario is

$$H_o : g_1(t) = g_2(t) \qquad for\ t \in [a,b),$$

against the alternative

$$H_1 : g_1(t) \geqslant g_2(t) \quad for\ t \in [a,b) \text{ with strict inequality for some } t \in [a,b),$$

where $g_1(.)$ and $g_2(.)$ denote any reliability measure of population 1 and 2, respectively. Note that the null hypothesis H_0 being tested is a hypothesis of equality between two reliability functions for all $t \in [a,b)$. While an extensive amount of literature is devoted to discussion of parametric and non-parametric hypothesis tests that are constructed to compare survival functions of two or more processes (e.g., see Lee and Wang, 2003, for a comprehensive survey), non-parametric hypothesis testing procedures for comparisons of MRL and EIT curves are scarce. In the literature, various non-parametric tests have been proposed to compare different functions related to lifetime random variables. For example, tests have been introduced to conduct comparisons of lifetime distribution functions by Andersen et al. (1993); Cao and Van Keilegom (2006), for hazard functions by Chikkagouder and Shuster (1974); Kochar (1979, 1981); Cheng (1985), while Berger et al. (1988); Aly (1997) introduce in the context of MRL functions of two populations. However, none exists in the context of EIT functions apart from the testing procedures that we intend to present in this chapter. The non-parametric hypothesis testing procedures that we intend to discuss here were proposed by Jayasinghe (2013); Jayasinghe and Zeephongsekul (2017). These involve fixed-design local polynomial regression to statistically compare the EIT and MRL functions of two populations. In Section

4.3.1 of this chapter, we consider the EIT function comparison tests, while Section 4.3.2 is concerned with MRL function comparison tests. The methodology of constructing the corresponding test statistics, decision rules, and asymptotic properties of the proposed test statistics will be presented for each testing procedure.

4.3.1 Statistical Comparison of Expected Inactivity Time Functions of Two Populations

The EIT function given by Eq. (4.2) of two or more aging processes, when making decisions regarding reliability, may require a statistical comparison. This allows a comparison between mean times that has elapsed since the occurrence of a certain event, given that it has occurred before time t of the aging processes concerned. In the tests introduced by Jayasinghe (2013); Jayasinghe and Zeephongsekul (2017) that permit EIT comparison of two aging processes: $e_i(t)$'s, $i = 1,2$, the null hypothesis is

$$H_0 : e_1(t) = e_2(t) \quad \text{for all } t \in [a,b] \tag{4.22}$$

vs. the alternative hypothesis

$$H_1 : e_1(t) \geqslant e_2(t) \text{ for } t \in [a,b] \text{ with strict inequality for some } t \in [a,b]. \tag{4.23}$$

It must be noted here that $a = \max(a_1, a_2)$ and $b = \min(b_1, b_2)$, with $a_i = \inf\{t : F_i(t) > 0\}$ and $b_i = \sup\{t : F_i(t) < 1\}$, for $i = 1,2$, where $F_i(t)$ is the cumulative distribution function of the ith aging process.

The tests proposed by Jayasinghe (2013); Jayasinghe and Zeephongsekul (2017) are based on the following weighted measure of deviation between $e_1(t)$ and $e_2(t)$:

$$\rho(t) = \sqrt{F_1(t).F_2(t)}\left(e_1(t) - e_2(t)\right). \tag{4.24}$$

The weight is dependent on $F_1(t)$ and $F_2(t)$, and these represent the proportions failed by t of the aging processes 1 and 2, respectively, and suppose T_{1i} for $i = 1,...n_1$ and T_{2i} for $i = 1,...n_2$ are samples from the two aging processes. Two test statistics were considered for testing the null hypothesis in (4.22): the Cramér–von Mises and Kolmogorov–Smirnov statistics. The Cramér–von Mises type test statistic is

$$T_{CM}(\rho) = \sqrt{\frac{n_1 n_2}{n_1 + n_2}} \int_a^b \hat{\rho}(t; \rho) dt \tag{4.25}$$

and the Kolmogorov–Smirnov type test statistic:

$$T_{KS}(p) = \sqrt{\frac{n_1 n_2}{n_1 + n_2}} \sup_{a \le t \le b} \hat{\rho}(t; p) \tag{4.26}$$

The term $\hat{\rho}(t; p)$ in these two test statistics refers to the pth order local polynomial estimator of the function $\rho(t)$, defined in Eq. (4.24) based on a fixed-design non-parametric regression model as introduced in Jayasinghe (2013). To fit the fixed-design model, an equally spaced mesh, $t_1, t_2, ..., t_N$, over $[a, b]$ is set with

$$t_i = a + (i-1)\Delta \tag{4.27}$$

where the bin width $\Delta = \dfrac{b-a}{N-1}$ and $N = n_1 + n_2$. Then, the pth order local polynomial estimator of this function is given by

$$\hat{\rho}(t; p) = e_1^T (T_p^T W_N T_p)^{-1} T_p^T W_N Y_N, \tag{4.28}$$

where e_1^T, W_N, T_p are as defined in Section 4.2.2 and

$$Y_N^T = \{y_i\}_{1 \le i \le N} = \{\sqrt{\hat{F}_1(t_i) \cdot \hat{F}_2(t_i)} (\hat{e}_1(t_i) - \hat{e}_2(t_i))\}_{1 \le i \le N} \tag{4.29}$$

Here, $\hat{e}_i(t)$, $\hat{F}_i(t)$ for $i = 1, 2$ are the empirical EIT and empirical cumulative distribution functions of the two processes, which can be estimated using estimators introduced in Section 4.2.1.

Note that Eq. (4.28) can be rewritten:

$$\hat{\rho}(t; p) = \sum_{i=1}^{N} L_N \left(\frac{t_i - t}{b} \right) y_i \tag{4.30}$$

where $L_N(u) = e_1^T S_N^{-1} \{1, uh, ..., \dfrac{(uh)^p\}^T K(u)}{b}$ is a symmetric weight function with h as the bandwith and any kernel function satisfies assumption **A2** listed under Section 4.2.2.1 is denoted as $K(.)$. Here, t_i is the ith design point in the grid associated with the fixed design regression model where $S_N = T_p^T W_N T_p$. The test statistic $T_{CM}(p)$ is approximated by a Riemann sum, which runs over z_j, $j = 1,..., M$' with grid width d, the distance between two consecutive points.

$$T_{CM}(p) \approx d \sqrt{\frac{n_1 n_2}{n_1 + n_2}} \sum_{j=1}^{M} \sum_{i=1}^{N} L_N \left(\frac{t_i - z_j}{h} \right) y_i \qquad (4.31)$$

Similarly, test statistic $T_{KS}(p)$ is approximated using a similar approach:

$$T_{KS}(p) \approx \sqrt{\frac{n_1 n_2}{n_1 + n_2}} \; \max_{j=1,...,M} \sum_{i=1}^{N} L_N \left(\frac{t_i - z_j}{h} \right) y_i \qquad (4.32)$$

Further variations of the test statistics can be derived by changing the order p in the preceding formulas, i.e., LL, LQ, and LC, CM, and KS test statistics can be obtained by letting $p = 1, 2, 3$, respectively. The choice of order mentioned in Section 4.2.2 is dependent on the behavior of the functions under comparison. To get an indication, a visual aid (a graph of $d \times \hat{p}(z_j; p)$ vs z_j) can be produced using LPR estimators and utilized. This will facilitate the researcher or the reliability practitioner to study the deviation between the estimated EIT functions of the two samples over the joint domain of the lifetime random variable under consideration before conducting the test. To select the bandwidths required when computing the test statistics, the AICC method is proposed due to its simplicity and efficacy. The test statistics proposed can be modified to accommodate right censored data:

$$\hat{p}^*(t; p) = e_1^T (T_p^T W_N T_p)^{-1} T_p^T W_N Y_N^* \qquad (4.33)$$

where $Y_N^* = \{y_i^*\}_{1 \leqslant i \leqslant N} = \left\{ \sqrt{\left(1 - \widehat{\overline{F}}_1^*(t_i)\right) \cdot \left(1 - \widehat{\overline{F}}_2^*(t_i)\right)} \left(\hat{e}_1^*(t_i) - \hat{e}_2^*(t_i)\right) \right\}_{1 \leqslant i \leqslant N}$ and e_1, T_p, and W_N is as defined in Eq. (4.28). The survival functions were estimated in the two samples separately by Kaplan–Meier estimators which are denoted by $\widehat{\overline{F}}_1^*(t_i)$ and $\widehat{\overline{F}}_2^*(t_i)$. Consequently, we have Kaplan–Meier type empirical estimators of the two samples: $\hat{e}_1^*(t_i) = \int_{t_i}^{\infty} \frac{\left(1 - \widehat{\overline{F}}_1^*(u)\right)}{\left(1 - \widehat{\overline{F}}_1^*(t_i)\right)} du$ and $\hat{e}_2^*(t_i) = \int_{t_i}^{\infty} \frac{\left(1 - \widehat{\overline{F}}_2^*(u)\right)}{\left(1 - \widehat{\overline{F}}_2^*(t_i)\right)} du$

4.3.1.1 Critical Values of the Test Statistics

The critical value of each variation of the test is required to be determined, which subsequently will allow us to construct the decision rules of the test. This requires derivation of the asymptotic distribution of the test statistics. Critical values based on asymptotic distribution is recommended when sample sizes are large. When samples are not large, a procedure based on bootstrapping is proposed by Jayasinghe (2013).

4.3.1.1.1 Asymptotic Properties

Define the Gaussian process:

$$Y(t) = \sqrt{\frac{n_2}{n_1 + n_2}} \sqrt{F_2(t)F_1(t)} W_{\sigma_1^2(t)} - \sqrt{\frac{n_1}{n_1 + n_2}} \sqrt{F_1(t)F_2(t)} W_{\sigma_2^2(t)} \quad (4.34)$$

where $W_{\sigma_1^2(t)}$ and $W_{\sigma_2^2(t)}$ are two independent Wiener processes with variances $\sigma_1^2(t)$ and $\sigma_2^2(t)$, respectively, with $\sigma_j^2(t) = Var\left(X_j \mid X_j < t\right)$ for $j = 1, 2$.

A Wiener process is formally defined as (cf. Stark and Woods, 2002):

Wiener process: *Wiener process is a continuous-time stochastic process characterized by four properties:*

1. $W_0 = 0$.
2. The function $t \to W_t$ is almost surely everywhere continuous.
3. W_t has independent increments, i.e., for any $t_1 < t_2 < s_1 < s_2$, $W_{t_2} - W_{t_1}$ and $W_{s_2} - W_{s_1}$ are independent random variables.
4. $W_t - W_s \sim N(0, t - s)$ for $0 \leq s < t$.

Following is a summary of the derivation of the asymptotic distribution of $\sqrt{\frac{n_1 n_2}{n_1 + n_2}}\ \theta(t; p)$ as given by Jayasinghe and Zeephongsekul (2013b). In addition to assumption **A2** stated under Section 4.2.2.1, these assumptions are made in the process:

A9 $n_2 / N \to c \in (0,1)$, therefore $n_1/N \to (1 - c) \in (0,1)$, as $N \to \infty$.
A10 $h \to 0$ as $N \to \infty$.
A11 $Nh \to \infty$ and $Nh^2 \to 0$, $N \to \infty$,

where $N = n_1 + n_2$.

Then, under H_0, given by Eq. (4.22), and with assumptions **A2, A9–A11,**

$$\sup_{a \le t < b} \left| \sqrt{\frac{n_1 n_2}{n_1 + n_2}} \hat{\rho}(t; p) - \Upsilon(t) \right| \xrightarrow{p} 0 \qquad (4.35)$$

Also, with

$$\mathbb{B}(t) = \sqrt{F_1(t) F_2(t)} \left[\sqrt{c} \ W_{\sigma_1^2(t)} - \sqrt{(1-c)} \ W_{\sigma_2^2(t)} \right]$$

we observe that

$$\lim_{N \to \infty} \sup_{a \le t < b} \left| \sqrt{\frac{n_1 n_2}{n_1 + n_2}} \hat{\rho}(t; p) - \mathbb{B}(t) \right|$$

$$\le \lim_{N \to \infty} \sup_{a \le t < b} \left| \sqrt{\frac{n_1 n_2}{n_1 + n_2}} \hat{\theta}(t; p) - \Upsilon(t) \right| + \lim_{N \to \infty} \sup_{a \le t < b} \left| \Upsilon(t) - \mathbb{B}(t) \right| \xrightarrow{p} 0 \quad (4.36)$$

where by Eq. (4.35), the first term converges in probability to zero, and the second term converges to zero by assumption **A9**. Therefore, since convergence in probability implies convergence in distribution, Jayasinghe (2013) obtains

$$\sqrt{\frac{n_1 n_2}{n_1 + n_2}} \ \hat{\rho}(t; p) \xrightarrow{d} \mathbb{B}(t) \qquad (4.37)$$

Further,

$$\int_a^b \mathbb{B}(t) \ dt \overset{d}{=} N\left(0, \sigma_{CM}^2\right)$$

where $W_{\sigma_i^2(t)}$'s for $i = 1, \ 2$ are two independent Wiener processes and

$$\sigma_{CM}^2 = c \ Var\left(\int_a^b \sqrt{F_1(t) F_2(t)} W_{\sigma_1^2(t)} \ dt\right)$$

$$+ (1 - c) \ Var\left(\int_a^b \sqrt{F_1(t) F_2(t)} W_{\sigma_2^2(t)} \ dt\right) \qquad (4.38)$$

Since $E\left(\int_a^b \sqrt{F_1(t)F_2(t)}W_{\sigma_i^2(t)}\ dt\right) = 0$ for a given population i,

$$\mathrm{Var}\left(\int_a^b \sqrt{F_1(t)F_2(t)}W_{\sigma_i^2(t)}\ dt\right)$$

$$= 2\int_a^b \sqrt{F_1(s)F_2(s)}\int_a^s \sqrt{F_1(t)F_2(t)}\min\left(W_{\sigma_i^2(t)},W_{\sigma_i^2(s)}\right)\ dt\ ds \qquad (4.39)$$

Therefore,

$$\sigma_{CM}^2 = 2\int_a^b\int_a^s \left(c\ \min\left(\sigma_1^2(t),\sigma_1^2(s)\right) + (1-c)\ \min\left(\sigma_2^2(t),\sigma_2^2(s)\right)\right)$$

$$\sqrt{F_1(s)F_2(s)}\sqrt{F_1(t)F_2(t)}\ dt\ ds \qquad (4.40)$$

The variance σ_{CM}^2 is estimated by $\hat{\sigma}_{CM}^2(p)$, for which $F_i(s)$, $i = 1,2$ and $\sigma_i^2(t)$, $i = 1,2$ are replaced by their local polynomial estimators. Thus it follows from Eq. (4.37) that the approximate asymptotic distribution of Cramér–von Mises type test statistic $T_{CM}(p)$ is

$$T_{CM}(p) \sim N\left(0,\hat{\sigma}_{CM}^2(p)\right)$$

Thus the null hypothesis will be rejected in favor of the alternative hypothesis if

$$T_{CM}(p)/\sqrt{\tilde{\sigma}_{CM}^2(p)} > z_{1-\alpha}$$

where $(1-\alpha)$th percentile of the standard normal distribution is given by $z_{1-\alpha}$.

In the case of KS test statistic,

$$\sup_{a\le t < b} \mathbb{B}(t) \overset{d}{=} \sup_{a\le t < b} W_{\sigma_{KS}^2(t)},$$

where

$$\sigma_{KS}^2(t) = F_1(t)F_2(t)\left(c\sigma_1^2(t) + (1-c)\ \sigma_2^2(t)\right) \qquad (4.41)$$

Noting the definition of $T_{KS}(p)$, by Eq. (4.37):

$$T_{KS}(p) \sim \sup_{a \le t < b} W_{\hat{\sigma}^2_{KS}(t;p)}$$

where $\hat{\sigma}^2_{KS}(t;p)$ is a plug-in local polynomial estimator of $\sigma^2_{KS}(t)$ [Eq. (4.41)], which is obtained by substituting the local polynomial estimators for each $F_i(s)$ and $\sigma^2_i(t)$, where $i = 1, 2$. However,

$$\sup_{a \le t < b} W_{\sigma^2_{KS}(t)} = \sup_{a' \le s \le b'} W_s$$

where $a' = \inf\{\sigma^2_{KS}(t) : a \le t < b\}$, which is taken as zero, and $b' = \sup\{\sigma^2_{KS}(t) : a \le t < b\}$ is estimated by $\hat{b}' = \max\{\hat{\sigma}^2_{KS}(t;p)\}$. Hence, H_0 in favor of the alternative H_1 can be rejected if

$$T_{KS}(p) > Q_\alpha(p)$$

where for a given significance level α, the critical value $Q_\alpha(p)$ is set based on the distribution of $T_{KS}(p)$. However, from the result on page 92 of Billingsley (1999):

$$P(\sup_{0 \le s \le b'} W_s > x) = \frac{2}{\sqrt{2\pi b'}} \int_x^\infty e^{-\frac{z^2}{2b'}} dz \qquad (4.42)$$

$Q_\alpha(p)$ can be determined for a given α value by observing that

$$\int_{Q_\alpha(p)}^\infty e^{-\frac{z^2}{2\hat{b}'}} dz = \sqrt{\frac{2\pi\hat{b}'}{4}} \left(1 - erf\left(\sqrt{\frac{1}{2\hat{b}'}} Q_\alpha(p)\right)\right) \qquad (4.43)$$

where $erf(x) = \frac{2}{\pi} \int_0^x e^{-t^2} dt$ is the Gauss error function (cf. Greene, 1993).

Consequently, mathematical software can be used to find $Q_\alpha(p)$ by solving the next equation:

$$erf\left(\sqrt{\frac{1}{2\hat{b}'}} Q_\alpha(p)\right) = 1 - \alpha \qquad (4.44)$$

4.3.1.1.2 Bootstrapping Approach for Calculation of the Critical Value

For smaller samples, the critical values using bootstrapping can be established. As the first step, the two samples are pooled, i.e., sample 1, $T_{11}, T_{12}, ..., T_{1n_1}$, with sample 2, $T_{21}, T_{22}, ..., T_{2n_2}$ to create the pooled sample:

$$Z = \left\{ Z_1, ..., Z_{n_1+n_2} \right\} = \left\{ T_{11}, ..., T_{1n_1} \right\} \cup \left\{ T_{21}, ..., T_{2n_2} \right\}$$

Then, from the pooled sample, Z, two independent samples are derived by resampling with replacement randomly, $T_{11}^*, T_{12}^*, ..., T_{1n_1}^*$ and $T_{21}^*, T_{22}^*, ..., T_{2n_2}^*$. Assuming that these two samples are drawn from the two populations concerned, we compute the test statistics $T_{CM}^*(p)$ and $T_{KS}^*(p)$. Suppose, the desired critical level or the level of confidence for the test is $1 - \alpha$. This resampling and estimation process from Z is repeated many times, and then, based on the empirical distribution of the computed test statistics, the critical points of the two tests, $t_{CM,\alpha}^*$ and $t_{KS,\alpha}^*$, are then determined such that

$$P\left(T_{CM}^*(p) \geqslant t_{CM,\alpha}^*(p) \right) = \alpha \quad \text{and} \quad P\left(T_{KS}^*(p) \geqslant t_{KS,\alpha}^*(p) \right) = \alpha$$

Then the null hypothesis is rejected if the test statistic

$$T_{CM}(p) > t_{CM,\alpha}^*(p)$$

or

$$T_{KS}(p) > t_{KS,\alpha}^*(p)$$

4.3.2 Statistical Comparison of Mean Residual Life Functions of Two Populations

Comparison of mean residual lives [cf. Eq. (4.5)] of two items of equipment (or systems) may be required when making decisions in reliability engineering. Several non-parametric tests already exist in the literature to test the equality of MRL functions of two populations (e.g., see Berger et al., 1988; Aly, 1997) apart from the procedure proposed by Jayasinghe (2013), which will be presented in this chapter in detail. The tests proposed by Berger et al. (1988), however, tests $H_0: m_1(t) \leq m_2(t)$

for some $t \in [T_1, T_2)$ vs. $H_1 : m_1(t) > m_2(t)$ for all $t \in [T_1, T_2)$. The null hypothesis in this test checks the hypothesis only at a specified age t in a specified time interval $t \in [T_1, T_2)$, and not rejecting of the null hypothesis can mean either $m_1(t) = m_2(t)$ at that $t \in [T_1, T_2)$ or $m_1(t) < m_2(t)$ at that $t \in [T_1, T_2)$. However, hypotheses being tested in the test proposed by Aly (1997) check

$$H_0 : m_1(t) = m_2(t) \quad \text{for all } t \in [a, b] \tag{4.45}$$

vs. the alternative hypothesis:

$$H_1 : M_1(t) \geqslant m_2(t) \quad \text{for } t \in [a, b] \text{ with strict inequality}$$
$$\text{for some } t \in [a, b] \tag{4.46}$$

The test statistic proposed in Aly (1997)'s test measures the deviation based on the empirical estimator of the function

$$\theta(t) = \sqrt{\overline{F}_1(t) . \overline{F}_2(t)} \left(m_1(t) - m_2(t) \right) \tag{4.47}$$

where $a = \max(a_1, a_2)$ and $b = \min(b_1, b_2)$, with $a_i = \sup\{t : \overline{F}_i(t) < 1\}$ and $b_i = \inf\{t : \overline{F}_i(t) > 0\}$, for $i = 1, 2$, where $\overline{F}_i(t)$ is the survival function of the ith population. A measurement similar to this has also been used by Hollander and Proschan (1975) to develop a hypothesis test, which can test the monotonicity properties of a MRL function. The weights in $\theta(t)$, i.e., $\overline{F}_1(t)$ and $\overline{F}_2(t)$, represent the proportions alive at t in the two populations. The empirical nature of this measure consequently affects the performance of the test statistic since empirical estimators can over-/undercalculate the value of the test statistic. This directly affects the decisions made by the hypothesis tests. This was observed through the performance analysis carried out by Jayasinghe (2013).

For testing the null and alternative hypotheses associated with the test proposed by Aly (1997), Jayasinghe (2013) introduces a more efficient testing procedure based on fixed-design local polynomial regression. The corresponding Cramér–von Mises type test statistic is given by

$$\tilde{T}_{CM}(p) = \sqrt{\frac{n_1 n_2}{n_1 + n_2}} \int_a^b \hat{\theta}(t; p) \, dt \tag{4.48}$$

and its Kolmogorov–Smirnov type test statistic has the form

$$\tilde{T}_{KS}(p) = \sqrt{\frac{n_1 n_2}{n_1 + n_2}} \, \sup_{a \leq t < b} \, \hat{\theta}(t; p) \tag{4.49}$$

In these two test statistics, $\hat{\theta}(t; p)$ refers to the pth order local polynomial estimator of the weighted deviation measure $\theta(t)$ and the pth order local polynomial estimator of the function $\theta(t)$ is given by

$$\hat{\theta}(t; p) = e_1^T (T_p^T W_N T_p)^{-1} T_p^T W_N Y_N \tag{4.50}$$

where

$$Y_N^T = \{y_i\}_{1 \leq i \leq N} = \{\sqrt{\widehat{\overline{F}}_1(t_i).\widehat{\overline{F}}_2(t_i)} \left(\widehat{m}_1(t_i) - \widehat{m}_2(t_i)\right)\}_{1 \leq i \leq N}$$

and the empirical MRL and survival functions of the two populations are denoted by $\widehat{m}_i(t)$, $\widehat{\overline{F}}_i(t)$ for $i = 1, 2$. Eq. (4.50) can be rewritten:

$$\hat{\theta}(t; p) = \sum_{i=1}^{N} L_N \left(\frac{t_i - t}{h}\right) y_i \tag{4.51}$$

where y_i's are as defined in Eq. (4.50).

The integral in the CM statistic can be approximated by a Riemann sum with width d and size of the grid M, as suggested in the CM statistic calculation relevant to EIT comparisons. By letting $p = 1, 2, 3$, LL, LQ, and LC, CM, and KS test statistics of the MRL tests can be derived, respectively. The choice of order can be determined by studying the behavior of the empirical MRL functions of the populations concerned.

To visually investigate the deviation between the MRL functions of the two samples over t prior to conducting the test, a graph of $d \times \hat{\theta}(z_j; p)$ vs. z_j can be utilized. To select the bandwidth required when computing the test statistics, the AICC method (cf. Hurvich et al. (1998)) is suggested by Jayasinghe and Zeephongsekul (2017). To handle right censored data, $\hat{\theta}(t; p)$ in test statistics can be modified:

$$\hat{\theta}^*(t; p) = e_1^T (T_p^T W_N T_p)^{-1} T_p^T W_N Y_N^* \tag{4.52}$$

where $\mathbf{Y_N^*} = \{y_i^*\}_{1 \leqslant i \leqslant N} = \{\sqrt{\widehat{\overline{F}}_1^*(t_i).\widehat{\overline{F}}_2^*(t_i)}\left(\widehat{M}_1^*(t_i) - \widehat{M}_2^*(t_i)\right)\}_{1 \leqslant i \leqslant N}$ and $\mathbf{e}_1$, $\mathbf{T_p}$,

$\mathbf{W_N}$ are as defined in Eq. (4.50). Empirical estimators for the MRL functions of

the two populations, $\widehat{M}_1^*(t_i) = \int_{t_i}^{\infty} \dfrac{\widehat{\overline{F}}_1^*(u)}{\widehat{\overline{F}}_1^*(t_i)}\,du$ and $\widehat{M}_2^*(t_i) = \int_{t_i}^{\infty} \dfrac{\widehat{\overline{F}}_2^*(u)}{\widehat{\overline{F}}_2^*(t_i)}\,du$ can be

derived by the corresponding Kaplan–Meier estimators of the survival function,

$\widehat{\overline{F}}_1^*(t_i)$ and $\widehat{\overline{F}}_2^*(t_i)$.

4.3.2.1 Critical Values of the Test Statistics

Two types of critical values will be presented as proposed in Jayasinghe (2013): using

the asymptotic distribution of $\sqrt{\dfrac{n_1 n_2}{n_1 + n_2}}\,\hat{\theta}(t;p)$ first for larger samples and the other

for relatively smaller samples using bootstrapping. The Gaussian process is relevant
to the present case:

$$\Theta(t) = \sqrt{\frac{n_2}{n_1 + n_2}}\sqrt{\overline{F}_2(t)\overline{F}_1(t)}W_{\tilde{\sigma}_1^2(t)} - \sqrt{\frac{n_1}{n_1 + n_2}}\sqrt{\overline{F}_1(t)\overline{F}_2(t)}W_{\tilde{\sigma}_2^2(t)} \quad (4.53)$$

where $W_{\tilde{\sigma}_1^2(t)}$ and $W_{\tilde{\sigma}_2^2(t)}$ are two independent Wiener processes with variances

$\tilde{\sigma}_1^2(t)$ and $\tilde{\sigma}_2^2(t)$, respectively, with $\tilde{\sigma}_j^2(t) = Var\left(X_j | X_j > t\right)$ for $j = 1,2$. Under

assumptions **A2, A12–A14** and assuming that H_0 given by Eq. (4.45) holds.

$$\sup_{a \leq t < b}\left|\sqrt{\frac{n_1 n_2}{n_1 + n_2}}\,\hat{\theta}(t;p) - \Theta(t)\right| \xrightarrow{p} 0 \quad (4.54)$$

Then, noting

$$\mathbb{A}(t) = \sqrt{\overline{F}_1(t)\overline{F}_2(t)}\left[\sqrt{c}\,W_{\tilde{\sigma}_1^2(t)} - \sqrt{(1-c)}\,W_{\tilde{\sigma}_2^2(t)}\right]$$

$$\lim_{N \to \infty}\sup_{a \leq t < b}\left|\sqrt{\frac{n_1 n_2}{n_1 + n_2}}\,\hat{\theta}(t;p) - \mathbb{A}(t)\right|$$

$$\le \lim_{N\to\infty} \sup_{a\le t<b} \left| \sqrt{\frac{n_1 n_2}{n_1 + n_2}}\, \hat{\theta}(t; p) - \Theta(t) \right| + \lim_{N\to\infty} \sup_{a\le t<b} \left| \Theta(t) - \mathbb{A}(t) \right| \xrightarrow{p} 0 \quad (4.55)$$

in which the first term converges to zero in probability by the result given by Eq. (4.54), and the second term converges to zero by assumption **A12**. However,

$$\sqrt{\frac{n_1 n_2}{n_1 + n_2}}\, \hat{\theta}(t; p) \xrightarrow{d} \mathbb{A}(t) \quad (4.56)$$

since convergence in probability implies convergence in distribution. Further,

$$\int_a^b \mathbb{A}(t)\, dt \xoverset{d}{=} N\left(0, \tilde{\sigma}_{CM}^2\right)$$

where

$$\tilde{\sigma}_{CM}^2 = c\ Var\left(\int_a^b \sqrt{\bar{F}_1(t)\bar{F}_2(t)}W_{\tilde{\sigma}_1^2(t)}\, dt\right) + (1-c)\ Var\left(\int_a^b \sqrt{\bar{F}_1(t)\bar{F}_2(t)}W_{\tilde{\sigma}_2^2(t)}\, dt\right) \quad (4.57)$$

since $W_{\tilde{\sigma}_i^2(t)}$'s for $i = 1, 2$ are two independent Wiener processes. Then, for a given population i,

$$Var\left(\int_a^b \sqrt{\bar{F}_1(t)\bar{F}_2(t)}W_{\tilde{\sigma}_i^2(t)}\, dt\right)$$

$$= 2\int_a^b \sqrt{\bar{F}_1(s)\bar{F}_2(s)}\int_a^s \sqrt{\bar{F}_1(t)\bar{F}_2(t)}\min\left(\tilde{\sigma}_i^2(t), \tilde{\sigma}_i^2(s)\right)\, dt\, ds \quad (4.58)$$

following similar steps taken when deriving Eq. (4.39). Hence

$$\tilde{\sigma}_{CM}^2 = 2\int_a^b \int_a^s \left(c\ \min\left(\tilde{\sigma}_1^2(t), \tilde{\sigma}_1^2(s)\right) + (1-c)\ \min\left(\tilde{\sigma}_2^2(t), \tilde{\sigma}_2^2(s)\right)\right)$$

$$\sqrt{\bar{F}_1(s)\bar{F}_2(s)}\sqrt{\bar{F}_1(t)\bar{F}_2(t)}\, dt\, ds \quad (4.59)$$

The variance $\tilde{\sigma}_{CM}^2$ is estimated by $\hat{\tilde{\sigma}}_{CM}^2(p)$ in which $\bar{F}_i(s)$, $i = 1, 2$ and $\tilde{\sigma}_i^2(t)$, $i = 1, 2$ are estimated by local polynomial estimators with appropriate orders. Hence the asymptotic distribution of the CM test statistic will be

$$\tilde{T}_{CM}(p) \sim N\left(0, \hat{\tilde{\sigma}}^2_{CM}(p)\right)$$

Then, H_0 can be rejected in favor of the alternative hypothesis H_1 if

$$\tilde{T}_{CM}(p) / \sqrt{\hat{\tilde{\sigma}}^2_{CM}(p)} > z_{1-\alpha}$$

where $z_{1-\alpha}$ denotes the $(1-\alpha)$th percentile of the standard normal distribution with α significance level. Note that in the KS test

$$\sup_{a \le t < b} \mathbb{A}(t) \overset{d}{=} \sup_{a \le t < b} W_{\tilde{\sigma}^2_{KS}(t)}$$

where

$$\tilde{\sigma}^2_{KS}(t) = c\,\bar{F}_1(t)\bar{F}_2(t)\tilde{\sigma}^2_1(t) + (1-c)\bar{F}_1(t)\bar{F}_2(t)\tilde{\sigma}^2_2(t) \qquad (4.60)$$

Hence

$$\tilde{T}_{KS}(p) \sim \sup_{a \le t < b} W_{\hat{\tilde{\sigma}}^2_{KS}(t;p)},$$

where $\hat{\tilde{\sigma}}^2_{KS}(t;p)$ is obtained by substituting the local polynomial estimators for survival and variance components. However,

$$\sup_{a \le t < b} W_{\tilde{\sigma}^2_{KS}(t)} = \sup_{a' \le s \le b'} W_{\tilde{s}},$$

where $a' = \inf\{\tilde{\sigma}^2_{KS}(t): a \le t < b\} = 0$ and $b' = \sup\{\tilde{\sigma}^2_{KS}(t): a \le t < b\}$. Estimation of b' is done by $\hat{b}' = \max\left\{\hat{\tilde{\sigma}}^2_{KS}(t;p)\right\}$. Then the decision rule according to Jayasinghe and Zeephongsekul (2017) is set to reject H_0 in favor of the alternative H_1 if

$$\tilde{T}_{KS}(p) > \tilde{Q}_\alpha(p)$$

where $\tilde{Q}_\alpha(p)$ is the critical value of the distribution of $\tilde{T}_{KS}(p)$ for a given significance level α. Then, for a given α, $\tilde{Q}_\alpha(p)$ can be determined by solving the following:

$$\int_{\tilde{Q}_\alpha(p)}^{\infty} e^{-\frac{z^2}{2\hat{b}'}}\,dz = \sqrt{\frac{2\pi\hat{b}'}{4}}\left(1 - erf\left(\sqrt{\frac{1}{2\hat{b}'}}\tilde{Q}_\alpha(p)\right)\right) \qquad (4.61)$$

4.3.2.2 *Using Bootstrapping to Calculate the Critical Value*

Critical values based on bootstrapping can be derived by following similar steps as recommended in Section 4.3.1 relevant to the EIT tests. Hence, after pooling and resampling, if the desired confidence level for the test is $1 - \alpha$, the critical points, $\tilde{t}^*_{CM,\alpha}$ and $\tilde{t}^*_{KS,\alpha}$, of the two tests can be computed by

$$P\left(T^*_{CM}\left(p\right) \geq \tilde{t}^*_{CM,\alpha}\left(p\right)\right) = \alpha \text{ and } P\left(T^*_{KS}\left(p\right) \geq \tilde{t}^*_{KS,\alpha}\left(p\right)\right) = \alpha$$

Then the null hypothesis is rejected if the test statistic

$$\tilde{T}_{CM}\left(p\right) > \tilde{t}^*_{CM,\alpha}\left(p\right)$$

or

$$\tilde{T}_{KS}\left(p\right) > \tilde{t}^*_{KS,\alpha}\left(p\right)$$

4.3.3 *Evaluating Efficiency of the Proposed Hypothesis Tests*

In the case of MRL tests, it is also required to compare the tests in Jayasinghe (2013) with those introduced by Aly (1997). In the tests by Aly (1997):

$$T_{CM_A} = \sqrt{\frac{n_1 n_2}{n_1 + n_2}} \int_a^b \hat{\theta}(t)\,dt \tag{4.62}$$

and

$$T_{KS_A} = \sqrt{\frac{n_1 n_2}{n_1 + n_2}} \sup_{a < t \leqslant b} \hat{\theta}(t) \tag{4.63}$$

where $\hat{\theta}(t)$ is an empirical estimator, which is a step function:

$$\hat{\theta}(t) = \begin{cases} \hat{\theta}(Z_i) & \text{for } Z_i \leq t < Z_{i+1}, \ i = 0, 1,..., \ N-1 \\ 0 & \text{for } t \geq Z_N, \end{cases} \tag{4.64}$$

where $Z_1, ..., Z_N$ are the order statistics of the combined sample with $Z_0 = 0$. There exists several performance measures for comparing performances between two hypothesis tests. Here we discuss a few in brief as given in Jayasinghe (2013).

Suppose that T_A and T_B are the test statistics of two tests A and B whose efficiency we wish to compare. Then, as mentioned by Nikitin (1995), the relative efficiency of T_A with respect to the test T_B is defined as

$$e_{A,B}(\alpha, \beta, \omega) = \frac{N_A(\alpha, \beta, \omega)}{N_B(\alpha, \beta, \omega)} \tag{4.65}$$

In this expression, $N_A(\alpha, \beta, \omega)$ and $N_B(\alpha, \beta, \omega)$ are the minimal sample sizes required, respectively, for test A and test B to ascertain a power of β with significance level of α for a alternative value of parameter ω. The value of $e_{A,B}(\alpha, \beta, \omega)$ is difficult to calculate explicitly. Hence, a limiting value of $e_{A,B}(\alpha, \beta, \omega)$ is being calculated instead. Three well-known limiting values are proposed for $e_{A,B}(\alpha, \beta, \omega)$ based on different limiting approaches: the Bahadur, Hodges–Lehmann, and Pitman asymptotic relative efficiencies (ARE). The limiting value of $e_{A,B}(\alpha, \beta, \omega)$ is calculated by the Bahadur asymptotic relative efficiency (BARE) by letting the significance level, $\alpha \to 0$:

$$\text{BARE}(\beta, \omega) = \lim_{\alpha \to 0} e_{A,B}(\alpha, \beta, \omega) \tag{4.66}$$

whereas in Hodges–Lehmann method, it is calculated by letting the power of the test $\beta \to 1$:

$$\text{HLARE}(\alpha, \omega) = \lim_{\beta \to 1} e_{A,B}(\alpha, \beta, \omega) \tag{4.67}$$

In Pitman's method (PARE), the limiting value is calculated by letting $\omega \to \omega_{H_0}$ where ω_{H_0} is the value of ω under null hypothesis, i.e.,

$$\text{PARE}(\alpha, \beta, \omega_{H_0}) = \lim_{\omega \to \omega_{H_0}} e_{A,B}(\alpha, \beta, \omega) \tag{4.68}$$

Practically, calculation of a limiting value is justifiable since only small significance levels ($\alpha \to 0$), high powers ($\beta \to 1$), and close alternatives ($\omega \to \omega_{H_0}$) are the scenarios we are mostly concerned with when comparing two statistical tests. If the limiting value of any of these three ARE measures is a value greater than 1, then it can be concluded that Test A is more efficient than Test B. Further, it has been identified that the Bahadur ARE does not depend on β the required power of the tests, that the Hodges–Lehmann ARE does not depend on α, that the set Type II error of the tests and PARE do not depend on either. PARE is a constant [cf. page 3 of Nikitin (1995)]. Jayasinghe (2013) used Pitman asymptotic relative efficiency (PARE) and rejection probability to compare different testing procedures.

In the case of CM, a MRL test proposed by Jayasinghe (2013), for a given power β and Type II error α:

$$P(\frac{\tilde{T}_{CM}(p)}{\sqrt{\hat{\tilde{\sigma}}_{CM}^2(p)}} > Z_{1-\alpha} \mid H_1 \text{ is true}) = 1 - \beta \tag{4.69}$$

With $c' = \dfrac{n_2}{N}$ by Eqs. (4.48) and (4.59), then it results in

$$\tilde{T}_{CM}(p) = \sqrt{N}\sqrt{c'(1-c')}\int_a^b \hat{\theta}(t; p) \, dt \tag{4.70}$$

and

$$\hat{\tilde{\sigma}}_{CM}^2(p) = 2\int_a^b \int_a^s \left(c' \min\left(\tilde{\sigma}_1^2(t; p), \tilde{\sigma}_1^2(s; p)\right) + (1-c')\min\left(\tilde{\sigma}_2^2(t; p), \tilde{\sigma}_1^2(s; p)\right) \right)$$

$$\sqrt{\bar{F}_1(s; p)\bar{F}_2(s; p)}\sqrt{\bar{F}_1(t; p)\bar{F}_2(t; p)} \, dt \, ds \tag{4.71}$$

Therefore,

$$\frac{\tilde{T}_{CM}(p)}{\sqrt{\hat{\tilde{\sigma}}_{CM}^2(p)}} = \sqrt{N}\sqrt{c'(1-c')}\frac{\int_a^b \hat{\theta}(t; p) \, dt}{\sqrt{\hat{\tilde{\sigma}}_{CM}^2(p)}} \tag{4.72}$$

Recall that test statistic $\tilde{T}_{CM}(p)$, when standardized, has an asymptotically standard normal distribution. Hence the minimal sample size required for the CM MRL test proposed by Jayasinghe (2013) such that it attains Type II error of α and power of β for a given c' is

$$N_{CM}(p) = \hat{\tilde{\sigma}}_{CM}^2(p) \frac{(Z_{1-\alpha} + Z_{1-\beta})^2}{c'(1-c')\omega^2} \tag{4.73}$$

where $\omega = \int_a^b \hat{\theta}(t\ p)\ dt$. Similarly, for the CM MRL test introduced by Aly (1997), i.e. CM_A,

$$N_{CM_A} = \hat{\sigma}_A^2 \frac{(Z_{1-\alpha} + Z_{1-\beta})^2}{c'(1-c')\ \omega^2} \tag{4.74}$$

where $\omega = \int_a^b \hat{\theta}(t)\,dt$ and $\sqrt{2}_A^2$ is the variance of the converging distribution of CM_A. Hence, Pitman's ARE, which compares efficiencies of CM MRL tests per Jayasinghe (2013), and Aly (1997), which is obtained by letting $\omega \to \omega_{H_0}$ in Eqs. (4.73) and (4.74), are given by

$$\text{PARE}\left(\alpha, \beta, \omega_{H_0}; p\right) = \frac{\hat{\sigma}_A^2}{\hat{\tilde{\sigma}}_{CM}^2(p)} \tag{4.75}$$

Then, if $\text{PARE}\left(\alpha, \beta, \omega_{H_0}; p\right) > 1$, it can be concluded that the tests by Jayasinghe and Zeephongsekul (2017) are asymptotically relatively efficient compared to the CM test by Aly (1997).

Similarly, for the KS MRL test proposed by Jayasinghe (2013):

$$P(\tilde{T}_{KS}(p) > B_{1-\alpha} \mid H_1 \text{ is true}) = 1 - \beta \tag{4.76}$$

where $B_{1-\alpha}$ is the $(1-\alpha)$th percentile of the folded normal distribution. By Eqs. (4.49) and (4.60), we have that

$$\tilde{T}_{KS}(p) = \sqrt{N}\sqrt{c'(1-c')}\ \sup_{a \leqslant t < b} \hat{\theta}(t; p) \tag{4.77}$$

and

$$\hat{\tilde{\sigma}}_{KS}^2(t; p) = c'\ \bar{F}_1(t; p)\bar{F}_2(t; p)\tilde{\sigma}_1^2(t; p) + (1-c')$$
$$\bar{F}_1(t; p)\bar{F}_2(t; p)\tilde{\sigma}_2^2(t; p) \tag{4.78}$$

Hence, Pitman's ARE for KS MRL test comparison between the two KS MRL tests per Jayasinghe and Zeephongsekul (2017) and Aly (1997) is

$$\text{PARE}\left(\alpha, \beta, \omega_{H_0} ; p\right) = \frac{(A_{1-\alpha} + A_{1-\beta})^2}{(B_{1-\alpha} + B_{1-\beta})^2} \tag{4.79}$$

where $A_{1-\alpha}$ is the $(1-\alpha)$th percentile of the distribution of the KS_A method's test statistic. Then, if $\text{PARE}\left(\alpha, \beta, \omega_{H_0} ; p\right) > 1$, it can be concluded that the KS test by Jayasinghe and Zeephongsekul (2017) is asymptotically relatively efficient compared to the KS test proposed by Aly (1997).

4.3.4 Practical Performance

An extensive simulation study was conducted by Jayasinghe (2013) to evaluate the performance of the tests they proposed. When selecting the underlying distributions of e_1/e_2 and m_1/m_2, the parameters of the selected lifetime distributions were carefully varied across five experiments to facilitate an investigation of varying degree of deviations among them.

Rejection probability was used as the performance evaluation measure of EIT tests by Jayasinghe (2013). The results of EIT comparison hypothesis tests revealed that both CM and KS types for all LL, LQ, and LC tests perform well in identifying all types of deviations tested in the simulation study, i.e., null, small, large deviations, especially when the critical value is determined based on the asymptotic distribution of the relevant test statistic. The performance of tests proposed by Jayasinghe (2013) improves as the deviation becomes larger, as expected. Further, it was observed that both CM and KS tests tend to perform better in identifying the deviations better with similarly sized sample sizes.

In the case of MRL comparison hypothesis tests by Jayasinghe (2013), it was revealed through rejection probabilities that, with the critical value determined based on the bootstrapping approach, both types of tests, i.e., CM and KS, regardless of whether it's LL, LQ, or LC tests, tend do a significantly better job in identifying models with small/large deviations compared to the CM and KS tests introduced by Aly (1997). The results also portrayed that the performance improves as the deviation between the two functions being compared becomes larger. This observation was clearly apparent when the sample sizes were approximately equal in both CM and KS tests. However, with the critical values determined based on asymptotic distribution, the performances of LPR CM tests and the Aly's CM test were found to be similar when tested for null deviation. When comparing performances between CM ans KS tests, in general, it was revealed that when converging distribution of the test statistics was used to determine the critical value, performances of

LPR CM tests were better than LPR KS tests. Pitman's ARE results demonstrated that the efficiency of both CM and KS for all LL, LQ, and LC tests when compared to Aly's CM and KS tests is higher. This result was true regardless of the sizes of the samples. In most experiments, as the deviations become larger, the relative efficiency measure that compares LPR tests to Aly's tests tend to increase. Further, the relative efficiency measure of LPR CM tests (compared to Aly's CM test) were in general higher than the relative efficiency measure of LPR KS tests (compared to Aly's KS test), and it can be concluded that CM MRL tests are more efficient than KS MRL tests.

4.4 Conclusion

This chapter presented two classes of non-parametric estimators, empirical and smooth non-parametric estimators for three popular and important component reliability measures. The smooth estimators proposed by Jayasinghe (2013) utilized a fixed-design local polynomial approach. Each empirical estimator was shown by the authors as asymptotically unbiased, variance of each empirical estimator converges to zero asymptotically, and the covariance of each empirical estimator converges to zero asymptotically. On the other hand, LPR estimators were also shown to be consistent and asymptotically normal under several assumptions. The choice of bandwidth, which influences the efficacy of the local polynomial estimation, was determined by minimizing the AMISE. In the context of EIT and RHR estimators, simulation experiments that were performed by Jayasinghe (2013); Jayasinghe and Zeephongsekul (2011, 2013b) indicated that these LPR non-parametric estimators performed much better compared to the relevant empirical estimator. Simulation experiments done for the case of MRL estimators by Jayasinghe (2013); Jayasinghe and Zeephongsekul (2013a) indicated local polynomial estimators with higher orders, on some occasions, i.e., LQ and LC, especially if the sample size is small. It was also revealed that the LPR estimators perform well in estimating MRL functions compared to other existing empirical and kernel-based estimators particularly when the underlying MRL models are constant, bathtub-shaped, upside-down bathtub-shaped MRL functions.

Hypothesis testing procedures based on fixed-design local polynomial regression due to Jayasinghe (2013); Jayasinghe and Zeephongsekul (2017) were also presented for comparing the MRL and EIT functions of two populations. Cramer–von Mises (CM) and Kolmogorov–Smirnov (KS) type test statistics were presented. Decision rule construction was demonstrated based on the critical values derived using the asymptotic distributions of the test statistics and bootstrapping approach. It was noticed through the simulation study conducted by Jayasinghe (2013);

Jayasinghe and Zeephongsekul (2017) that both CM and KS type tests, regardless of the order of the LPR test, are efficient in identifying null, small, and large deviations.

References

B. Abdous and A. Berred. Mean residual life estimation. *Journal of Statistical Planning and Inference*, 132(1):3–19, 2005.

I.A. Ahmad and M. Kayid. Characterizations of the RHR and MIT orderings and the DRHR and IMIT classes of life distributions. *Probability in the Engineering and Informational Sciences*, 19(4): 447–461, 2005.

E.A. Aly. Nonparametric tests for comparing two mean residual life functions. *Lifetime Data Analysis*, 3:353–366, 1997.

P.K. Andersen, O. Borgan, R.D. Gill, and N. Keiding. *Statistical Models Based on Counting Processes*. Springer Series in Statistics, 1993.

M. Asadi and A. Berred. Properties and estimation of the mean past lifetime. *Statistics*, 46(3): 1–13, 2011.

F.G. Badia and M.D. Berrade. Advances in mathematical modeling for reliability, chapter On the reversed hazard rate and mean inactivity time of mixtures, pages 103–110. Delft University Press, Amsterdam, The Netherlands, 2008.

D. Bagkavos and P. Patil. Local polynomial fitting in failure rate estimation. *IEEE Transactions on Reliability*, 57(1):41–52, 2008.

R.L. Berger, D.D. Boos, and F.M. Guess. Tests and confidence sets for comparing two mean residual life functions. *Biometrika*, 44:103–115, 1988.

P. Billingsley. *Convergence of Probability Measures*. Wiley Interscience, second edition, 1999.

H.W. Block and H. Joe. Tail behavior of the failure rate functions of mixtures. *Lifetime Data Analysis*, 3:269–288, 1997.

H.W. Block and T.H. Savits. Burn-in. *Statistical Science*, 12:1–19, 1997.

H.W. Block, T. H. Savits, and H. Singh. The reversed hazard rate function. *Probability in the Engineering and Informational Sciences*, 12:69–90, 1998.

R. Cao and I. Van Keilegom. Empirical likelihood tests for two-sample problems via nonparametric density estimation. *Canadian Journal of Statistics*, 34(1):61–77, 2006.

N.K. Chandra and D. Roy. Some results on reversed hazard rate. *Probability in the Engineering and Informational Sciences Archive*, 15(1):95–102, 2001.

K.F. Cheng. Tests for the equality of failure rates. *Biometrika*, 72:211–215, 1985.

M.S. Chikkagouder and J.S. Shuster. Comparison of failure rates using rank tests. *Journal of American Statistical Association*, 69:411–413, 1974.

L. Eeckhoudt and C. Gollier. Demand for risky assets and the monotone probability ratio order. *Journal of Risk and Uncertainty*, 11(2):113–22, September 1995.

J. Fan and I. Gijbels. Adaptive order polynomial fitting: Bandwidth robustification and bias reduction. *Journal of Computational and Graphical Statistics*, 4(3):213–227, 1995.

J. Fan, Q. Yao, and H. Tong. Estimation of conditional densities and sensitivity measures in nonlinear dynamical systems. *Biometrika*, 83:189–206, 1996.

M. S. Finkelstein. On the reversed hazard rate. *Reliability Engineering and System Safety*, 78(1): 71–75, 2002.

S. Goliforushani and M. Asadi. On the discrete mean past lifetime. *Metrika*, 68(2):209–217, 2008.

W.H. Greene. *Econometric Analysis*. Prentice-Hall, fifth edition, 1993.

F. M. Guess, X. Zhang, T. M. Young, and R. V. Leon. Using mean residual life functions for unique insights. *International Journal of Reliability and Applications*, 6(2):79–85, 2005.

A. Guillamon, J. Navarro, and J. Ruiz. Nonparametric estimator for mean residual life and vitality function. *Statistical Papers*, 39(3):263–276, 1998.

R.D. Gupta and A.K. Nanda. Some results on reversed hazard rate ordering. *Communications in Statistics: Theory and Methods*, 30(11):2447–2457, 2001.

M. Hollander and F. Proschan. Tests for mean residual life. *Biometrika*, 62:585–593, 1975.

C.M. Hurvich, J.S. Simonoff, and C.-L. Tsai. Smoothing parameter selection in non-parametric regression using an improved akaike information criterion. *Journal of Royal Statistical Society. Series B (Statistical Methodology)*, 60(2):271–293, 1998. 26

C.L. Jayasinghe. Nonparametric approach to reliability and its applications. PhD thesis, RMIT University, 2013.

C.L. Jayasinghe and P. Zeephongsekul. Nonparametric estimation of the reversed hazard rate function for uncensored and censored data. *International Journal of Reliability, Quality and Safety Engineering*, 18(5):417–429, 2011. doi: https://doi.org/10.1142/S02185 39311004160.

C.L. Jayasinghe and P. Zeephongsekul. On the nonparametric smooth estimation of the reversed hazard rate function. *Statistical Methodology*, 9(3):364–380, 2012.

C.L. Jayasinghe and P. Zeephongsekul. Local polynomial fitting of the mean residual life function. *IEEE Transactions on Reliability*, 62(2):317–328, 2013a. doi: 10.1109/TR.2013.2255774.

C.L. Jayasinghe and P. Zeephongsekul. Nonparametric smooth estimation of the expected inactivity time function. *Journal of Statistical Planning and Inference*, 143(5):911–928, 2013b. ISSN 0378-3758. doi: https://doi.org/10.1016/j.jspi.2012.12.002. URL www. sciencedirect.com/science/article/pii/S0378375812003515.

C.L. Jayasinghe and P. Zeephongsekul. Non parametric hypothesis tests for comparing reliability functions. *Communications in Statistics—Theory and Methods*, 46(8):3698–3717, 2017. doi: 10. 1080/03610926.2015.1071392. URL https://doi.org/10.1080/03610926.2015. 1071392

M. Kayid and I.A. Ahmad. On the mean inactivity time ordering with reliability applications. *Probability in the Engineering and Informational Sciences*, 18(3):395–409, 2004.

N. Keiding. Age-specific incidence and prevalence: A statistical perspective. *Journal of the Royal Statistical Society. Series A (Statistics in Society)*, 154(3):371–412, 1991.

N. Keiding and R.D. Gill. Random truncation models and markov processes. Annals of Statistics, 18(2):582–602, 1990.

J. Keilson and U. Sumita. Uniform stochastic ordering and related inequalities. *Canadian Journal of Statistics*, 10(3):181–198, 1982.

M. Kijima and M. Ohnishi. Stochastic orders and their applications in financial optimization. *Mathematical Methods of Operations Research*, 50:351–372, 1999.

G.A. Klutke, P.C. Kiessler, and M.A. Wortman. A critical look at the bathtub curve. *IEEE Transactions on Reliability*, 52(1):125–129, 2003.

S.C. Kochar. Distribution-free comparison of two probability distributions with reference to their hazard rates. *Biometrika*, 66:437–441, 1979.

S.C. Kochar. A new distribution-free test for the equality of two failure rates. *Biometrika*, 68: 423–426, 1981.

C. Kundu and A.K. Nanda. Some reliability properties of the inactivity time. *Communications in Statistics—Theory and Methods*, 39(5):899–911, 2010.

C. Kundu, A.K. Nanda, and S.S. Maiti. Some distributional results through past entropy. *Journal of Statistical Planning and Inference*, 140(5):1280–1291, 2010.

E.T. Lee and J. Wang. *Statistical Methods for Survival Data Analysis*. John Wiley & Sons, 2003.

X. Li and M. Xu. Some results about MIT order and IMIT class of life distributions. *Probability in the Engineering and Informational Sciences*, 20(3):481–496, 2006.

X. Li and M. Xu. Reversed hazard rate order of equilibrium distributions and a related aging notion. *Statistical Papers*, 49:749–767, 2008.

A.K. Nanda, H. Singh, N. Misra, and P. Paul. Reliability properties of reversed residual lifetime. *Communications in Statistics—Theory and Methods*, 32(10):2031–2041, 2003.

Y. Nikitin. *Asymptotic efficiency of nonparametric tests*. Cambridge University Press, 1995. 27

E. Ortega. A note on some functional relationships involving the mean inactivity time order. *IEEE Transactions on Reliability*, 58(1):172–178, 2009.

Kyung S. Park. Effect of burn-in on mean residual life. *IEEE Transactions on Reliability*, 34(5): 522–523, 1985.

S. Rajarshia and M.B. Rajarshib. Bathtub distributions: a review. *Communications in Statistics—Theory and Methods*, 17:2597–2621, 1988.

R. Reinertsen. Residual life of technical systems; diagnosis, prediction and life extension. *Reliability Engineering and System Safety*, 54:23–24, 1996.

M. Shaked and G.J. Shanthikumar. Stochastic orders. Springer, New York, 2007. M. Siddiqui. Residual lifetime distribution and its applications. *Microelectronics Reliability*, 34 (2):211–227, 1994.

H. Stark and J. Woods. *Probability and Random Processes with Applications to Signal Processing*. Prentice Hall, New Jersey, 2002.

G.S. Watson. Smooth regression analysis. *Sankhya: The Indian Journal of Statistics, Series A* (1961–2002), 26(4):359–372, 1964.

E.T. Wondmagegnehu, J. Navarro, and P.J. Hernandez. Bathtub shaped failure rates from mixtures: a practical point of view. *IEEE Transactions on Reliability*, 54(2):270–275, 2005.

G. Yang. Estimation of a biometric function. *Annals of Statistics*, 6(1):112–116, 1978.

W.Y. Yun, D.N. Murthy, and N. Jack. Warranty servicing with imperfect repair. *International Journal of Production Economics*, 111(1):159–169, 2008.

Chapter 5

Reliability Analysis of Relation between Urbanization, Vegetation Health, and Heat Island Through Markov Chain Model

Asutosh Goswami,[1] Shubhanita Dasgupta
Charkrabarty,[2] Suhel Sen,[2] and Priyanka Majumder[1]
[1]Department of Earth Sciences and Remote Sensing,
JIS University, Agarpara, Kolkata, India
[2]Department of Geography, Lovely Professional University, Phagwara,
Punjab, India

5.1 Introduction

Urbanization is a major indicator of development of the modern world. Since Independence, urbanization in India has been gaining momentum [1]. According to the census of 1901, about 11% of the total population lived in the urban areas, which is characterized by a meteoric rise in 2011 when about 31.16% of people lived in urban areas. The Kolkata Municipal Area in West Bengal is not an exception.

DOI: 10.1201/9781032624983-5

However, the rapid urban expansion of the city is characterized by large-scale construction of buildings and concretization of open spaces. All these tasks are often done at the expense of the vegetation cover within the city area [2]. As a result, there has been a decline in vegetation health and an increasing incidence of urban heat island effect. Initially, it was very difficult to study the temporal change of vegetation health, the scenario of urban heat island events, and the trend of urbanization. But presently, the advancement of GIS and remote sensing are helping scholars and researchers to use them as an indispensable tool to identify such changes over time. Thus this technology has become an important weapon for undertaking various urban development programs which ensures not only the overall development of the region but also takes into account the various environmental issues within and surrounding areas of the city and triggers the implementation of balanced planning over the area. Since its founding, Kolkata, formerly Calcutta, has experienced a rapid shift in terms of the management of its ambient air and water quality, urban morphology, and interactions with the environment. Kolkata became a hub of trade and capital throughout the nineteenth century, which marked the beginning of a new age of development in commerce; jobs, however, did not do so until 1960. Charnock saw the region's potential and established the foundation of British Calcutta at the Sutanuti's location, the villages of Govindapur and Kalikata on the eastern bank of the river Hugli [3]. The land use of an area is a mirror image of livelihoods. In rural areas, agricultural land plays a major role in the economy, and the built-up sector, viz., residential, commercial, and industrial sectors, control the economic activities in the urban area. Land use change occurs for different reasons in different places and times. In the twenty-first century, rapid urbanization not only is causing changes in land use, but it also is becoming a threat to the city environment and ecology. Therefore, land use change needs special attention for evaluation. The ongoing city project in Kolkata is causing a change of land use purpose and such changes greatly influence the inhabitants of the rural-urban fringe areas. When agricultural land is converted into residential, commercial area or other urban functional areas, it triggers a flow of people from different parts of the state (West Bengal) and other parts of India [4]. The suburbs continue to grow, but the inner city made up of the oldest neighborhoods is slowly stagnating and even starting to shrink in population. Between 2001 and 2011, the city of Kolkata lost about 76,000 people, although this is only a small percentage of its population of 4.5 million in 2001, it signals a new trend that must be examined more closely on a neighborhood scale. This data corrects the view that India's largest cities are growing rapidly when in fact several reasons explain their slowdown. As in the West, the improvement of the transport network has played a role in promoting outbound movement from the city center to the suburbs and beyond, facilitating living and work in better environmental conditions and on cheaper land. An equally important reason for the slowdown is land constraints at the heart of the cities over the years, which means that new development had to happen outside of existing urban areas [5].

In the Western world, the development of urbanization accelerated after the industrial revolution, which resulted in the growth of infrastructure, including communication and transportation systems, significantly accelerated the transition from rural to urban life. The concentration of people in urban areas and dominance improved provision of non-agricultural activities in metropolitan centers and social comforts like infrastructure for health and education emerged as defining characteristics of urban communities after societal industrialization [6]. The cities of today have the capacity to be thriving, convivial, and civilization-enhancing hubs. They might provide accessibility to creativity, innovation, variety, and information, as well as to better health, greater literacy, and a higher standard of living. They can represent the variety and vitality of human endeavors. The cities can be exceptional engines of economic and social advancement in many respects because they provide efficiencies, comforts, and possibilities that cannot be obtained anywhere else. In general, city dwellers earn more money and enjoy better health and easier lives than those in rural settings. In the past, cities have been the centers of economic activity and the producers of significant amounts of wealth [7–8]. Public spaces reflect the everyday routines of residents as well as tourist interests. Their design indicates the values that the community holds and helps to create impressions and perceptions of the city. This is especially true for cities like Kolkata, which have undergone numerous memories, events, and transitions. Apart from colonial ideals, Kolkata's public spaces drew inspiration from the neighborhood or paraculture of regular get-togethers and football tournaments, among other things, which eventually aided patriotic movements [9]. Accordingly, the connection between them has likewise changed. Metropolitan life and the related utilitarian situation are critical dynamic cycles and are the principal factor for metropolitan monetary advancement. This climate is under the umbrella of the metropolitan climate, which is described by the presence of high-thickness private and business structures, surface canvassed in asphalt, and a few other metropolitan related factors. Proficient utilization of land should be possible by vertical development and manageable eco-climate [10]. Urban including peri-urban planning is one of the biggest challenges most third world cities will have to face in the coming decades. In old industrialized or post-industrialized countries, it is clear that the urban peri-urban is a zone of social and economic change and spatial restructuring, whereas in most recently industrialized developing countries, the urban peri-urban area is often in a states of disorderly urbanization leading to urban sprawl [11]. Since 2007, urban areas have predominated as places where people live, making the trend of urbanization one of the most important tendencies around the world in the twenty-first century. The historical past has undergone changes that include size, pace, and altering geographic patterns of urbanization. The world in development (particularly in Asia and Africa) has already arrived at the fast-moving, high-growth stage of the numerous issues and difficulties are associated with the urbanization process, including changes in the rural–urban split [12]. Urbanization is a new peculiarity in mankind's set of experiences. The interaction and qualities of urbanization shifts start with one country, then move on to the next. Modern unrest has brought about urbanization in Western Europe and North America in 1900 years, however in Asia, Africa, and Latin America, it is an outcome of colonial rule. To that end, the example and pattern of urbanization of creating nations is very exceptional [13]. Kolkata is situated in the Bengal Delta area of India, which is center point of various tropical diseases. Tropical illnesses are irresistible and communicable in nature. They are created by the passage of illness-causing parasites into the human body. The methods for the transmission of these illnesses are unique, some being communicated straightforwardly from one individual to other, with others going through at least one intermediary transporter, called "vectors" [14]. The hot and damp climate is friendly to the spread of various irresistible infections. Kolkata is a weak zone for the assault of different irresistible and transferable sicknesses. Chance of this assault is exasperated with the undesirable adjustment by the sped-up pace of human mediation of the actual climate. The metropolitan setup of Kolkata is constrained by individuals who satisfy their various requirements with development of houses, tall structures, streets, ventures, markets, business, business units, etc. Fast populace development in the urban communities and towns is the significant trademark highlighted in India since the twentieth century [15]. Urbanization is presently a consuming issue all around the world, and it is related to numerous interconnected things. Urbanization is viewed as one of the critical elements of the course of financial turn of events. Be that as it may, there is a distinction between the effects of urbanization on the financial improvement of created nations and that of non-industrial nations. The attribute of urbanization in created nations is not quite the same as in non-industrial nations. Urban communities in the created world are considered the driving force of development, whereas in emerging nations, the urban communities are considered parasites, removing assets from country regions [16]. In spite of the fact that India is one of the less urbanized nations of the world with just 27.78% of the populace living in towns, India is confronting a serious emergency of metropolitan development at the present time. Even as urbanization has been an instrument of monetary, social, and political advancement, it has prompted serious financial issues. Urbanization is an interaction that prompts the development of urban communities because of industrialization and financial development [17]. Metropolitan settlements are grown by impacting the indigenous habitat so enormously that individuals tend to see the city just as a work site and as a financial and social focus; the metropolitan region in this manner has changed into a very clogged and contaminated human habitat. This results in huge increases of vehicles, ecological stress, and perpetual harm to the environment [18]. Urban sprawl or urban expansion is the unplanned or the undesirable development of a city towards its contiguous provincial regions at the expense of metropolitan natural quality because of high populace pressure, lower land rates at the peripheral parts, improvement of foundations, rises in the way of life, lack of metropolitan preparation, and so on [19]. At present, the populace of the Kolkata Metropolitan Area (KMA) is developing at an extremely quicker rate, spreading the impact of human residence to the nearby suburban lands. As an ever increasing number of individuals are deciding to live in regions contiguous to the fundamental city center, land esteem is expanding and ascending beyond reasonable cutoff points of neighborhood inhabitants [20]. Public spaces are viewed as a fundamental element of prosperous urban communities as they support the feeling of local area, personality, and culture. Understanding their importance, the Mexican government has grown new administrative frameworks. Urbanization implies the course of an area to be urbanized. It is exceptionally fast on account of emerging nations, and it diminishes towards created nations. On account of non-industrial nations, metropolitan urban communities have been assuming a fundamental role in the higher developmental pace of urbanization. According to different specialists, urbanization has been ordered as a course of urbanization [21]. The present metropolitan framework in many parts of the world is portrayed by an area of improvement in a couple of kilometres of each metropolitan city, giving the metropolitan community an appearance of an island of improvement in an expanse of hardship [22]. This is valid for India as well as for West Bengal. Metropolitan and peri-metropolitan horticultural practices are corrupting spaces by creating scenes of remarkable metropolitan rambling and subsequent extension of developed regions. This study endeavours to detect the changing area of land use/land cover of Kolkata metropolitan area, India from 1999 to 2022 with special emphasis on the change trajectories of its metropolitan and peri-metropolitan farming as a contextual investigation utilizing free and open-source programming and multi-transient geospatial information base. As in other emerging nations, urbanization is also expanding in India. Metropolitan occupants are supposed to represent almost 40% of the total populace by 2021, and a significant part of the metropolitan populace is presumed to live in the huge urban communities. West Bengal likewise gives a very comparative picture. Since freedom, the province of West Bengal has seen a consistent pace of urbanization, with the level of metropolitan populace in West Bengal continuously higher than the gross normal [22]. Several studies have focused on the problem of UHI impact on the whole ecosystem, especially vegetation health. Earlier studies have regarded the UHI effect as the difference in energy balance between the rural and urban areas [23]. Generally, heat energetics of the earth-atmosphere system is characterized by short-wave radiation exchange during the day and long-wave radiation at night [24]. The energy gained by the earth is lost through conduction and convection, so that sensible heat is converted into latent heat. It has been observed that air temperatures in a city are generally higher than in the surrounding peri-urban or rural areas [25]. This is mainly because sensible heat flux is higher due to the presence of concrete structures [26], which have high heat trapping capacity. The absence or scarcity of vegetation ensures that the latent heat flux is lower. Moreover, heat is added from other sources, like industrial and vehicular combustion, air conditioners, etc. [27], apart from solar energy. The heat island effect can be measured on both horizontal and vertical scales and is affected by geographical location, seasonality [28], and the size and density of the urban area. The vertical extent of the heat energetics can be studied with respect to two distinct layers, i.e., the urban canopy layer (UCL) and the urban boundary layer (UBL) [23]. The UCL, a microscale phenomenon, is the first layer of an urban heat island, which extends from the ground surface to the roof or vegetation level [29], where air flow is restricted by surface roughness. The UBL, a mesoscale phenomenon, is the second layer, situated above the UCL and extending to the layer of temperature inversion. Although the UHI effect takes place at the surface, the process controlling it takes place in the UBL [30]. The UBL can be divided into a roughness sublayer (RSL), which is characterized by turbulence in mean air flow and the inertial sublayer (ISL), where turbulence is uniform [30]. The depth of the UBL increases during the daytime over the urban area, depending on the availability of the sensible heat and stability of air flow. This leads to the doming of the mixed layer (ML), which is a zone of strong turbulence and mixing. Towards the lee side of this dome, a rural boundary layer (RBL), which cuts off the hot urban air, forms a zone of urban plume. During the night, the UHI is well developed, and the ML exists at the surface. This problem is compounded with the increase in density of urban areas [31]. Spatial variations exist due to the presence of waterbodies [32] and vegetation, which play a significant role in reducing the UHI effect locally. Studies conclude that the presence of hotter LST (land surface temperature) pixels in satellite images of urban built-up areas, whereas cooler LST pixels are found to be concentrated in urban areas [33]. Moreover, a strong relationship seems to exist between high LST and impervious surfaces. Studies indicate that urbanization has resulted in an inverse relationship between impervious surface [34] and vegetation cover and has also led to alterations in the LST patterns [35]. However, rapid urbanization occurs at the cost of natural vegetation cover [36] leading to vegetation degradation [37, 38], fragmentation of the surface, and formation of irregular spaces [39]. Urbanization also affects the plant–herbivore relationship due to the negative effect on water availability and fragmentation of habitats [40]. This, in turn, has a negative impact on the ecological and evolutionary processes. The threats of global warming and subsequent climate change makes the situation of cities in the period of globalization and post-globalization even further complicated [41], due to which alternative ecosystems are seen to emerge. Indian cities are also undergoing land use and land cover (LULC) changes in urban areas both horizontally and vertically. The high rate of migration leads to huge population pressure in the cities, which then tend to expand in a haphazard and unplanned manner. Studies have revealed a huge decline of vegetation and waterbodies between 1973 and 2017 [42]. Urban vegetation health is an emerging issue in study of impact of UHI. In India, studies conducted in cities like Bengaluru [43] yield interesting results. The surface UHI effect can be studied using remote sensing with the help of thermal remote sensing data from satellite images [44, 45]. Using LULC maps, obtained from satellite data, the temperature vegetation index (TVX) can be calculated.

Studies have shown that over time the number of pixels in low-temperature areas of dense vegetation decreases, while an increase is seen in high-temperature areas of sparse vegetation [46]. This method can be used for monitoring LULC changes to understand UHI effect. NDVI, or normalized difference vegetation index, which can be calculated using satellite data, giving a clear understanding of vegetation health. NDBI, or normalized difference built-up index, is used to highlight urban areas, with respect to the differences in the reflectance values of short-wave infrared and near-infrared regions [47]. NDBI increases with the increase in built-up areas, whereas NDVI values decrease [48]. Studies using the method of maximum normalized difference vegetation index (NDVImax) shows that urbanized areas, especially those that are newly developed, have significantly lower NDVI values [49] and that older urban centers show a greening trend. Studies using NDVI in mountainous areas have shown that the rapidly increasing rate of urbanization has a detrimental effect on vegetation restoration [50]. This may result in a pronounced UHI effect in future, even in mountainous urban centers. An automated temperature-sensor network, along with remotely sensed data impact of UHI effect on plant health, has also been studied [51].

The present study highlights the urbanization issues in Kolkata (Figure 5.1) along with its geo-environmental consequences mainly on the natural vegetation of the study area. The predicted rate of expanding urban centers and its overwhelming consequences has been thoroughly computed by the Markov chain decision support system with analytical hierarchy process (AHP) at the back of the informational fundamentals.

5.2 Materials and Methods

5.2.1 Normalized Difference Vegetation Index (NDVI)

NDVI is a mathematical pointer that utilizes the apparent and close infrared groups of the electromagnetic range and is taken on to examine remote detecting estimations and survey whether the target being noticed contains live green vegetation. Researchers notice the tones (frequencies) of apparent and close infrared daylight reflected by the plants to decide the thickness of green on a fix of land. When daylight strikes vegetation and bare soil, certain frequencies of this range are ingested and different frequencies are reflected. The shade in plant leaves, chlorophyll, unequivocally retains apparent light (0.4–0.7 μm) for use in photosynthesis. The cell construction of the leaves, then, again, unequivocally reflects close infrared light (0.7–1.1 μm). The more leaves a plant has, the more these frequencies of light are impacted, separately.

The National Oceanic and Atmospheric Administration advanced very high resolution radiometer (NOAA AHVRR) sensor has five locators, two of which are dedicated to the frequencies of light running from 0.55–0.70 to 0.73–1.0 mm. With

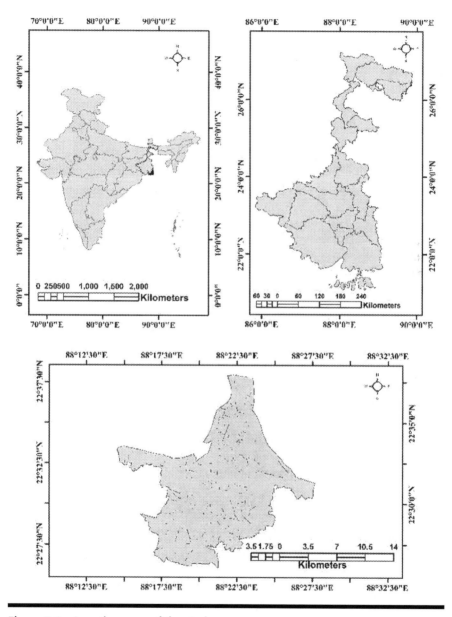

Figure 5.1   Location map of the study area.

AHVRR's identifiers, analysts can quantify the force of light falling off the earth in apparent and close infrared frequencies; furthermore, they can evaluate the photosynthetic limit of the vegetation in a given pixel (an AVHRR pixel is 1 km²) of land surface. By and large, assuming there is significantly more reflected radiation in close to infrared frequencies than in noticeable frequencies, then, at that point, the vegetation in that pixel is probably going to be thick and may contain a backwoods of some sort. In the event that almost no distinction in the power of apparent and close infrared frequencies is reflected, then the vegetation is presumably scanty and may be comprised of field, tundra, or desert. NDVI is determined from the visible and near-infrared light reflected by vegetation. Solid vegetation ingests the majority of the noticeable light that hits it and mirrors a huge part of the close infrared light. Undesirable or inadequate vegetation mirrors more noticeable light and less close infrared light. Hence the NDVI is a detector of plant "greenness" or photosynthetic movement and is one of the most usually utilized for vegetation vigor. Vegetation records depend on the perception that various surfaces mirror various kinds of light in unexpected ways. Photographs of artificially dynamic vegetation, specifically, retain the vast majority of the red light that hits the surface while reflecting a large part of the close to infrared light. Vegetation that is dead reflects more red light and less close to infrared light. Similarly, non-vegetated surfaces have a considerably more even reflectance across the light range.

The work has been done by adopting geospatial techniques using software like ERDAS Imagine 2015 and ArcGIS 10.3. In order to accomplish the task, Landsat Enhanced Thematic Mapper (ETM+) and Landsat Thematic Mapper images of the study area were downloaded from USGS Earth Explorer website (https://earthexplo rer.usgs.gov/) for the four years of 1999, 2009, 2019, and 2022. Landsat ETM+ has eight bands, while Landsat TM images have seven bands. Sensor features among Landsat TM and ETM+ are same from band 1 to band 5. In ETM+, band 6 has two sub-bands: high and low. Panchromatic band (band 8) is available only in ETM+. The satellite images of the following date were downloaded to fulfill the task (Table 5.1).

NDVI is an algorithm that helps in the estimation of the amount of ground green vegetation cover from the reflectance of the red (R) and the near-infrared (NIR) bands. NDVI values range from –1 to +1. NDVI values ranging from 0.3 to 0.6 are considered to be stressed vegetation, while values exceeding 0.6 are considered to be healthy vegetation. The NDVI map is prepared using the following formula (Equation 5.1):

$$NDVI = (NIR - R)/ (NIR + R) \qquad (5.1)$$

Table 5.1 Details of Satellite Images Downloaded

Acquisition Date	Sensor and Satellite	Reference System/ Path/Row
1999/05/31	Landsat 5 TM	UTM–45N/138/44
2009/05/10	Landsat 5 TM	UTM-45N/138/44
2019/04/28	Landsat 7 ETM+	UTM-45N/138/44
2022/03/19	Landsat 9	UTM-45N/138/44

5.2.2 *Normalized Difference Built-Up Index (NDBI)*

Land experiences an exceptional addition in the reflectance from band 4 to band 5. However, vegetation has marginally bigger or more modest DN esteem (not calculable) on band 5 than on band 4. And this interesting augmentation should be visible between these groups. This empowers the development region to be isolated from residual covers and consequently NDBI. The normalized separation of band 5 and band 4 results in positive values for development pixels. The proportion is relegated another worth of either 0 on the off chance that the input pixel had a negative record or 264 on the off chance that its feedback file was bigger than 0. As indicated by the aftereffects of Table 5.1, deduction of NDBI and NDVI will prompt just developed region and fruitless pixels, while the remainder of pixels with upsides of 0 or –264, permitting the developed region to be planned naturally. The normalized difference built-up index (NDBI) helps in the extraction of built-up features, and its value ranges from –1 to +1. The NDBI map was prepared using Equation 5.2:

$$\text{NDBI} = (\text{SWIR} - \text{NIR}) / (\text{SWIR} + \text{NIR}) \tag{5.2}$$

where SWIR is short wave infrared and NIR is near-infrared.

5.2.3 *Land Surface Temperature Method*

Land surface temperatures (LST) were determined utilizing the information from the groups of the LANDSAT-8 satellite picture. The 10th and 11th groups of the TIRS (thermal infrared sensor) are accessible in the satellite. Reflection values are utilized and changed to appraise the temperature as computerized numbers (DN). These qualities are then switched over completely to reflectance values from DN to equal the ground surface temperature with the situation underneath. It was changed to computerized number values over completely to °C by taking away 273.15 worth from Ts values in Kelvin (Equation 5.3).

$$\text{LST} = \text{ST}/1 + \text{W}^*(\text{ST}/\text{p})^*\text{In}(\text{e}) \tag{5.3}$$

where ST is satellite temperature, W is wavelength of radiance emitted (11.5 μm), $p = h^*\text{C}/\text{S}$ (1.438*10^–2mk), h = Planck's constant (6.626*10^–34JS), s = Boltzmann constant (1.38*10^–23J/K), C = speed of light (2.998*10^8 m/s), p = 14380.

The thermal band was used to generate radiance data using ArcGIS 10.3 software, and then land surface temperature maps were generated using the algorithm mentioned in the Landsat 7 handbook. The land use maps were prepared using ERDAS Imagine 2015 software with the maximum likelihood principle. Finally, relationships were drawn between the NDVI, NDBI, and heat island maps to decipher the relation between urbanization, vegetation health, and urban heat island effect of Kolkata municipal corporation area.

5.2.4 Analytical Hierarchy Process (AHP)

The AHP is an overall hypothesis of estimation that is determined by making correlations utilizing mathematical decisions from the flat-out size of numbers. This is fundamental when both objective elements should be viewed, as in a very similar pool. AHP gives a method for determining and incorporating family member scales deliberately. The different variables are organized in a pecking order and estimated by the component and subfactor addressed inside these designs. It is utilized to get proportion scales from both discrete and nonstop matched correlations [52]. The expanding utilization of the AHP has been the inspiration for this review to investigate the present status of its approach. The technique is for evaluating the best instrument for every choice circumstance and reflecting every member's perspective accurately [53]. It is the method of thinking about every component in the relating level and aligning them on the mathematical size of numbers that demonstrates how often a more significant or prevailing component supersedes a component depending on the factor for which they are looked at.

Stage 1: A nine-point mathematical scale is utilized for the correlation. The force, or pair wise ranking, is as follows: 1 = equivalent significance; 2 = powerless or slight; 3 = moderate significance; 4 = moderate in addition to; 5 = solid significance; 6 = solid in addition to; 7 = exceptionally amazing; 8 = incredibly solid; 9 = outrageous significance. Or 1.1–1.9 can be used on the off chance that the exercises are very close.

Stage 2: The pairwise correlations of different elements created at stage 1 are coordinated into a square grid. The corner-to-corner components of the grid are as follows: I column is better than considering the J segment if the worth of component (I, J) is multiple; in any case, the J section is better than that in the I column. The (J, I) component of the framework is the proportional of the (I, J) component.

Stage 3: The central eigenvalue and the relating standardized right eigenvector of the examination framework give the family member the significance of the different measures being looked at. The components of the standardized eigenvector are named loads concerning the standards or subcriteria and evaluations with regard to the other options.

Stage 4: For all the subfactors, nine credits were distinguished: magnificent/awesome/great/better than expected/normal/beneath normal/not poor/poor/extremely poor. For each subfactor, the magnificent quality got a load of 0.9, the above-average weight of 0.6, and the extremely unfortunate load of 0.1.

Stage 5: The rating of every option is increased by the loads of the subfactor and amassed to get neighborhood evaluations concerning each variable. The nearby evaluations are then, at that point, increased by the loads of the variable and collected to get combined efficiency. The AHP produces weight values for every option in view of making a decision about the significance of one option over another regarding a typical. This study involves the utilization of multi-models direction (MCDM) devices, specifically the AHP. AHP is utilized to explain diverse decision contention and to connect with a staggered order design of objectives, models, subcriteria, and choices. A strategy in getting the ideal expert measures right off the bat is to distinguish the models for advisor determination. The cycle associated with AHP fundamentally includes the appraisal of standards and sub-rules by pertinent specialists in their particular field. Among the key commitments given by AHP is that it can decide the most predominant measures and sub-models for each given objective. The main stage in AHP is to fabricate a various leveled structure that comprises objectives, measures, and sub-models. Then the AHP model is created through a pair wise survey that will be evaluated by the specialists. Hence the aftereffects of the survey will be registered also; determining the mathematical mean before it is shaped to the framework structure and the heaviness of each standards is acquired. In particular, the AHP strategy can decide to the degree to which reactions are reliable or conflicting through the consistency record.

5.2.5 Markov Chain Model

Here, the Markov decision model is proposed to display the ways of behaving of partners (government, occupants, and nature), and of the communications between them. Government, the focal chief in managing the environmental issues, at each time step, n, makes a move (i.e., speculation choice) towards x^n and gets reactions from the occupants y^n; furthermore, the nature z^n through the expense c^n. Then this normal and financial framework moves to another state S^n in view of the past state S^{n-1}, government's activity x^n, and the ascent level r^n. The framework state comprises the sets of city's foundation state s^n and the ascent level n, i.e., $S^n = (s^n, \text{'}n\text{'})$. The public authority's venture choices additionally decide the condition of the city framework s^n, which is demonstrated as Equation 5.10:

$$(S_t - 1, l_{t-1}) \tag{5.4}$$

$$I_t = 0, r_t = r_1 \tag{5.5}$$

$$(S_t - 1, l_{t-1} + r_1) \tag{5.6}$$

$$X_t = 1, r_t = r_2 \tag{5.7}$$

$$(S_{t-1} + 1, l_{t-1} + r_2) \tag{5.8}$$

$$X_t = q, \, r_t = r_3 \tag{5.9}$$

$$(S_{t-1} + q, l_{t-1} + r_3) \tag{5.10}$$

Here 0 and l0 are individually the underlying framework state, and the underlying ocean level of the city. With regard to reenactments, these are two user-defined numbers addressing the current states toward the start of the reproductions. The framework state plainly fulfills the Markov property: $P(S_t|S_t-1,\ldots., S_0) = P(St|S_{t-1})$.

5.2.5.1 Governmental Model

At each time step, e.g., a year, the public authority chooses the level of its venture $x^n \in \{0, 1, 2, \ldots., q\}$ for framework improvement, where q is a limited positive number (Equation 5.11).

$$C_N = \sum_{n=0}^{N} a^n_g \left[\alpha X_n - \beta y_n + z_n \right] \tag{5.11}$$

$x^n = 0$ methods follow no venture at step n. Thus there are $q + 1$ potential activities for the public authority at each time step. The mathematical worth of $x^n = m$ can be deciphered as spending m unit directly towards the framework improvement or on the other hand the mth activity among q various activities with expanding cost and viability. Conceivable government activities incorporate but are not restricted to building seawalls, raising streets, broadening ocean side, building customary or flat levees, setting stormwater siphons, further developing sewage frameworks, migrating coastline properties, and so forth. The scope of x^n is intended to cover the genuine expenses from the least expensive speculation like cleaning the lines to the most costly venture like purchasing grounds and property to move the shoreline occupants and organizations. The complete expense cn to the specialist at each time n comprises the venture cost, cost from nature, and the inhabitants' commitment to the speculation. Since the public authority's venture choice and the inhabitants' commitment choice have whole number qualities, we model the all-out cost as $c^n = \alpha x^n - \beta y^n + z^n$ utilizing boundaries α and β to plan the choices to financial values. The three unique elements in the expense definition are joined by changing the boundaries α, β and the boundaries of the probabilistic model presented for the nature's cost z^n in Section 5.2.5.

5.2.6 Finding Supportive Policy

We showed that the ideal strategy is given by a number of limits, but totally determining the ideal arrangement with insightful articulations for limits doesn't appear to be manageable because of countless boundaries connected with the issue. Thus we next propose a reinforcement learning (RL) calculation as the ideal strategy for mimicked situations. In particular, to gain proficiency with the ideal strategy, a profound RL calculation is required due to the constant urban environmental qualities, which cause a boundless number of potential states. The profound Q organization (DQN) calculation, which is a well-known decision for profound RL, addresses well the limitless layered state space issue (Equation 5.12). It uses a profound organization to gauge the ideal activity esteem capability.

$$Q\left(S_t, l_t, X_t\right) = E\left[C_t + a_g \min_x Q\left(S_t + X_t, l_{t+1}, X\right) \mid X_t\right] \qquad (5.12)$$

5.3 Result and Discussion

5.3.1 Temporal Analysis of Land Use and Land Cover of Kolkata Municipal Area

The Kolkata Municipal Area has undergone significant changes in land use and land cover over the period of 1999, 2009, 2019, and 2022 (Figure 5.2). The detailed discussion of land use and land cover maps of the study area has been incorporated in the following section, which reveals that out of the total 20342.9 hectares of land area, about 4543.83 hectares were under waterbodies in the year 1999 including marshes, ponds, lakes, river, etc. and thus accounted for about 22.34% of total land area. About 3488.94 hectares was under vegetation cover, accounting for about 17.15% of total area. Built-up areas covered about 12310.10 hectares, accounting for about 60.51% of total area (Figure 5.2[A]). Thus in 1999 there has been a dominance of built-up area among all the land use and land cover types. The land use and land cover map in 2009 reveals that out of the total 20342.9 hectares of land area, about 2183.76 hectares were under waterbodies and thus accounted for about 10.73% of total land area, indicating a sharp decline in the spatial coverage of waterbodies in comparison to the year 1999. The decline in waterbodies can be interpreted as a result of increasing spatial coverage of built-up areas, which accounted for 72.44% of total area (Figure 5.2[B]). Thus in 2009 there has also been a dominance of built-up area among all the land use and land covers. The situation is found to be improving in 2019 when 2538.94 hectares of area has been detected to be dominated by waterbodies, including marshes, ponds, lakes, rivers, etc. and thus accounted for about 12.48% of total land area (Figure 5.2[C]). It is due to increasing awareness among everyday people and government reading about the conservation of waterbodies. Out of the total area of 20342.9 hectares, about 1473.18 hectares are found to be under vegetation cover, accounting for about 7.24% of total area. There is almost 8% (80% of the total area) increase in the built-up coverage in the time span from 2009 to 2019. The increasing trend in spatial coverage of built-up area is also found to be continuing in 2022 (Figure 5.2[D]). Only at an interval of 3 years, i.e., from 2019 to 2022, built-up areas have experienced an increase of 1.7% at the cost of declining waterbodies and vegetation cover. Through the temporal analysis of the

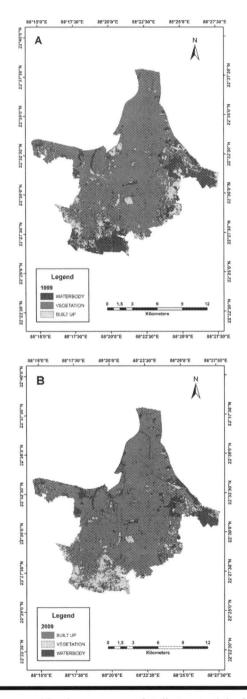

Figure 5.2   Land use and land cover map of Kolkata Municipal Area in (A) 1999;
(B) 2009; (C) 2019; and (D) 2022.

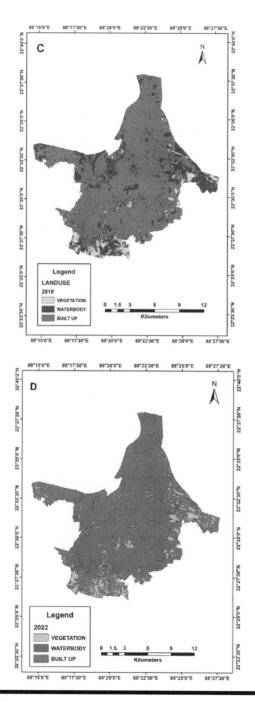

Figure 5.2   (Continued)

land use and land cover maps of Kolkata Municipal Area, it can be seen that built-up areas have registered an increasing trend from 1999 to 2022. In 1999, the total built-up area was 12310.10 hectares which increased to 14735.90 hectares in 2009 and further increased to become 16330.8 hectares in 2019 and finally jumped to become 17361.9 hectares in 2022. This can be attributed to the large scale of urbanization and concretization of the study area over the given time periods. Vegetation of the study area has registered a declining trend over the same time period with 3488.94 hectares in 1999, slightly declining to 3423.24 hectares in 2009, and has undergone a sharp decline to about 1473.18 hectares in 2019. But area coverage of vegetation increased to 2663 hectares in 2022 as there was suspension of human activities due to the pandemic lockdown, and the city environment had the chance to restore itself. Destruction of vegetation within the study area for developmental projects like the expansion of roadways and construction of buildings and large-scale promoting activity has led to this decreased vegetation of the study area. Area under waterbodies has undergone continuous fluctuations when the area decreased between 1999 and 2022 and has registered a rise between 2009 and 2019.

5.3.2 Temporal Analysis of Normalized Difference Vegetation Index (NDVI) of Kolkata Municipal Area

The scenario or status of vegetation health can be analyzed from the temporal analysis of NDVI images. Within the Kolkata Municipal Area, vegetation health has been declining significantly. The maximum NDVI value has declined from 0.56 in 1999 to 0.52 in 2022 (Figure 5.3). The rate of decline in the highest NDVI value is found to be maximum in 2019 with the NDVI value of 0.43 as a result of drastic change in land use and land cover patterns. Major developmental activities in the city at the cost of natural environment have taken place within the time period from 2009 to 2019. However, the NDVI value is found to be improving in 2022 as result of increasing awareness by KMC about the geo-environmental environs of the city.

5.3.3 Temporal Analysis of Normalized Difference Built-Up Index (NDBI) of Kolkata Municipal Area

Scenario of urbanization of the study area has been analyzed through the preparation of NDBI maps. The study clearly shows that there has been a remarkable rise in the NDBI values with time from 1999 to 2022, and a rising trend is exhibited. The NDBI value of Kolkata Municipal Area has risen from 0.35 in 1999 to 0.39 in 2009, finally reaching the maximum value of 1 in 2019 (Figure 5.4). The intensity of built-up potential has been found to be declining for the year 2022 when the computed NDBI value is detected as 0.3 (Figure 5.4), as a result of the rainwater harvesting system and rooftop gardening scheme, considering the fact of continuous rise in built-up areas within the city.

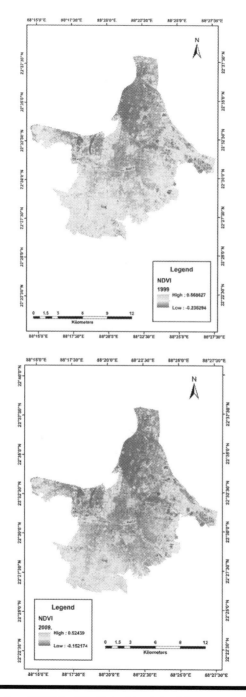

Figure 5.3 Scenario of NDVI of Kolkata Municipal Area (1999–2022).

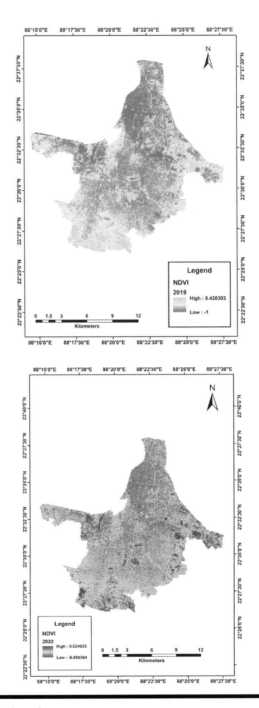

Figure 5.3 (Continued)

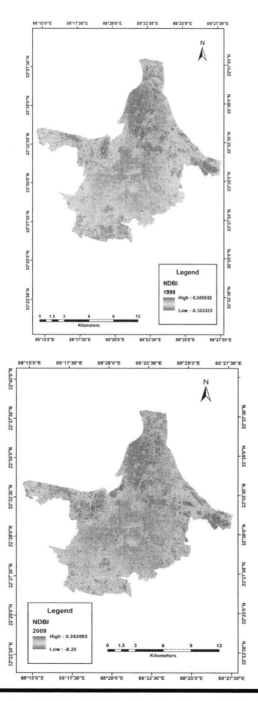

Figure 5.4 Scenario of NDBI of Kolkata Municipal Area (1999–2022).

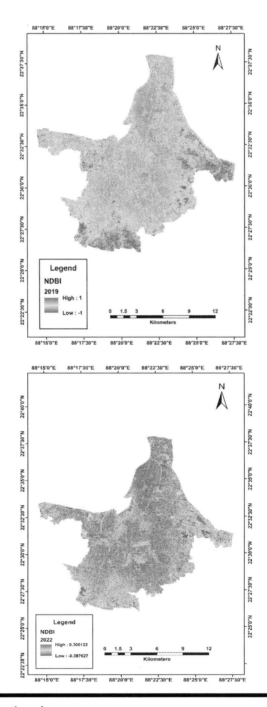

Figure 5.4   (Continued)

5.3.4 Scenario of Urban Heat Island of Kolkata Municipal Area From 1999 to 2022

The scenario of the urban heat island phenomena within the study area can be analyzed with the help of the land surface temperature maps. The maps reveal that in 1999, the maximum and minimum temperatures within the city were computed as 35.6517°C and 24.9737°C, respectively which increased to 37.6121°C and 26.2511°C, respectively, for the year 2009 (Figure 5.5). In 2019, the maximum temperature value increased to become 37.7551°C, while the minimum temperature declined to become 24.3641°C. The increasing trend in average maximum and minimum temperatures is also encountered in 2022 when these values are found to be 38.3°C and 26.87° C, respectively.

5.3.5 Analytical Hierarchy Process

The study employs AHP (Figure 5.6) to explain the role of different environmental factors in controlling the city climate. Five criteria have been selected based on the review of literature mainly framed on Kolkata city. The scale values 1 to 9 have been used to highlight the role of each parameter on the city's geo-environmental sustainability. The role of vegetation has always been a significant factor in determining the moisture condition in an area, particularly the city climate. Indices based on the vegetation health status are getting higher significance values (generally 3) in comparison to rainfall. The city temperature, more specifically with the inclusion of LST values, is getting due significance in estimating the hierarchy model of city environment. Making correlations among different significant parameters (Figure 5.7) indicates temperature and rainfall, NDVI, VCI and LST pair and is highly significant in forecasting the city weather behavior.

Figure 5.8 highlights the percentage weighting of different controlling parametric values. The maximum weightage is gained by the LST and rainfall factors with 27.6% assigned to each. The rainfall is undoubtedly a controlling factor for minimizing the role of urban heat island effect. On the contrary, LST values are crucial in deteriorating the city climate system, aggravated by the declining NDVI and rising NDBI phenomena. Again, the role of LST can be interpreted as a systematic and dependable factor if the urban environmental degradation is to be minimized. The graph indicates that, out of five factors, the role of temperature, particularly its higher occupancy over the pillar, is found to be maximum in determining the critical city weather pattern. It is followed by the factor of VCI (vegetation condition index). Though the altitudinal influence is more for LST parameter, its altitudinal coverage is found to be less in comparison to the temperature factor.

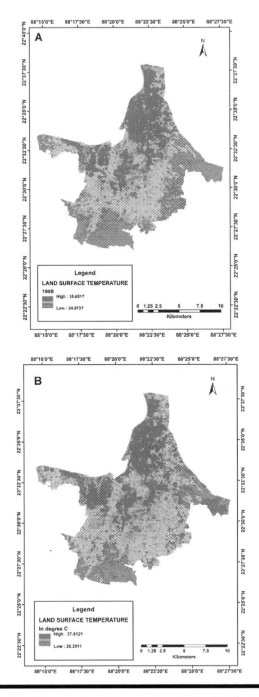

Figure 5.5 Scenario of land surface temperature (◦C) of Kolkata Municipal Area in (A) 1999; (B) 2009; (C) 2019; and (D) 2022.

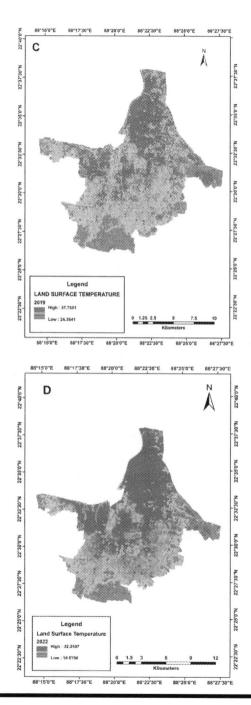

Figure 5.5   (Continued)

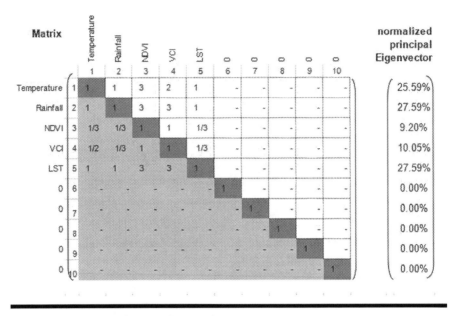

Figure 5.6 Analytical hierarchy matrix.

5.3.6 *Markov Chain*

The integrational advancement of the urban management has become obvious for all the major cities in the world. The major problem of the ongoing chain model is the number of sample size. Spatial measurements registered in thickness angles help in explaining spatio-fleeting examples of urbanization at neighborhood levels and in backing supportable metropolitan preparation and management choices. Measurements show an expansion in metropolitan pixels. Parameters measurements (like vegetation, waterbodies, LST, built-up intensity) feature a never ending suburbia at the edges and in the cushion locales, while total records feature the course of collection at the downtown area. The metropolitan example investigation through spatial measurements gave experiences about the spatial designs transiently and quantitatively. Figure 5.9, particularly the positive uprising bar graphs, highlights the more probable expansion of urban dimension of Kolkata city. The least variation found in the probabilistic model suggests the contiguous urban development and expansion within a very short time span. The measurements highlight the anthropogenic tensions on the scene. This indicates that the scene at the city fringe is exceptionally divided; furthermore, the city organization requires designs to be done in a staged way to give fundamental conveniences. Legitimate land use arrangements with temporal observing would support manageable preparation. The coexistence of financial exercises, biological honesty, infrastructural deficiencies, destitution mitigation, and populace development are presenting serious difficulties to metropolitan

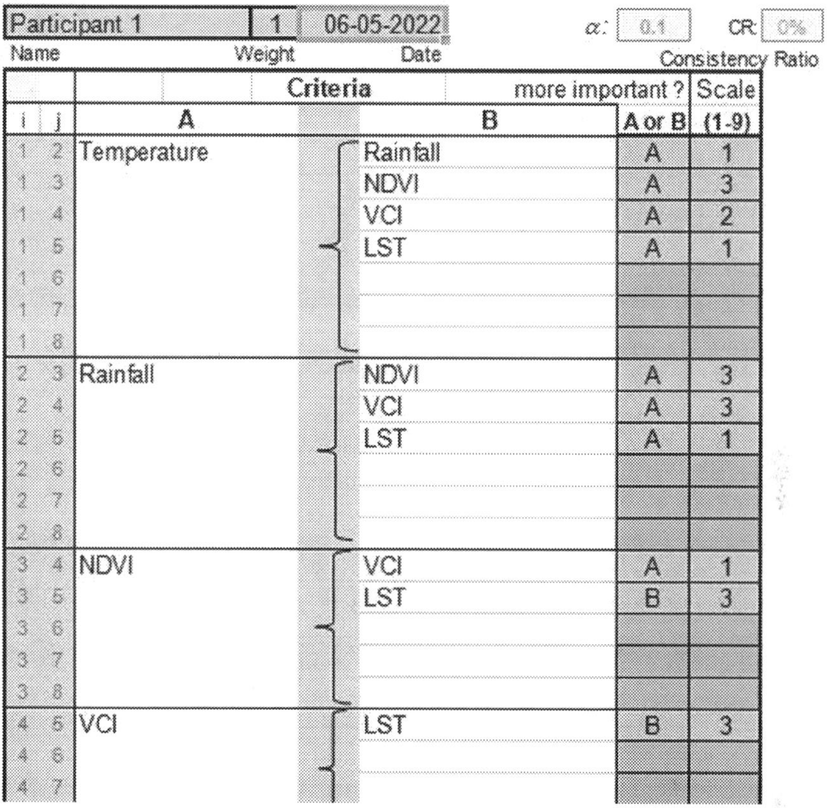

Participant 1 | 1 | 06-05-2022 | α: 0.1 | CR: 0%

Name | Weight | Date | Consistency Ratio

i	j	Criteria A	Criteria B	more important? A or B	Scale (1-9)
1	2	Temperature	Rainfall	A	1
1	3		NDVI	A	3
1	4		VCI	A	2
1	5		LST	A	1
1	6				
1	7				
1	8				
2	3	Rainfall	NDVI	A	3
2	4		VCI	A	3
2	5		LST	A	1
2	6				
2	7				
2	8				
3	4	NDVI	VCI	A	1
3	5		LST	B	3
3	6				
3	7				
3	8				
4	5	VCI	LST	B	3
4	6				
4	7				

Figure 5.7 Correlation between different parameters.

preparation. These require coordinated interdisciplinary investigations to comprehend the multidimensional and complex cooperation of metropolitan frameworks to examine the impacts of various measures.

5.4 Conclusion

Through the analysis of the relationships among vegetation health, urbanization, and urban heat island, it has been clearly revealed that vegetation health has exhibited a decline from 1999 to 2022, while urbanization and heat island phenomena have shown a rising trend within the same period. There is no doubt that urbanization is a precursor of development. However, urban development must be done in a balanced way so that both development and environmental issues can be taken care of. From this we can presume that certain instances of harm to the climate due to urbanization will occur from the regulation and the

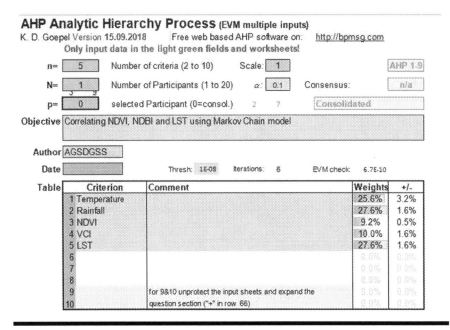

Figure 5.8   Weightage of different parameters.

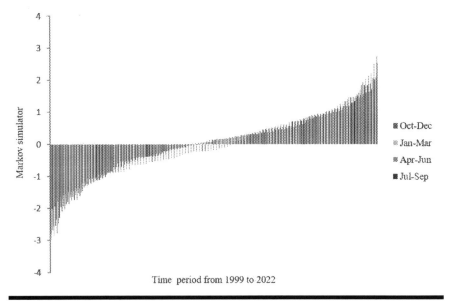

Figure 5.9   Markov chain analysis.

directing offices of the country. Disappointment with the present administration in urban communities has come about in the development of casual settlements and ghettos that comprise undesirable living and workplace conditions. Serious consideration ought to be given to the requirement for working on metropolitan methodologies to advance effectiveness in asset use. Dire consideration ought to be given to diminish the age of strong waste at the sources through obligatory principles and guideline change and assessment of motivating forces, along with training and willful consistency. Also, if satisfactory advances are not taken to forestall contamination, in order to improve personal satisfaction by making more social conveniences available, the existence of the metropolitan inhabitants of India may become even more hopeless; this might be the reason for well-being risks and horrendously awful demolition. So it is the obligation of government to make vital moves to forestall climate change by taking every conceivable measure. Furthermore, organizers need to likewise focus on these issues while safeguarding the climate. Efficiency in the operating room relies not just upon the clinic, patient, or cooperating agencies (which are either evenhanded or emotional); so, in light of the intricacy of our subject, it isn't difficult to measure and the communicate about it. The efficiency needs a computation technique, and AHP has a sound numerical premise, and its application is user-friendly. Thus AHP is an important means to plan a model to choose the total efficiency, efficiency rate, and, what's more, to pursue a choice in OT. It very well may be utilized for analysis in connection with other, more standard means. Besides, it could empower us to distinguish what is lacking in particular regions.

References

1. Roy, T.D., & Basak, A. (2020). The Emergence of the Urban Heat Island through Remote Sensing Approach: A case study of Greater Siliguri, West Bengal, India. In P.K Kundu (Eds.), *Sustainable Urbanisation in East India: Present Trends and Future Concerns* (1st ed., pp 349–357). Levant Books.
2. Adhikari, A.K., & Roy, T.B. (2020). Application of Geospatial Technology for Assessment of Urban Heat Island; A Case Study of Gangarampur Municipality, West Bengal, India. In P.K Kundu (Eds.), *Sustainable Urbanisation in East India: Present Trends and Future Concerns* (1st ed., pp 298–309). Levant Books.
3. Dey, F. (2021). Dynamics of urban growth and environmental challenges: a case of Kolkata, India. *Geography, Environment, Sustainability*, 3, 24–31. https://DOI-10.24057/2071-9388-2020-194
4. Biswas, A., & Singh, O. (2017). Rajarhat New Town an Urban Perspective: A Case Study of Urbanization, West Bengal, India. *International Journal of New Technology and Research*, 3(5), 39–44.
5. Shaw, A. (2015). Inner-city and Outer-city Neighborhoods in Kolkata: Their Changing Dynamics Post Liberalization. *Environment and Urbanization Asia*, 6(2), 139–153.

6. Rahaman, M., & Das, S. (2018). Urbanization of West Bengal: A Study of Inter-District Variation in Level of Urbanization. *International Journal of Creative Research Thoughts, 6*(2), 01–10.

7. Dasgupta, A. (2021). Relationship between population growth with changing land-use pattern and environmental changes in Kolkata, West Bengal. *Environmental Science. 11*(11), 57–61. https://DOI-10.36106/ijar

8. Grierson, D. (2007). The Urban Environment: Agendas and Problems. *The International Journal of Environmental, Cultural, Economic and Social Sustainability, 3*(1), 01–08. https://DOI-10.18848/1832-2077/CGP/v03i01/54314

9. Choudhury, D. (2017). Realties and Myths of Public Spaces: Conflict and Participation in Kolkata. *International Journal on Emerging Technologies, 8*(1), 337–343.

10. Dhali, M.K. (2016). Vertical Growth and Associated Socio-Functional changes after 21st Century: A micro study of Kolkata, India. *International Research Journal of Social Sciences, 5*(6), 16–23.

11. Karmakar, J. (2015). Encountering the reality of the planning process in peri-urban areas of Kolkata: Case study of Rajarhat. *Archives of Applied Science Research, 7*(5), 129–138.

12. Donner, H. (2012). Whose city is it anyway? Middle class imagination and urban restructuring in twenty first century Kolkata. *New Perspectives on Turkey, 46*, 129–155.

13. Mukherjee, J. (2015). Beyond the urban: rethinking urban ecology using Kolkata as a case study. *International Journal of Urban Sustainable Development, 7*(2), 131–146. https://DOI-10.1080/19463138.2015.1011160

14. Mukherjee, M. (2012). Urban growth and spatial transformation of Kolkata metropolis: a continuation of Colonial Legacy. *ARPN Journal of Science and Technology, 2*, 365–380.

15. De, M. (2017). Urban Ecology and Resurgence of Malaria in Kolkata, West Bengal in India. *Journal of Research in Environmental and Earth Science. 3*(5), 67–74.

16. Anisujjaman, M. (2015). Urbanisation and Human Development: A Study of West Bengal. *International Journal of Humanities and Social Science Invention, 4*(7), 01–08.

17. Rai, M.S. (2017). Impact of Urbanization on Environment. *International Journal on Emerging Technologies, 8*(1), 127–129.

18. Rahaman, M. (2019). Urbanization, Urban Green Space and Public Health: A Case Study of Kolkata. *International Journal of Research in Social Sciences, 9*(2), 1080–1093.

19. Banerjee, S. (2018). Urban Expansion of the City Kolkata since last 25 years using Remote Sensing. *International Journal of Research and Analytical Reviews, 5*(2), 422–429.

20. Sen, S. (2011). Effect of Urban Sprawl on Human Habitation in Urban Fringe and Peri-Urban Areas in Kolkata Metropolitan Area. *Institute of Town Planners, India Journal, 8* (4), 58–66.

21. Chatterjee, U., & Majumder, S. (2022). Impact of land use change and rapid urbanization on urban heat island in Kolkata city: A remote sensing based perspective. *Journal of Urban Management, 11*, 59–71. https://doi.org/10.1016/j.jum.2021.09.002

22. Bhowmick, S., & Sivaramakrishnan, L. (2021). Growth behaviour of census towns in Kolkata metropolitan region, West Bengal, India. *Transactions, 43*(1), 81–92.

23. Oke, T.R. (1982). The energetic basis of the urban heat island. *Quarterly Journal of the Royal Meteorological Society, 108*, 01–24.

24. Zhao, S., Liu, S., & Zhou, D. (2016). Prevalent vegetation growth enhancement in urban environment. *PNAS, 113*, 6313–6318. https://doi/10.1073/pnas.160 2312113

25. Bhatta, B. (2011). *Remote Sensing and GIS*. Oxford University Press, New Delhi.

26. Wei, S., Chen, Q., Wu, W., & Ma, J. (2021). Quantifying the indirect effects of urbanization on urban vegetation carbon uptake in the megacity of Shanghai, China. *Environmental Research Letters, 16*, 01–11. https://doi.org/10.1088/1748-9326/ ac06fd

27. Krpo, A., Salamanca, F., Martilli, A., & Clappier, A. (2010). On the Impact of Anthropogenic Heat Fluxes on the Urban Boundary Layer: A Two-Dimensional Numerical Study. *Boundary-Layer Meteorology, 136*, 105–127. https://doi.org/ 10.1007/s10546-010-9491-2

28. Guha, S., Govil, H., & Diwan, P. (2020). Monitoring LST-NDVI Relationship Using Pre-monsoon Landsat Datasets. *Advances in Meteorology, 2020*, 1–15. https:// doi.org/10.1155/2020/4539684

29. Macarof, P., & Statescu, F. (2017). Comparison of NDBI and NDVI as indicators of surface urban heat island effect in Landsat 8 imagery: a case study of Iasi. *Present Environment and Sustainable Development, 11*, 141–150. https://doi.org/10.1515/ pesd-2017-0032

30. Hamdi, R., Termonia, P., & Baguis, P. (2010). Effects of urbanization and climate change on surface runoff of the Brussels Capital Region: a case study using an urban soil–vegetation–atmosphere-transfer model. *International Journal of Climatology*. https://doi.org/10.1002/joc.2207

31. Li, Y., Schubert, S., Kropp, J.P., & Rybski, D. (2020). On the influence of density and morphology on the Urban Heat Island intensity. *Nature Communications, 11*, 01–08. https://doi.org/10.1038/s41467-020-16461-9

32. Yang, Li., Qian, F., Song, D.X., & Zheng, K.J. (2016). Research on Urban Heat-island Effect. *Procedia Engineering, 169*, 11–18. https://doi.org/10.1016/j.pro eng.2016.10.002

33. Mathew, A., Chaudhary, R., Gupta, N., Khandelwal, S., & Kaul. N. (2015). Study of Urban heat Island Effect on Ahmedabad City and Its Relationship with Urbanization and Vegetation Parameters. *International Journal of Computer & Mathematical Sciences. 4*, 126–135.

34. Sukopp, H. & Werner, P., 1983. Urban environments and vegetation. In W. Holzner, M.J.A. Werger, & I. Ikusima (Eds.), *Man's impact on vegetation*. Dr W. Junk Publishers, 247–260.

35. Weng, Q., & Lu, D. (2008). A sub-pixel analysis of urbanization effect on land surface temperature and its interplay with impervious surface and vegetation coverage in Indianapolis, United States. *International Journal of Applied Earth Observation and Geoinformation, 10*, 68–83.

36. Ali, K., Akhtar, N., Shuaib, M., Ali, S., Ghaffar, A., Shah, M., Khan, A., Hussain, F., Khan, Z., Kaleem, I., Nazir, A., & Iqbal. M. (2019). Impact of Urbanization on Vegetation: a Survey of Peshawar, Pakistan. *Polish Journal of Environmental Studies, 28*, 2523–2530. https://doi.org/10.15244/pjoes/89609

37. Liu, Y., Wang, Y., Peng, J., Du, Y., Liu, X., Li, S., & Zhang, D. (2015). Correlations between Urbanization and Vegetation Degradation across the World's Metropolises Using DMSP/OLS Night time Light Data. *Remote Sensing, 7*, 2067–2088. https://doi.org/10.3390/rs70202067

38. Mbaya, L.A., Abu, G.O., Makadi, Y.C., & Umar, D.M. (2019). Impact of urbanization on vegetation cover in Gombe Metropolis and Environs. *British Journal of Earth Sciences Research, 4*, 17–25.

39. Gui, X., Wang, L., Yao, R., Yu, D., & Li, C. (2019). Investigating the urbanization process and its impact on vegetation change and urban heat island in Wuhan, China. *Environmental Science and Pollution Research.* https://doi.org/10.1007/s11356-019-06273-w

40. Miles, L.S., Breitbart, S.T., Wagner, H.H., & Johnson, M.T.J. (2019). Urbanization Shapes the Ecology and Evolution of Plant-Arthropod Herbivore Interactions. *Frontiers in Ecology and Evolution, 7*(310). https://doi.org/10.3389/fevo.2019.00310

41. Esau, I., Miles, V.V., Davy, R., Miles, M.W., & Kurchatowa, A. (2016). Trends in normalized difference vegetation index (NDVI) associated with urban development in northern West Siberia. *Atmospheric Chemistry and Physics, 16*, 9563–9577. https://doi.org/10.5194/acp-16-9563-2016

42. Ramachandra, T.V., Sellers, J., Bharath, H.A., & Setturu, B. (2019). Micro level analyses of environmentally disastrous urbanization in Bangalore. *Environmental Monitoring and Assessment, 191*, 01–13. https://doi.org/10.1007/s10661-019-7693-8

43. Myint, S.W., Wentz, E.A., Brazel, A.J., & Quattrochi, D.A. (2013). The impact of distinct anthropogenic and vegetation features on urban warming. *Landscape Ecology, 28*, 959–978. https://doi.org/10.1007/s10980-013-9868-y

44. Rao, P., Hutyra, L.R., Raciti, S.M., & Finzi, A.C. (2013). Field and remotely sensed measures of soil and vegetation carbon and nitrogen across an urbanization gradient in the Boston metropolitan area. *Urban Ecosystems, 16*, 593–616. https://doi.org/10.1007/s11252-013-0291-6

45. Ahmed, H.A., Singh, S.K., Kumar, M., Maina, M.S., Dzwairo, R., & Lal, D. (2020). Impact of urbanization and land cover change on urban climate: Case study of Nigeria. *Urban Climate, 32*, 01–17. https://doi.org/10.1016/j.uclim.2020.100600

46. Amiri, R., Weng, Q., Mohammadi, A.A., & Alavipanah, S.K. (2009). Spatial–temporal dynamics of land surface temperature in relation to fractional vegetation cover and land use/cover in the Tabriz urban area, Iran. *Remote Sensing and Environment, 113*, 2606–2617. https://doi.org/10.1016/j.rse.2009.07.021

47. Kabano, P., Lindley, S., & Harris, A. (2021). Evidence of urban heat island impacts on the vegetation growing season length in a tropical city. *Landscape and Urban Planning, 206*, 01–09. https://doi.org/10.1016/j.landurbplan.2020.103989

48. Roy, S. 2020. Urban encroachment and its impact on indigenous agricultural practice: An overview of the Apatani Tribe, Arunachal Pradesh. In P.K Kundu (Eds.), *Sustainable Urbanisation in East India: Present Trends and Future Concerns* (1st ed., pp 282–297). Levant Books.

49. Munck, C., Pigeon, G., Masson, V., Meunier, F., Bousquet, P., Tremeac, B., Merchat, M., Poeuf, P., & Marchadier, C. (2012). How much can air conditioning increase air temperatures for a city like Paris, France? *International Journal of Climatology, 33*, 210–227. https://doi.org/10.1002/joc.3415.

50. Peng, L., Deng, W., & Liu, Y. (2021). Understanding the Role of Urbanization on Vegetation Dynamics in Mountainous Areas of Southwest China: Mechanism, spatio-temporal Pattern, and Policy Implications. *International Journal of Geo-Information, 10*, 590, 01–16. https://doi.org/10.3390/ijgi10090590

51. Zipper, S.C., Schatz, J., Singh. A., Kucharik, C.J., Townsend, P.A., & Loheide, S.P. (2016). Urban heat island impacts on plant phenology: intra-urban variability and response to land cover. *Environmental Research Letters, 11*, 01–12. https://doi.org/10.1088/1748-9326/11/5/054023

52. Ezzat, A.E.M., & Hamoud, H.S. (2016). Analytic hierarchy process as module for productivity evaluation and decision-making of the operation theater. *Avicenna Journal of Medicine, 6*, 03–07. https://doi.org/10.4103/2231-0770.173579

53. Schmidt, K., Anumann, I., Hollander, I., Damm, K. & Schulberg, J.M.G. (2015). Applying the Analytic Hierarchy Process in healthcare research: A systematic literature review and evaluation of reporting. *BMC Medical Informatics and Decision Making, 15*, 01–27. https://doi.org/10.1186/s12911-015-0234-7

Chapter 6

Modeling and IoT (Internet of Things) Analysis for Smart Precision Agriculture

Imtiaz Ahmed, Gousia Habib, and
Pramod Kumar Yadav
National Institute of Technology, Srinagar, India

6.1 Introduction

Agriculture and smart farming take on a new dimension with the Internet of Things (IoT). Rural farming and agricultural bases can be connected efficiently to fog computing and Wi-Fi-based long-distance networks found in the Internet of Things. In order to focus on the unique requirements, we propose a scalable network architecture for controlling and monitoring farming and agriculture in rural regions. In 2020, Montelone et al. found that, compared to the present IoT-based agricultural and agriculture solutions, the recommended method reduces network latency to a certain extent. This provides a recommendation for a sensing and actuating cross-layer-based channel access and routing system. Throughput, latency, and coverage area are taken into account in our analysis of the network structure. The foundation of human existence is agriculture, which provides food, cereals, and other raw materials (Phupattanasilp & Tong, 2019). Technology has a significant influence

DOI: 10.1201/9781032624983-6

in boosting output and reducing the need for additional labor. Smart farming and agriculture now have a viable solution to the Internet of Things (IoT), but this is still only a pipe dream as long as rural areas are not connected.

Rural areas can now be connected at low cost via the Wi-Fi-based long-distance (Wild) network. For a better and more efficient IoT in this area, fog computing and cloud computing solutions can be implemented in Wi-Fi devices with the expanded range. The responsibility for gathering the sensor data and transmitting it to an IoT cloud server falls on a border router (6LBR) (Singh et al., 2019). As a response to this issue, fog computing has arisen. These devices need a local solution station to support the long-range wire-free network. Accurately integrating information and control technology into agricultural activities is the practice of agriculture (PA). To achieve the highest optimization and profitability, PA uses a variety of technologies, including micro-electromechanical systems, wireless sensor networks (WSN), computer systems, and improved machinery. These technologies allow PA to modify traditional farming practices to the particular conditions of each point of the crop. Positive results are guaranteed when this strategy is used effectively.

These methods may be applied to hydroponic, indoor, and outdoor crops, among other things (Ahmed et al., 2018). These technologies are usually divided into three stages for management. The first is referred to as the determination stage, in which the type of crop is chosen, and its areas are categorized based on their homogeneity; the tools used in this stage to analyze each area's features are sensors. The second stage involves computer systems processing the acquired data. which provides processes to be used in each area. Finally, cutting-edge machinery completes the execution stage. In the agricultural industry, new trends have recently arisen. PA has begun to take shape as a result of advancements in WSN and the shrinking of sensor boards. Nevertheless, despite significant advancements in a variety of technological fields, only a small portion of them is focused on the creation and use of unique low-cost systems for agricultural applications. Agricultural industries have historically had access to information technologies, but they have not been widely adopted in settings due to prohibitively expensive systems and challenges in deploying, managing, and maintaining these installations (Ferrández-Pastor et al., 2016). New platforms specifically designed to break through these obstacles are required in this area. This chapter offers a solution based on a heterogeneous and scalable platform that can gather, process, store, and monitor data from crop producing systems using a mobile ubiquitous approach. Ubiquitous sensor networks (USNs) and the Internet of Things (IoT) paradigms were used in the development of this strategy. The platform is focused (Fizza et al., 2022) on agricultural land automation maintenance and aims to regulate the factors that affect how well a crop develops, including substrate and ambient temperature, brightness, air humidity, water PH level, and others. (See Figure 6.1.)

Consequently not tailored to each farmer's unique requirements for his or her intended use. In this work, a user-centered design approach for intelligent and tailored services is proposed, where each farmer chooses its own installation leveraging

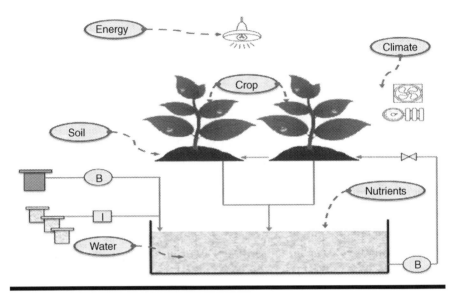

Figure 6.1 Agricultural production subsystems.

the distributed computing's Internet of Things technologies using the edge and fog paradigms (Figure 6.2) (Kashyap et al., 2021). This method's utility was tested in an automated greenhouse after being developed for several use situations.

To get beyond these restrictions and anticipate yield productivity using a neural network prediction approach for informed decisions, we propose an IoT-based smart agriculture monitoring system:

1. We outline the elements and necessary elements of the sensing environment.
2. The IoT data collection process's methodology is made clear.
3. PCA is suggested as a method for choosing and reducing feature data for use in processing and data management.
4. A prediction model that incorporates prior information will enable farmers to make wise decisions to boost productivity.

We have outlined the many steps that connect data analytics and the IoT in Figure 6.3. Precision agriculture may be made practicable by combining machine learning and IoT data analytics (Chanak, 2020). First, linked sensor devices use apps to interact with one another in the managing IoT data sources stage. As an example, the interaction of devices such as CCTV cameras, drones, environmental sensors, soil sensors, plant sensors, etc. creates vast volumes of data in several formats. This generated data may be saved on the cloud using standard hardware. Data is complicated in the second go because of its volume, pace, and variety, depending on the requirements of the precision agricultural application.

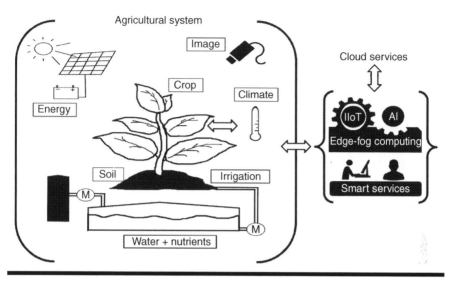

Figure 6.2   Agricultural system.

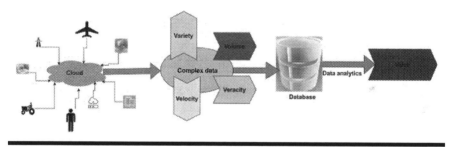

Figure 6.3   Relationship between data analytics and the Internet of Things.

6.1.1 How IoT in Agriculture Has Left Its Mark

The Internet of Things in Agriculture is a continuation of the green revolution. Farmers can benefit from IoT adoption in two ways. It has helped farmers cut costs while simultaneously increasing yields by empowering their decision making with precise data, Using industrial IoT in agriculture, sensors are now utilized throughout the entire farming process. The sensors are now connected to the cloud via a cellular or satellite network. As a result, we have access to real-time sensor data, which helps us make wise decisions (Mekala & Viswanathan, 2017). Farmers may now instantly monitor the water level in their tanks, which increases the effectiveness of irrigation with the use of Industrial IoT in the agricultural sector. The growth of IoT technology serves as a reminder of the length of time and labor required to cultivate a vegetable from seed to harvest.

6.1.2 Application of IoT in Agriculture

Sustainable farming practices are the foundation of the high-tech, productive smart farming technique of food production. It is a method of applying modern technology and connected devices to agriculture. The Internet of Things (IoT) is a crucial element of smart farming, which reduces the need for farmers and producers to conduct physical labor while simultaneously boosting production in all areas. Given the dependency of contemporary agricultural developments on agriculture, the Internet of Things has greatly benefited from efficient water utilization, input optimization, and many others (Kour & Arora, 2020). What made a difference were the substantial benefits that have lately transformed agriculture. The total agricultural system is improved through IoT-based smart farming by continually monitoring the land. By utilizing sensors and connections, the Internet of Things in agriculture has decreased the extravagant use of resources like water and electricity and has saved farmers' time. While controlling numerous parameters like humidity, temperature, soil, etc., it offers clear real-time observation.

The following are some benefits of using contemporary technology, like the Internet of Things, in agriculture.

6.1.3 Environmental Factors

Climate has a big impact on farming. Furthermore, inaccurate climate information substantially reduces agricultural yield, both in quantity and quality. IoT technologies, on the other hand, inform you of present weather conditions. Sensors have been put both within and outside the agricultural fields. They collect environmental data that is used to choose the best crops for the particular climatic conditions. In order to monitor real-time meteorological variables like humidity, rainfall, temperature, and more, the whole Internet of Things (IoT) ecosystem is made up of sensors (Brunelli et al., 2020). Each of these parameters may be detected by a variety of sensors, which can be configured to match your demands for smart farming. These sensors monitor the condition of the crops and the environment. See Figure 6.4.

If any uncomfortable weather is found, an alarm is sent. It is no longer necessary for people to be present during unfavorable weather, which eventually increases output and helps farmers to benefit more from agriculture.

6.1.4 Precision Farming

Precision farming is one of the most well-known applications of IoT in agriculture. It enhances the accuracy and control of agricultural practices by utilizing smart farming applications, including animal monitoring, vehicle tracking, field observation, and inventory monitoring. The goal of precision farming is to analyze sensor data and take the right action. Precision farming uses sensors to help farmers gather data, analyze it, and make decisions quickly and with knowledge. Many precision

Figure 6.4   Climate environment temperature.

Figure 6.5   Precision farming IOT.

agricultural techniques, such as vehicle tracking, irrigation management, and live-stock management (Gaddam et al., 2020), all greatly increase production and effect-iveness. To increase operational effectiveness, precision farming may be used to analyze soil conditions and other pertinent characteristics. In addition, you can look at the connected devices' operational status in real time to see how they're doing. See Figure 6.5.

6.1.5 Smart Greenhouses

Our greenhouses are now smarter due to IoT, which enables weather stations to autonomously modify the environment's parameters in line with a precise set of instructions. The elimination of human involvement due to the deployment of IoT in greenhouses has reduced costs and increased accuracy throughout the process: for instance, building contemporary, inexpensive greenhouses with Internet of Things sensors powered by solar energy. These sensors collect and transmit real-time data,

Figure 6.6 Greenhouse.

allowing for exact real-time tracking of the greenhouse's condition (Kakamoukas et al., 2022). The sensors enable water usage and greenhouse conditions to be tracked via emails or SMS alerts. IoT is used for intelligent and autonomous irrigation. These sensors provide data that includes pressure, humidity, temperature, and light levels. See Figure 6.6.

6.1.6 Data Analytics

The typical database system is unable to accommodate the data collected by IoT devices. The core elements of the smart agricultural system are the end-to-end IoT platform and cloud-based data storage. These systems are believed to be essential in facilitating greater task performance. Sensors are the primary means of bulk data collecting in the IoT era. The data is reviewed and turned into meaningful information using analytics technology. Data analytics facilitates the examination of agricultural, animal, and meteorological factors. Better judgments might be made by leveraging the obtained data and technology developments. By capturing images of the crops, you may use IoT devices to track their condition in real time (Anand et al., 2021). By employing predictive analytics, you may obtain insights to enhance your harvesting decisions. Farmers can anticipate upcoming weather and crop harvesting with the use of trend analysis. By preserving the soil's fertility and the quality of their crops, IoT in the agricultural sector has helped farmers increase both the quantity and quality of their output. See Figure 6.7.

6.1.7 Agricultural Drones

As a result of technology advancements, agricultural drones have almost entirely changed agricultural operations. Drones are used for agricultural spraying, crop monitoring, field analysis, and crop health assessments. The agriculture industry

Figure 6.7   Data analytics for IOT.

Figure 6.8   Agriculture drone system.

has seen a rapid rise and makeover in drone technology, with proper strategy and planning based on real-time data. Drones with thermal or multispectral sensors can find the places where irrigation has to be adjusted (Lin et al., 2020). Once the crops have started to develop and reveal their condition of health, sensors calculate the vegetation index. Eventually, drones with intelligence help to reduce environmental effects. The results have been such that the amount of chemical entering ground-water has been significantly reduced. See Figure 6.8.

6.2 Related Work

PA monitors, quantifies, and reacts to agricultural variability both within and between fields. The primary gains are an increase in output and profitability. Better working circumstances have additional advantages. PA thus contributes to the broader objective of agricultural production sustainability. PA implementation has become feasible to advances in sensor technology and procedures that link mapped variables to appropriate farming management operations including growing, sowing, fertilization, herbicide application, and harvesting (Roy & De, 2022). Several sensors are now available that may be used as part of the PA deployment for data collecting or information dissemination. These devices are designed for both stationary and portable recording. To assess the state of soils, a variety of techniques are available, such as apparent EC sensors, gamma-radiometric soil sensors, and soil moisture tools, among others. Others monitor weather or microclimate information (thermometer, hygrometer, etc.). Special attention is paid to sensors that gauge the physiological status of crops (like nitrogen sensors). Sensors have historically played a key role in industrial operations because of their ability to track the physical qualities involved in the various production processes. They are interconnected via traditional wired networks. Although PA is accepted to provide benefits (Islam et al., 2022), a variety of factors may limit full integration

The Internet of Things (IoT) is the inter-networking paradigm that allows different devices (things) to offer intelligent services. IoT systems can be utilized to collect historical data over an extended period of time for integrated pest management applications. For immersive data applications, augmented reality (AR) superimposes virtual items with the surrounding environment. The emergence of smart farming can be used to anticipate an exponential expansion of AR when combined with the IoT. ElSayed et al. suggested using augmented reality to let users engage with information visually. Additionally, customers have the option of comparing data related to various actual objects. An IoT and AR system's tracking modules can be thought of as a core component. A good approach might be computer vision with the appropriate functions and algorithms. Markerless vision-based cameras might offer a low-cost, non-destructive way to monitor plant growth (Akhavan et al., 2022).

- Unfulfilled initial hopes and promises of benefits: The agricultural community has been quite supportive of using PA technology to regulate variability within paddocks. The largest obstacle to the adoption of PA is that people have grown frustrated with the technology, particularly the lack of assistance.
- Practically speaking, farmers must develop the confidence to manage variability and collaborate with PA experts.
- Technology's complexity and component incompatibility: Because more people are becoming aware of the advantages of the technology, it is anticipated that the pace of PA adoption will keep increasing. There are limitations to adapting due to technical difficulties with hardware and software as well as the equipment's incompatibility with current farming practices (Orozco-Lugo et al., 2022).

A WSN is a collection of sensors that may be positioned anywhere and that have wireless communication capabilities. In addition to communicating with one another and a base station, sensor nodes can also transmit data to distant systems for processing, visualizing, analyzing, and storing. The real-time data collected from the fields can give farmers a strong foundation on which to build future strategy changes. Some IoT-based applications may be accessible on our smartphones and assist in agricultural settings with crop control. The use of identifiable wireless technology in applications related to the environment and nature protection is one of the most potential market categories for the future. The current level of technology reveals a variety of issues that must be fixed in order to fully integrate the control and information technologies into routine agricultural activities. Increased productivity, efficiency, and profitability are now feasible in many agricultural production systems due to the development of WSN applications in PA.

Even though there are other, more nuanced definitions of the PA, its basic purpose is to "provide the correct treatment in the right place at the right time" (Fujita et al., 2022). Precision agriculture is an area of technology that integrates sensors, information systems, enhanced equipment, and informed management to maximize output while accounting for the unpredictability and uncertainty in agricultural systems. It is an approach to agricultural management that centers on keeping an eye on crop variability both within and between fields (Pfender et al., 2022). When developing the techniques and technologies that govern how, where, and when to employ sensors and machines, farmers and information and communication professionals should be involved. The user-centered strategies and Internet of Things communication technologies utilized in precision agriculture are updated in this section. Then different greenhouses are examined.

6.2.1 User-Centered Design Models

User-centered design (UCD) in the context of PA refers to a design methodology where farmers have a say in how the design develops. The user (agricultural specialist) has a variety of ways to get involved in the process. This phrase refers to a group of techniques for developing models on which to base customized designs. The user-centered design methodology challenges arbitrary presumptions about user behavior. It requires evidence that the design choices are successful. A properly executed user-centered design will result in applications that actively engage users. Any design choices made as a result of watching and listening to them won't be influenced by personal tastes. UX is one of the numerous areas on which UCD focuses (Sato et al., 2022). UX asserts that user-centered design is a process of product creation that ensures a product, a piece of software, or a website will be simple to use. The following concepts underlie user-centered design, according to the International Usability Standard (ISO 13407):

- Gathering requirements, comprehending them, and defining the use context
- Requirements specification, which outlines the needs of the user and the organization
- Creating designs, prototypes, and designs
- Evaluation, including user-based evaluation of the website

An explicit understanding of users, tasks, and settings forms the foundation of the design. All phases of design and development involve users. Iterative processes are used. User-centered evaluation guides and improves the design. The entire user experience is addressed in the design (Kakamoukas et al., 2022). The design team consists of individuals with diverse backgrounds and viewpoints.

6.2.2 Internet of Things: Protocols and Architectures

Layer-based architectures are used in IoT construction to connect a large number of devices to one another and to existing services. The basic Internet of Things model has a three-layer architecture, which is made up of Perception, Network, and Application Layers. IoT has several challenges, especially in the privacy and security domains. To overcome these issues, new standard designs must place a higher focus on a number of essential components including quality of services (QoS), data integrity, sustainability, secrecy, etc. IAB (Interactive Advertising Bureau) released a paper titled "Architectural Considerations in Smart Object Networking (Internet Architecture Board)." The recommendations in this paper can be used by the engineers building Internet-connected smart objects. Examples of various works that employ the layer concept in IoT architecture are shown in Table 6.1.

IoT protocols must be changed to comply with the new requirements. New protocols are being proposed that give several possibilities in diverse circumstances, while traditional protocols are being broadened. IoT today has a wide range of applications. Smart devices include wired and wireless connectivity options. Speaking about wireless, the main issue is the Internet of Things (IoT), and a range of wireless communication technologies and protocols, such as Internet Protocol Version 6 (IPv6) over Low Power Wireless Personal Area Networks (6LoWPAN), ZigBee, Bluetooth Low Energy (BLE), Z-Wave, and Near Field Communication, can be used to connect smart devices (NFC). Contrary to normal short-range network

Table 6.1 IoT Architecture: Layers

Layers Proposed	Characteristics
3	Perception, network, application
4	Things, edge, network, application
5	Business, application, service, object abstraction, objects

Table 6.2 IoT Protocols

Layer	Protocols
Session/application	MQTT, CoAP, AMQT, HTTP, SOAP, …
Network	6LowPAN, RPL, CORPL, IPSec, TCP/UDP, DTLS
Perception/things	WiFi, Bluetooth Low Energy, Z-Wave, ZigBee, LoraWan, IEEE 802.15.4, LTE, …

protocols, SigFox and Cellular are Low Power Wide Area Network technologies (LPWAN) regular procedures. Bella et al. (2022) provides a review and comparison of various IoT communication methods. Table 6.2 shows different protocols used at different layers.

The environment, the network properties, the amount of data to be transmitted, the level of security, and the kind of service requests are the most important considerations when choosing the optimal protocol. MQTT is a many-to-many communication protocol for sending and receiving messages among several clients, CoAP network is largely a one-to-one protocol for conveying state information between client and server. Because CoAP uses UDP instead of TCP, communication overhead is drastically minimized. RESTful services can be simply constructed and interact with the Internet utilizing the global HTTP protocol (Gupta, 2022) if restricted communication and battery consumption are not a concern. The MQTT protocol is more suited if the final applications that are being targeted demand frequent updates of the same information. Various protocols (including MQTT, HTTP, Bluetooth, Wi-Fi, etc.) can be used.

6.2.3 Internet of Things Technologies Applied on PA Scenarios

New hardware with wireless communication capabilities, including sensors, actuators, and computing nodes are being created based on advancements in electronics, computing, and telecommunications (Shim et al., 2021). These devices are smaller, more energy-efficient, autonomous, powerful, and less expensive. User-driven service modeling for IoT, as illustrated by examples of low-cost IoT devices used to collect, send, and receive remote commands in addition to sensor data, is suggested. The Internet of Things (IoT) relies on connections between devices to enhance their functionality and user experience, with communication being one of the key components of an effective IoT network. To find the best bidirectional sensor network made up of inexpensive sensors, the most common wired and wireless communication protocols will be examined, their characteristics, advantages, and disadvantages will be discussed, and a comparative study will be done.

IoT technology is advised for PA environments. Applications for IoT examines this paradigm as a precision agricultural approach. Tracking and monitoring farm parameters, as well as field and storage monitoring, are all part of smart farming. In the article "Internet of Things Platform for Smart Farming," a platform based on IoT technologies is described that can automatically gather data on the environment, soil, fertilization, and irrigation; correlate such data; filter out irrelevant data with the goal of assessing crop performance; compute crop forecasts; and generate personalized crop recommendations for any given farm. The platform (SmartFarmNet) may be used to integrate almost any IoT device, including commercially available sensors, cameras, weather stations, etc. The platform can also store data from these devices in the cloud for performance evaluation and suggestions.

6.2.4 Edge and Fog Computing Paradigms: Evolution of the Internet of Things, Cloud, and Machine Learning

Massive volumes of data are being generated by the Internet of Things (IoT), which may be too much for storage systems and analytical tools to manage. The fog and edge computing ideas extend cloud services to the network edge in order to decrease latency and network congestion. Both edge computing and fog computing bring knowledge and computing power closer to the data's source. By processing data on a fog node or Internet of Things gateway, fog computing pushes intelligence into local area networks (Kour & Arora, 2020). Edge computing pushes directly into devices the intelligence, processing power, and communication capabilities of an edge gateway or appliance. Cisco Systems predicts that there will be 50 billion linked devices by the year 2020. This is feasible, and the edge and fog computing concepts will support a large number of new IoT applications. For smart city services, a fog computing system based on radio access networks is recommended.

6.2.5 Automated Greenhouse Technologies

The type of installation at various greenhouses has been examined, and knowledgeable users have been consulted during visits to the southeast of Spain. Although all of the sensors and actuators were present in the most automated greenhouse possible, not all of them could be connected. Self-assembled greenhouses have two sizable subsystems that cannot communicate with one another. These subsystems install many controls and technology, including:

■ Nutrition and irrigation and
■ Ventilation and air conditioning.

In these buildings, the irrigation system's irrigation water temperature sensor is independent of the air conditioning system's ambient temperature sensor. The main subsystems of the various automated greenhouses are shown in Figure 6.9.

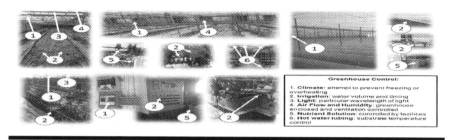

Figure 6.9 Automated greenhouses: key components of modern facilities.

6.3 Materials and Methods

Modern agricultural facilities are separated into separate, unconnected subsystems: irrigation, light, climate, soil, crop, and energy. Each subsystem's core automation functions are provided by industrial logic programmable controllers and specialized sensors. A new set of functionalities centered on information access, control, and monitoring are made possible by the internet and electronic devices like smartphones. Examples of recent innovations include human interfaces on cellphones that are connected to web servers. Farmers and agricultural technicians have information that can be translated into professional norms for device control. These rules are actually set and put into action on programmable devices, but they are static rules, which means they don't change as new circumstances arise or with the unique characteristics of each installation (Yuan et al., 2019).

The farmer must select how to establish the guidelines, including what pH the irrigation water must have and how much water should be programmed in the irrigation process, among other things. Additionally, there is no interoperability because each rule only affects a certain subsystem (i.e., irrigation or climate).

This chapter suggests new methods for facility design and development in light of the setting. The goal is for the farmer to engage in the automated processes and for the subsystems to work together. Additionally, a system that automates the application of rules and decision making while taking into account installation behavior is suggested. Figure 6.10 depicts the phases of the suggested model.

- Analysis: In this step, two types of consumers are recognized (agriculture user expert and ICT technician). To identify the primary processes to control, experts in the field of agriculture are surveyed. These concerns are all connected to ICT specialists in a participative design. The outcomes of this initial strategy are the elements needed for service design and control. A user-centered methodology is used in this phase to document the needs of the farmer (Cui et al., 2021).

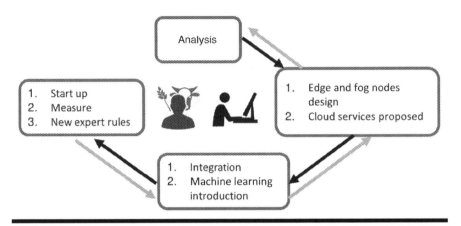

Figure 6.10   Shows a user-centered paradigm that incorporates edge and fog communication levels into its design. This approach integrates cloud services with machine learning procedures.

- Design: Edge, fog, and cloud services make up the model's three levels of architecture. Using these tiers, this phase entails designing an altered architecture. In Figure 6.11, the modified architecture is displayed.
- Data analysis and integration: During this phase, subsystems for installation and integration are created. To develop services for machine learning based on expert rules with farmers, data analysis is suggested.
- Start-up, evaluation, and feedback: Tests and evaluations are started. The initial expert guidelines incorporate farmer oversight. With the use of feedback procedures, new rules are created. Machine learning platforms and artificial intelligence systems are used to create automated and customized rules.

6.3.1 User-Centered Analysis and Design

Two cases are dealt with: an agricultural establishment with certain existing automated facilities and a new agricultural installation. Both use the same technique. To determine new procedures regulation, experts in the field of agriculture are consulted. This initial method identifies the necessary items (objects), their connections, and potential services. After being identified, objects and services must be connected to the required technology for control and communication (IoT protocols). Changes are made to the human interface. Expert rules and intelligent services are examined (edge and fog computing proposal). The methods for setup, maintenance, and use are then developed. All of this was developed with the help of an information technology specialist and an agriculture technician user.

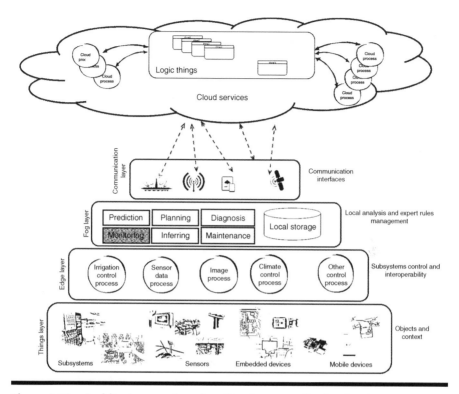

Figure 6.11   Architecture: various functional communication levels.

6.3.2 Data Analysis: Configuration of Edge and Fog Computing

There are three stages in the evolution of edge and fog computing:

■ Connection: Numerous heterogeneous, real-time connections between terminals and devices, as well as autonomous network formation and operation, will facilitate edge computing. Furthermore, it is important to guarantee the security, reliability, and interoperability of connections. This phase is used for remote automated soil parameter and ambient conditions data reading.

■ Edge computing device data treatment: In this stage, new edge node capabilities are implemented through data analysis and automatic services. Applications of this phase include data filtering, climate data forecasting, classification services, and event detection.

■ Fog computing node services: These are made feasible by IoT connectivity protocols and AI technology. Fog computing nodes carry out intelligent

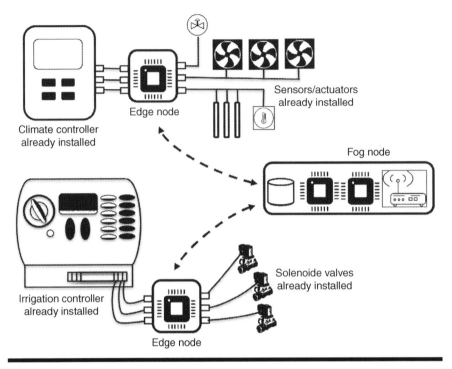

Figure 6.12   Potential architecture for automated facilities that interconnects all subsystems using fog nodes and edge nodes among installed devices.

computation and analysis as well as dynamic, real-time self-optimization and policy changes. Forecasting water consumption, intelligent detection, and unattended production are applications of this phase.

Figure 6.12 shows the architecture utilized with edge and fog nodes. When automated subsystems are already built, it is crucial to interleave embedded devices (edge nodes) between controllers, sensors, and actuators. With the help of this equipment, guided learning can begin while the initial services are maintained. New algorithms are tested and approved on edge and fog nodes, and several services are available on each node.

6.3.3 Things and Communication

Control devices, also known as connected devices, or items like sensors and actuators need be defined in order to employ IoT paradigms for communication and information structure creation. In order to assess the needs for development, agricultural subsystems, including crop, soil, climate, water, nutrients, and energy, need also be considered [6]. During this time, sensors allow for the collection of a wide range of

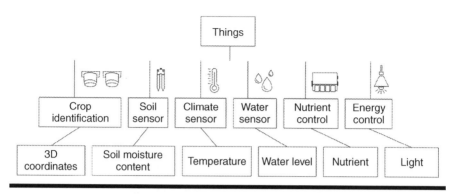

Figure 6.13 Architecture implemented services proposed.

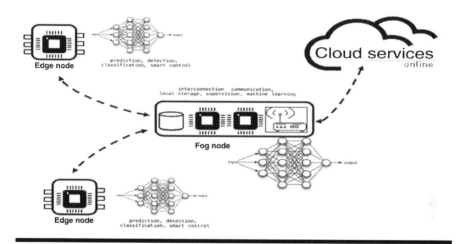

Figure 6.14 Three-dimensional system.

sensor data, including crop coordinates, soil moisture content, temperature, water level, nutrients, and brightness. A farmer manager, for instance, can use numerous types of equipment, such as multi-cameras, that are positioned throughout the farm (as in Figure 6.13) to view the same thing from several perspectives. This will enable virtual visualization by identifying the coordinates of crops. Due to its accuracy and stability, an IoT-based multi-camera was used in our case study to measure coordinates. In order to visualize the virtual contents, a WSN (wireless sensor network) was developed (Guillon et al., 2021). See Figure 6.14.

A hierarchy of agricultural production in our AR-IoT system is made up of farm regions (FARM REGION VO), a farmer manager (FARMER), sensor devices (SENSOR), and crops (PLANT). Several lots make up the farm (FARM LOT VO).

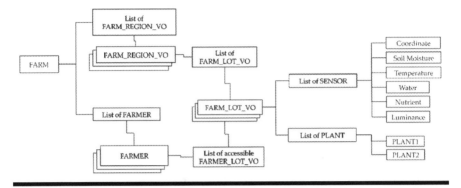

Figure 6.15   Hierarchical information structure.

The farm manager is given access codes for a number of lots (FARMER LOT VO). Control and sensor devices make up the things (SENSOR). As seen in Figure 6.15, each crop (PLANT) is listed by crop type (e.g., PLANT1). The development of rules for the farmer, plant, and farm comes first. This level makes an effort to ensure that a message is gotten, saved, and periodically retransmitted. All sensors and actuators are necessary in this scenario. New messages are created, and changes to control procedures are made. A farmer is able to determine the location of a crop as well as its growing area. For instance, PLANT1 is situated singly, but PLANT2 is situated in a group.

6.3.4 Network Platform: Development and Design

When the internet network was first built using the client-server model, the client was always the one who initiated requests. Devices initiate the dialogue when they need to push data to the cloud. The server must push data to a client in Internet of Things (IoT) applications without the client first asking for it. Web developers have created a few solutions to address this issue. The three alternatives listed here, in our opinion, are better suited for the embedded world:

■ Short polling: This is a method in which the client connects to the server repeatedly (when new data is available to communicate). This is the simplest method to code. It is not recommended for real time.
■ Long polling: Until it has something to say, the server does not respond to the client's request. This enables real-time push notifications from the cloud to devices. This approach consumes more energy and increases the chance of the connection failing.
■ Adapted protocols: To make use of more recent protocols, such as low latency, small packet sizes, and reliable communication over unstable networks, is the

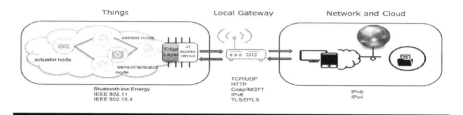

Figure 6.16   Use of the device-to-gateway IoT model (RFC7452).

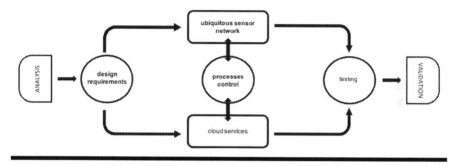

Figure 6.17   Planning a design or development project.

goal of constrained application protocol (CoAp) and message queue telemetry transport (MQTT).

The two-way communication channel supports the push notifications that these protocols offer. They are therefore suitable for Internet of Things (IoT) projects that call for real-time control of connected devices (Fedushko et al., 2019). For creating new apps, firmware libraries and embedded device examples are needed, which often use HTTP-based connections. A communication paradigm with *n* to *m* nodes is possible in ubiquitous networks (Figure 6.16). Any node has the ability to query other nodes and be queried by them. Additionally, any node can act as a base station (skin node) that can send data via a gateway device to distant processing locations.

6.3.5 Platform Development

When building a monitoring and control installation for PA situations, design recommendations should be considered. The flow diagram in Figure 6.17 is the proposed reference model for building these types of installations using the IoT paradigm. To determine the necessity for development, this model's elements—analysis, control, etc.—are connected to agricultural subsystems (crop, soil, water, etc.). Things (sensors, actuators, and devices) are deployed in an ecosystem that

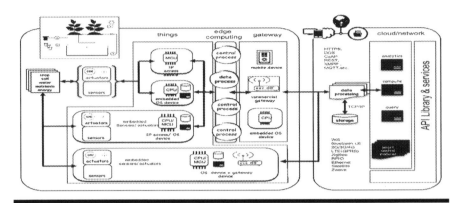

Figure 6.18 The ubiquitous thing layer is made up of IP access devices, sensors, and actuators.

leverages IoT principles to create cloud services and communicate. This ecosystem is based on a network of omnipresent sensors.

The envisioned ecology is depicted in Figure 6.18. In line with the IoT ecosystem's platform design paradigm, PA procedures are designed in accordance with the following stages:

■ Analysis: The fundamental objectives for the project should be established by agronomists and information and communication technologies (ICT) specialists. In this phase, scenarios, goals, and technological requirements are identified (Viloria et al., 2019).

■ Design specifications: On the IoT platform, specifications for design have already been defined. These specifications include low cost, interoperability, standard communication protocols, ease of access and maintenance, modularity and scalability, and non-proprietary dependencies. These criteria are connected to the agricultural installation's requirements that were examined in this phase. Agricultural and ICT technicians propose a design that is based on objects and their needs (computing and communication). Agricultural practices and things have definitions.

■ A ubiquitous sensor network should have well-defined sensors, actuators, and communication and processing capabilities, as well as the intermediary network access nodes.

■ A suggestion must be made using data from a variety of sources. By facilitating communication with a control center or other external entities, these nodes provide USN network access. The architecture for the communication layer is put forth in this phase.

■ Control processes: Agronomists define agricultural activities with fundamental and sophisticated rules between things. ICT professionals suggest a technology platform (middleware) to make a USN useful in the specific application. Relationships between things and control rules are modeled (Li et al., 2021).

■ Edge computing: This allows for knowledge creation and analysis at the data source. In this work, the edge is the layer that sits between data sources and cloud data centers.

Monitoring data from cloud services is accessed via a human–machine interface (HMI). IoT platforms compel all Internet-enabled devices to immediately begin and push data from them. The availability of such platforms and services demonstrates the state of commercial IoT technology. Examples of IoT service providers include Azure [45], Ubidots [46], and ThingSpeak [47]. These platforms share similar architectural designs and typically offer the identical resources. Messages are exchanged between clients and an IoT server via an application programming interface (API). All of these platforms offer prebuilt HMI dashboard designs for data monitoring. Processes are put in place on the fog node to transmit fresh data to each dashboard via API services (Li et al., 2021). The data structure that is sent between your devices and the Ubidots is described in the API documentation. The irrigation schedule can be mechanized in crop productions in the future, first under human supervision and eventually automatically. The models' inputs are biophysical factors (plant, soil, canal flow, and meteorological conditions) that are measured during the growth seasons. It will accumulate data on plant phenology (stages of growth), soil moisture, and environmental variables. The evaluation of irrigation choices is crucial since it can aid in the prediction of immediate irrigation requirements. Knowing the outcomes of the automated processes can assist canal operators better control water deliveries, avert unforeseen delays, and prevent operating circumstances that raise canal losses. Information on these demands can also be useful for assessing anticipated agricultural supplies in the future. Knowing the future cannot ever be conceivable.

6.4 Conclusions and Future Work

The most recent agricultural PA and IoT technologies settings have been examined in this article. Farmers may find it challenging to implement PA. Cultural perceptions, a lack of technological know-how in the area, infrastructure limitations, knowledge and technical gaps, and expensive start-up expenses are a few of these. The design and incorporation of these technology into farmers' facilities must involve them. There must be a means to enable such integration in order to implement this solution. In this paper, a novel approach to involving farmers in the creation of new solutions is proposed. It makes use of low-cost sensor technology and cutting-edge communication paradigms. The technological foundation of the suggested technique is an architecture based on two additional tiers of nodes for communication and processing.

Each level carries out a group of related functionalities. The suggested architecture can be implemented in both newly constructed facilities and automated systems. The technique opens up new opportunities for the creation of intelligent and connected control in already automated systems. In a greenhouse, an experiment has been conducted. In this work, communication nodes that have already been established are used to design a novel service based on a decision tree paradigm. The irrigation and temperature control subsystems are interoperable with the suggested model's capabilities, which also let the farmer design new integrated control rules. The farmer can evaluate modifications to the new dispersed communication paradigm. This experiment launches a brand-new working methodology.

References

Ahmed, N., De, D., & Hussain, I. (2018). Internet of Things (IoT) for Smart Precision Agriculture and Farming in Rural Areas. *IEEE Internet of Things Journal*, 5(6), 4890–4899. https://doi.org/10.1109/JIOT.2018.2879579

Akhavan, Z., Esmaeili, M., Sikeridis, D., & Devetsikiotis, M. (2022). Internet of Things-enabled Passive Contact Tracing in Smart Cities. *Internet of Things (Netherlands)*, 18, 100397. https://doi.org/10.1016/j.iot.2021.100397

Anand, T., Sinha, S., Mandal, M., Chamola, V., & Yu, F. R. (2021). AgriSegNet: Deep Aerial Semantic Segmentation Framework for IoT-Assisted Precision Agriculture. *IEEE Sensors Journal*, 21(16), 17581–17590. https://doi.org/10.1109/JSEN.2021.3071290

Bella, G., Biondi, P., & Bognanni, S. (2022). Multi-service threats: Attacking and protecting network printers and VoIP phones alike. *Internet of Things (Netherlands)*, 18(August 2021), 100507. https://doi.org/10.1016/j.iot.2022.100507

Brunelli, D., Albanese, A., Acunto, D., & Nardello, M. (2020). *Energy Neutral Machine Learning Based IoT Device for Pest Detection in Precision Agriculture. December 2019*, 10–13.

Chanak, P. (2020). *Internet-of-Things–Enabled Smart Villages: An Overview.* 12–18.

Cui, Y., Lin, K., Chen, Y., & Zhu, J. (2021). A quantum-inspired model for statistical analysis of repairable systems. *Computers and Industrial Engineering*, 161(August), 107613. https://doi.org/10.1016/j.cie.2021.107613

Fedushko, S., Gregus Ml, M., & Ustyianovych, T. (2019). Medical card data imputation and patient psychological and behavioral profile construction. *Procedia Computer Science*, 160, 354–361. https://doi.org/10.1016/j.procs.2019.11.080

Ferrández-Pastor, F. J., García-Chamizo, J. M., Nieto-Hidalgo, M., Mora-Pascual, J., & Mora-Martínez, J. (2016). Developing ubiquitous sensor network platform using internet of things: Application in precision agriculture. *Sensors (Switzerland)*, 16(7). https://doi.org/10.3390/s16071141

Fizza, K., Jayaraman, P. P., Banerjee, A., Georgakopoulos, D., & Ranjan, R. (2022). Evaluating Sensor Data Quality in Internet of Things Smart Agriculture Applications. *IEEE Micro*, 42(1), 51–60. https://doi.org/10.1109/MM.2021.3137401

Fujita, M., Iida, Y., Hattori, M., Yamanaka, T., Matsuda, N., Ito, S., & Kikuchi, H. (2022). Proposal of anonymization dictionary using disclosed statements by business operators.

Internet of Things (Netherlands), *18*(January), 100490. https://doi.org/10.1016/j.iot.2021.100490

Gaddam, A., Wilkin, T., Angelova, M., & Gaddam, J. (2020). Detecting sensor faults, anomalies and outliers in the internet of things: A survey on the challenges and solutions. *Electronics (Switzerland)*, *9*(3), 1–15. https://doi.org/10.3390/electronics9030511

Guillon, D., Villeneuve, E., Merlo, C., Vareilles, E., & Aldanondo, M. (2021). ISIEM: A methodology to deploy a knowledge-based system to support bidding process. *Computers and Industrial Engineering*, *161*(August), 107638. https://doi.org/10.1016/j.cie.2021.107638

Gupta, S. (2022). Non-functional requirements elicitation for edge computing. *Internet of Things (Netherlands)*, *18*(January), 100503. https://doi.org/10.1016/j.iot.2022.100503

Islam, M. D., Shen, H., & Badsha, S. (2022). Integrating blockchain into supply chain safeguarded by PUF-enabled RFID. *Internet of Things (Netherlands)*, *18*(June 2021), 100505. https://doi.org/10.1016/j.iot.2022.100505

Kakamoukas, G. A., Sarigiannidis, P. G., & Economides, A. A. (2022). FANETs in Agriculture–A routing protocol survey. *Internet of Things (Netherlands)*, *18*, 100183. https://doi.org/10.1016/j.iot.2020.100183

Kashyap, P. K., Kumar, S., Jaiswal, A., Prasad, M., & Gandomi, A. H. (2021). Towards Precision Agriculture: IoT-Enabled. *IEEE Sensors Journal*, *21*(16), 17479–17491.

Kour, V. P., & Arora, S. (2020). Recent Developments of the Internet of Things in Agriculture: A Survey. *IEEE Access*, *8*, 129924–129957. https://doi.org/10.1109/ACCESS.2020.3009298

Li, J., Dai, J., Issakhov, A., Almojil, S. F., & Souri, A. (2021). Towards decision support systems for energy management in the smart industry and Internet of Things. *Computers and Industrial Engineering*, *161*(September), 107671. https://doi.org/10.1016/j.cie.2021.107671

Lin, N., Wang, X., Zhang, Y., Hu, X., & Ruan, J. (2020). Fertigation management for sustainable precision agriculture based on Internet of Things. *Journal of Cleaner Production*, *277*. https://doi.org/10.1016/j.jclepro.2020.124119

Mekala, M. S., & Viswanathan, P. (2017). A Survey: Smart agriculture IoT with cloud computing. *2017 International Conference on Microelectronic Devices, Circuits and Systems, ICMDCS 2017*, *2017-January*, 1–7. https://doi.org/10.1109/ICMDCS.2017.8211551

Orozco-Lugo, A. G., McLernon, D. C., Lara, M., Zaidi, S. A. R., González, B. J., Illescas, O., Pérez-Macías, C. I., Nájera-Bello, V., Balderas, J. A., Pizano-Escalante, J. L., Perera, C. M., & Rodríguez-Vázquez, R. (2022). Monitoring of water quality in a shrimp farm using a FANET. *Internet of Things (Netherlands)*, *18*(xxxx), 100170. https://doi.org/10.1016/j.iot.2020.100170

Pfender, J., Valera, A., & Seah, W. K. G. (2022). Reassessing caching performance in information-centric IoT. *Internet of Things (Netherlands)*, *18*(January), 100479. https://doi.org/10.1016/j.iot.2021.100479

Phupattanasilp, P., & Tong, S. R. (2019). Augmented reality in the integrative internet of things (AR-IoT): Application for precision farming. *Sustainability (Switzerland)*, *11*(9). https://doi.org/10.3390/su11092658

Roy, S. K., & De, D. (2022). Genetic Algorithm based Internet of Precision Agricultural Things (IopaT) for Agriculture 4.0. *Internet of Things (Netherlands)*, *18*, 100201. https://doi.org/10.1016/j.iot.2020.100201

Sato, G., Sakuraba, A., Uchida, N., & Shibata, Y. (2022). A new road state information platform based on crowed sensing on challenged network environments. *Internet of Things (Netherlands)*, *18*, 100214. https://doi.org/10.1016/j.iot.2020.100214

Shim, J., Cho, S., Kum, E., & Jeong, S. (2021). Adaptive fault detection framework for recipe transition in semiconductor manufacturing. *Computers and Industrial Engineering*, *161*(August), 107632. https://doi.org/10.1016/j.cie.2021.107632

Singh, S., Alam, P., Kumar, P., & Kaur, S. (2019). Internet of Things for Precision Agriculture Applications. *Proceedings of the IEEE International Conference Image Information Processing*, *2019-November*, 420–424. https://doi.org/10.1109/ICIIP47 207.2019.8985688

Viloria, A., Lezama, O. B. P., & Varela, N. (2019). Method for estimating height in people using multivariable statistics. *Procedia Computer Science*, *160*, 224–228. https://doi.org/10.1016/j.procs.2019.11.091

Yuan, Y., Sun, X., Liu, Z., Li, Y., & Guan, X. (2019). Approach of personnel location in roadway environment based on multi-sensor fusion and activity classification. *Computer Networks*, *148*, 34–45. https://doi.org/10.1016/j.comnet.2018.10.022

Chapter 7

Engineering Challenges in the Development of Artificial Intelligence and Machine Learning Software Systems

Mohammad Idrees Bhat,[1] Syed Irfan Yaqoob,[1] and Mohammad Imran[2]

[1]*School of Computer Science, MIT-World Peace University, Pune, India*

[2]*NTT DATA Information Processing Services Private Limited, Bangalore, India*

7.1 Introduction

Over the years, an enormous amount of research work related to artificial intelligence and machine learning (AI/ML) has been carried out in an attempt to imitate human behavior. In other words, AI/ML aims at designing/developing complex algorithms (software) that try to automate human intelligence and learning. That is why AI/ML applications/services and tools are becoming value propositions (add-ons) in almost all industrial products, for example, in e-commerce, education, lifestyle/social media, navigation, robotics, human resource, health critical safety-critical systems, agriculture, gaming, automobiles, and finance, to name just a few.

DOI: 10.1201/9781032624983-7

If we say that AI/ML has revolutionized how software industries and enterprises develop/design software and tools, run businesses, improve product efficiency and profitability etc., it would not be an exaggeration.

Broadly speaking, AI/ML software development differs from traditional development with respect to (1) process knowledge, i.e., the lack of best/standard/agreed-upon practices and workflows; (2) customer business, i.e., domain-specific knowledge; and (3) data-oriented challenges, i.e., data quality, labeling, preparation, validation, accuracy, security, storage, structure/design and analysis, etc. (Mattos et al., 2017; Acm et al., 2017; Erik Brynjolfsson & Tom Mitchell; Byrne, 2017; Estado, 2019; Lin et al., 2014; Martin & Schreckenghost, 2004; Quirchmayr, 1992; Nascimento et al., 2020; Ishikawa, 2019; Shcherbakov et al., 2014; Kim & Zimmermann, 2015; Rahman et al., 2019). Moreover, agreeing on the success metrics before the commencement of any project without any delay can be difficult; in the domain of AI/ML, the task is all the more difficult. These differences make AI/ML systems more data dependent in terms of both behavior and requirement (Estado, 2019).

Furthermore, in the traditional software development life cycle (SDLC), different phases (i.e., planning, design, prototyping, development, testing, deployment, and maintenance) and workflows are mature enough to accommodate any new practice. In contrast, AI/ML development is still in its infancy (Amershi et al., 2019; Byrne, 2017; Estado, 2019; M. Kim et al., 2017; M. Kim & Zimmermann, 2015; Rahman et al., 2019). However, it is strongly argued that AI/ML development will also evolve/mature (with best practices/workflows) with the passage of time. In fact, if we search the term "AI/ML" on search engines, we are witnessing an innumerable works/studies and industrial products on a daily basis. More importantly, among the various works (Byrne, 2017; Erik Brynjolfsson & Tom Mitchell, 2017; Nascimento et al., 2020) are those devoted to finding solutions circumvent the engineering challenges. Nevertheless, it still remains a challenge to fully understand these challenges.

Although, in the literature (Byrne, 2017; Braiek & Khomh, 2020; Erik Brynjolfsson & Tom Mitchell, 2017; Ghofrani et al., 2019; Arpteg et al., 2018; Rahman et al., 2019; Amershi et al., 2019; Kim et al., 2018), researchers/practitioners have listed various challenges and have come up with different solutions, these solutions are not generalized, i.e., the solutions are case specific or application specific. More importantly, there is lack of knowledge (or clarity) about the challenges themselves, much less proposing any generalized solution. Hence, it is extremely important to have a consolidated, generalized, and superficial knowledge about challenges at the outset. Therefore, this chapter attempts to overcome this lack of knowledge. Note that, for coherence, relevance, and consistency, we followed the categorization of challenges given in (Nascimento et al., 2020). Further arguments are clearly summarized and cross-referenced.

7.2 Categories of Challenges in AI/ML Software Systems

7.2.1 Software Testing and Quality Assurance

In general, testing is intended to uncover the errors that creep in unintentionally during the design and construction of software systems/models or to verify whether the model meets the expected objectives. In contrast to traditional software development, AI/ML models are constructed inductively (De Silva & Alahakoon, 2022). That is, the behavior of the model is generated/designed from training data. Therefore, besides noisy data, the potential causes for undesired behavior in AI/ML include execution environment, design mis-specification, poor choice of model, program code, numerical instability, and non-convex objectives (Giray, 2021; Selsam et al., 2017). Traditional development testing techniques, i.e., code/test coverage, and mutation/property testing, etc., try to increase the structural coverage of the program code. Therefore, they are not competent to be used in forms of AI/ML (deep/reinforcement learning etc.), where program codes are data hungry/dependent (Braiek & Khomh, 2020; Giray, 2021; J. Kim et al., 2019; Paul Amma & Jeff Offutt, 2016; Schröder & Schulz, 2022; Selsam et al., 2017).

The inductive nature of AI/ML systems also makes it difficult and challenging to identify and localize the bugs in a program code. More importantly, AI/ML models expect huge amounts of data, hence extending the canvas of testing, heterogeneity, management, manipulation, quality, integration, labeling, estimation, statistical drifts, effort and budget (Sculley et al., 2015; Kruchten & Eds, 2018; Munappy et al., 2019). Furthermore, a limited amount of explainability, predictability, and interpretability make it difficult to understand the implementation and conceptual errors that may lead to unexpected behaviors and ultimately hinder real-world deployment. In fact, there is no agreement on correctness and testing criteria of an AI/ML model (Braiek & Khomh, 2020; Kruchten & Eds, 2018; Ma et al., 2018). It is also strange that AI ethics and scalability are the most neglected and poorly researched areas (Vakkuri et al., 2019, 2020; Amershi et al., 2019; Bryson & Winfield, 2017; Walz & Firth-Butterfield, 2019; Vakkuri & Kemell, 2019). Overall, more effort and research are needed to investigate the causes of vulnerabilities, interpretability, and systematic testing for system correctness and predictability. More importantly, to integrate AI/ML models into full-fledged software systems, ethics (for responsible use) and scalability are indispensable.

7.2.2 Model Development

As stated, AI/ML services are extended as value propositions in industrial products in order to keep pace with current changing scenarios (Rahman et al.,

2019; Alaswad & Poovammal, 2022; Amershi et al., 2019; Byrne, 2017; M. Kim et al., 2018). Hence, it is extremely important to have huge, labeled multiple amounts of relevant, trusted, and processed data (feature engineered), in order to build complex, suitable, and appropriate models (the AI/ML algorithmic pipeline). Thereafter, rigorous testing, performance computation, and evaluations are performed for selecting the best performing/tuned model. Next is maintaining and managing the model after deploying it into real-world environments/production. Finally, it is difficult to compute the correctness of outputs of the model against each individual input (Alaswad & Poovammal, 2022; Grünewälder, 2015; Ishikawa, 2019; Nascimento et al., 2020).

7.2.3 *Project Management and Infrastructure*

With the penetration of AI/ML applications in industrial products, it is vital for project managers (PM) to understand these projects technically, ethically, and have firm grip on communicating the decisions taken by these applications (Alshangiti et al., 2019; Vakkuri & Kemell, 2019; Martin & Schreckenghost, 2004; Ishikawa, 2019; Selsam et al., 2017).

Project managing challenges start with data management. That is, the degree of cleanness, preparation, and relevance of huge data is directly proportional to the accuracy of predictions of AI/ML models. Moreover, managing coordination across the different platforms and technologies is also considered a key monitoring challenge. Next, a PM must have specialization in mathematical and statistical model building, evaluation, tuning, and model fitting (Vakkuri & Kemell, 2019; Alshangiti et al., 2019; Hilllaz et al., 2016; Martin & Schreckenghost, 2004.; Selsam et al., 2017; B et al., 2017; Ishikawa, 2019). Finally, communicating and explaining model technicalities, decisions, and ethical requirements of the end users are some of the nontrivial tasks. Failing at these steps leads to poor estimation of time and resource management (Amershi et al., 2019; B et al., 2017; Munappy et al., 2019).

The most important challenge that must be addressed before the commencement of building any AI/ML model is the agreement on the acquisition, installation, and configuration of the required infrastructure, i.e., hardware, platform, and project-specific tools (B et al., 2017; Hilllaz et al., 2016; Nascimento et al., 2020). According to (Hilllaz et al., 2016), software teams communicate with each other informally. Furthermore, tracking progress is hampered by poor logging and tracking mechanisms.

7.2.4 *Requirement Engineering*

In contrast to traditional development, the engineering requirements (RE) for AI/ML models have introduced a new set of challenges thanks to their data dependence, visible debt, un-explainability/unpredictability, limited support, and less coordination among teams. More importantly, dynamic and vague customer requirements and their complex specifications and validations have led to inadequate modeling (Bhat M.I. et al., 2022., Alaswad & Poovammal, 2022; M. Kim et al., 2018; Lavicza et al., 2021; Mattos et al., 2017; Nascimento et al., 2020; Rahman et al., 2019; Sculley et al., 2015; Xie et al., 2011).

7.2.5 Architecture Design and Integration

As stated, AI/ML models/services are added as value propositions; therefore, the challenges accumulate in the effort to carry out smooth component (i.e., AI/ML model, data and existing software) interaction, system maintenance, monitoring, accommodating requirement change, and evolution of the system. Hence, poor understanding of these architectural dependences results in a lack of reliability and perceptiveness, degradation, and unintended entanglements in the overall system (Amershi et al., 2019; Kruchten & Eds, 2018; Nascimento et al., 2020; Ozkaya, 2021; Lwakatare et al., 2019; Sculley et al., 2015; Tamir & Kandel, 1995). These challenges become manifold once we integrate different modules of AI/ML, for instance, in cloud computing and in the Internet of Things (IoT).

7.2.6 Model Deployment

Deploying AI/ML models are considered one of the difficult decisions that enterprises/organizations have to take. For example, in Algorithmia (2020), it is stated that 64% of organizations delay their product deployment for months and that 38% of organizations waste 50% of engineers'/developers' time in this process. There are innumerable number for reasons for these delays, such as, absence of well-defined examples or no clarity in all the deployment steps. For example, there is no agreement on choosing the appropriate requirements for production, effective organizational and infrastructure setup, success metrics, and *how to handle differences in scale, size, and change in behavior.* Also, how to maintain the model before and after its deployment is not clear (Stephen Oladele, 2023).

7.2.7 Engineering

According to the saying, that "there is always a difference in a priori expectations and posterior results," the same is true in the case of engineering AI/ML models. At the outset, there are high expectations with respect to accuracy levels, high throughput at functional levels, high repeatability, and predictability, etc. But as the development cycle starts, it faces various hiccups/bottlenecks in meeting these a priori expectations. For example, there is no consensus on high productiveness—what are the defined and unifying processes, patterns, tools and practices? (Prescient Technologies, 2023, Nascimento et al., 2020, Bhat M.I. et al., 2022). Also, overdependence on data results in provenance-, quality-, reproducibility-, and monitoring-related engineering problems. Overall, the role of the AI/ML engineer/developer is still evolving/changing; i.e., all the steps are not fully defined (Dice Guest, 2020; Bhat, M.I & B Sharada, et al., 2022; Oladele et al., 2023).

7.3 Summary

Artificial intelligence and machine learning (AI/ML) services/models are state-of-the-art in almost all software engineering practices and industrial products. In contrast to traditional development, the inductive nature of AI/ML introduces a new set of challenges. Starting from data management, these challenges can be summarized as: data acquisition, preparation, scale, relevance, customer requirements, quality, etc. In model development, the selection of the appropriate algorithm, data labeling, tuning of the selected model, training and testing of the model are the main challenges. Next, in the realm of quality, a software engineer has to ensure, while building the AI/ML model, predictability, explainability, reliability, bug detection, heterogeneity in testing, etc. To supervise overall development, a project manager must understand the technical details in depth, acquire, install, configure necessary architecture, and integrate the required infrastructure. Above all, maintaining coordination among different teams is the prime management skill that the project manager has to master. Afterward, in requirement engineering, we must ensure that we accommodate dynamic customer requirements and always check whether a priori expectation is met by posterior results in the model. Finally, deployment is considered extremely difficult decision that enterprises have to take. And it is always delayed due to following reasons: lack of well-defined and agreed upon processes, requirements, organizational setup, and absence of success metric.

References

Acm, I., Zhang, Y., Zhang, T., Jia, Y., Sun, J., Xu, F., & Xu, W. (2017). *DataLab: Introducing Software Engineering Thinking into Data Science Education at Scale.* https://doi.org/10.1109/ICSE-SEET.2017.7

Alaswad, F., & Poovammal, E. (2022). Software quality prediction using machine learning. *Materials Today: Proceedings*, *62*(xxxx), 4714–4720. https://doi.org/10.1016/j.matpr.2022.03.165

Algorithmia. (2020). *2021 Enterprise Trends in Machine Learning.* tinyurl.com/ml-trends-web%0Ahttps://info.algorithmia.com/hubfs/2020/Reports/2021-Trends-in-ML/Algorithmia_2021_enterprise_ML_trends.pdf?hsLang=en-us

Alshangiti, M., Sapkota, H., Murukannaiah, P. K., Liu, X., & Yu, Q. (2019). Why is Developing Machine Learning Applications Challenging? A Study on Stack Overflow

Posts. *International Symposium on Empirical Software Engineering and Measurement, 2019-Septe*(February 2020). https://doi.org/10.1109/ESEM.2019.8870187

Amershi, S., Begel, A., Bird, C., DeLine, R., Gall, H., Kamar, E., Nagappan, N., Nushi, B., & Zimmermann, T. (2019). Software Engineering for Machine Learning Applications. *Icse, 2020*, 1–10. https://fontysblogt.nl/software-engineering-for-machine-learning-applications/

Arpteg, A., Brinne, B., Crnkovic-Friis, L., & Bosch, J. (2018). Software engineering challenges of deep learning. *Proceedings–44th Euromicro Conference on Software Engineering and Advanced Applications, SEAA 2018*, 50–59. https://doi.org/10.1109/SEAA.2018.00018

Bhat, M.I., Sharada, B., Imran, M., Obaidullah, S. (2022). Automatic Segmentation of Handwritten Devanagari Word Documents Enabling Accurate Recognition. In: Chbeir, R., Manolopoulos, Y., Prasath, R. (eds) Mining Intelligence and Knowledge Exploration. MIKE 2021. Lecture Notes in Computer Science(), vol 13119. Springer, Cham. https://doi.org/10.1007/978-3-031-21517-9_8

Bhat, M.I., Sharada, B., Sinha, M.K. (2022). A Graph-Based Holistic Recognition of Handwritten Devanagari Words: An Approach Based on Spectral Graph Embedding. In: Santosh, K., Hegadi, R., Pal, U. (eds) *Recent Trends in Image Processing and Pattern Recognition. RTIP2R 2021.* Communications in Computer and Information Science, vol 1576. Springer, Cham. https://doi.org/10.1007/978-3-031-07005-1_25

Braiek, H. Ben, & Khomh, F. (2020). On testing machine learning programs. *Journal of Systems and Software, 164*. https://doi.org/10.1016/j.jss.2020.110542

Bryson, J., & Winfield, A. (2017). Standardizing Ethical Design for Artificial Intelligence and Autonomous Systems. *Computer, 50*(5), 116–119. https://doi.org/10.1109/MC.2017.154

Byrne, C. (2017). Development Work ows for Data Scientists. *O'Reilly.*

De Silva, D., & Alahakoon, D. (2022). An artificial intelligence life cycle: From conception to production. *Patterns, 3*(6), 100489. https://doi.org/10.1016/j.patter.2022.100489

Dice Guest. (2020). *Machine Learning Engineer: Challenges and Changes Facing the Profession.* Https://Insights.Dice.Com/2020/05/04/Machine-Learning-Engineer-Challenges-Changes-Facing-Profession/. https://doi.org/10.3233/JIFS-169712

Erik Brynjolfsson, & Tom Mitchell. (2017). What can machine learning do? Workforce implications. *Science, 358*(6370), 1530–1534. www.cs.cmu.edu/~tom/pubs/Science_WorkforceDec2017.pdf

Estado, S. De. (2019). Understanding Development Process of Machine Learning Systems: Challenges and Solutions. *2019 ACM/IEEE International Symposium on Empirical Software Engineering and Measurement (ESEM)*, 1–6.

Ghofrani, J., Kozegar, E., Bozorgmehr, A., & Soorati, M. D. (2019). Reusability in artificial neural networks: An empirical study. *ACM International Conference Proceeding Series, B*(i). https://doi.org/10.1145/3307630.3342419

Giray, G. (2021). A software engineering perspective on engineering machine learning systems: State of the art and challenges. *Journal of Systems and Software, 180*, 111031. https://doi.org/10.1016/j.jss.2021.111031

Grünewälder, S. (2015). Continuous integration of machine learning models with ease. ML/CI: Towards a rigorous yet practical treatment (*2019). Third International*

Conference on I-SMAC (IoT in Social, Mobile, Analytics and Cloud) (I-SMAC), 113, 13–21.

Hilllaz, C., Bellarnyz, R., Ericksonz, T., & Burnett, M. (2016). Trials and tribulations of developers of intelligent systems: A field study. *Proceedings of IEEE Symposium on Visual Languages and Human-Centric Computing, VL/HCC, 2016-Novem,* 162–170. https://doi.org/10.1109/VLHCC.2016.7739680

Ishikawa, F. (2019). How do Engineers Perceive Difficulties in Engineering of Machine-Learning Systems?–Questionnaire Survey. *2019 IEEE/ACM Joint 7th International Workshop on Conducting Empirical Studies in Industry (CESI) and 6th International Workshop on Software Engineering Research and Industrial Practice (SER&IP),* 2–9. https://doi.org/10.1109/CESSER-IP.2019.00009

Kim, J., Feldt, R., & Yoo, S. (2019). Guiding Deep Learning System Testing Using Surprise Adequacy. *Proceedings–International Conference on Software Engineering, 2019-May,* 1039–1049. https://doi.org/10.1109/ICSE.2019.00108

Kim, M., & Zimmermann, T. (2015). *The Emerging Role of Data Scientists on Software Development Teams on Software Development Teams.* 1–12.

Kim, M., Zimmermann, T., Deline, R., & Begel, A. (2017). *Data Scientists in Software Teams: State of the Art and Challenges.* 5589(c), 1–16. https://doi.org/10.1109/TSE.2017.2754374

Kim, M., Zimmermann, T., Deline, R., & Begel, A. (2018). Data Scientists in Software Teams: State of the Art and Challenges. *IEEE Transactions,* 2754374. http://web.cs.ucla.edu/~miryung/Publications/tse2017-datascientists.pdf

Kouba, Z., Lažansky, J., Marik, V., Quirchmayr, G., Retschitzegger, W., Vlcek, T., Wagner, R. (1992). *Software development for cim–a case study. Annual Review in Automatic Programming, 16,* 11–19.

Kruchten, P., & Eds, F. C. (2018). *Agile Processes in Software Engineering and Extreme Programming:* (Vol. 314). https://doi.org/10.1007/978-3-030-19034-7

Lavicza, Z., Fenyvesi, K., Lieban, D., Park, H., Hohenwarter, M., Mantecon, J. D., & Prodromou, T. (2021). Continuous Experimentation of Artificial Intelligence Software–A Research Agenda. *Business and Society, 60*(2), 420–453.

Lin, G., Zhu, H., Kang, X., Fan, C., & Zhang, E. (2014). Feature structure fusion and its application. *Information Fusion, 20*(1), 146–154. https://doi.org/10.1016/j.inffus.2014.01.002

Lwakatare, L.E., Raj, A., Bosch, J., Olsson, H.H., Crnkovic, I. (2019). *A Taxonomy of Software Engineering Challenges for Machine Learning Systems: An Empirical Investigation.* 1, 227–243. https://doi.org/10.1007/978-3-030-19034-7

Ma, L., Juefei-xu, F., Zhang, F., Sun, J., Xue, M., & Li, B. (2018). DeepGauge: Multi-Granularity Testing Criteria for Deep Learning Systems. *In Proceedings of the 2018 33rd ACM/IEEE International Conference on Automated Software Engineering (ASE, 12*(September 3–7).

Martin, C., & Schreckenghost, D. (2004). *Beyond the Prototype: The Design Evolution of a Deployed AI System.* American Association for Artificial Intelligence.

Mattos, D. I., Bosch, J., & Olsson, H. H. (2017). *Your System Gets Better Every Day You Use It: Towards Automated Continuous Experimentation. Ml.* https://doi.org/10.1109/SEAA.2017.15

Munappy, A., Bosch, J., Olsson, H. H., Arpteg, A., & Brinne, B. (2019). Data Management Challenges for Deep Learning. *Proceedings–45th Euromicro Conference on Software Engineering and Advanced Applications, SEAA 2019*, 140–147. https://doi.org/10.1109/SEAA.2019.00030

Nascimento, E., Nguyen-Duc, A., Sundbø, I., & Conte, T. (2020). Software engineering for artificial intelligence and machine learning software: A systematic literature review. *ArXiv, abs/2011.0.*

Ozkaya, I. (2021). *Overcoming Software Architecture Challenges for ML-Enabled Systems.* 1–19 (Carnegie Mellon University).

Paul Amma, & Jeff Offutt. (2016). *Introduction to Software testing* (Cambridge).

Prescient Technologies. (2023). *AI-ML Engineering Problems.* www.Pre-Scient.Com/Blogs/Artificial-Intelligence/Ai-Ml-Engineering-Problems.Html.

Rahman, M. S., Rivera, E., Khomh, F., Guéhéneuc, Y.-G., & Lehnert, B. (2019). Machine Learning Software Engineering in Practice: An Industrial Case Study. *ArXiv, abs/1906.0*, 1–21. http://arxiv.org/abs/1906.07154

Schröder, T., & Schulz, M. (2022). Monitoring machine learning models: a categorization of challenges and methods. *Data Science and Management*, 5(3), 105–116. https://doi.org/10.1016/j.dsm.2022.07.004

Sculley, D., Holt, G., Golovin, D., Davydov, E., Phillips, T., Ebner, D., Chaudhary, V., Young, M., Crespo, J. F., & Dennison, D. (2015). Hidden technical debt in machine learning systems. *Advances in Neural Information Processing Systems*, 2015-Janua, 2503–2511.

Selsam, D., Liang, P., & Dill, D. L. (2017). Developing bug-free machine learning systems with formal mathematics. *34th International Conference on Machine Learning, ICML 2017*, 6, 4661–4670.

Shcherbakov, M., Shcherbakova, N., & Brebels, A. (2014). Lean Data Science Research Life Cycle: A Concept for Data Analysis Software Development Lean Data Science Research Life Cycle: *A. Kravets et al. (Eds.): JCKBSE 2014, CCIS, 466*(December 2018), 708–716. https://doi.org/10.1007/978-3-319-11854-3

Stephen Oladele. (2023). *Model Deployment Challenges: 6 Lessons From 6 ML Engineers.* www.Mendeley.Com/Guides/Web-Citation-Guide/. https://doi.org/10.1109/ASE.2019.00080

Tamir, D. E., & Kandel, A. (1995). Logic programming and the execution model of Prolog. *Information Sciences–Applications*, 4(3), 167–191. https://doi.org/10.1016/1069-0115(95)90038-1

Vakkuri, V., & Kemell, K. K. (2019). Implementing AI ethics in practice: An empirical evaluation of the RESOLVEDD strategy. *Lecture Notes in Business Information Processing*, 370 LNBIP, 260–275. https://doi.org/10.1007/978-3-030-33742-1_21

Vakkuri, V., Kemell, K. K., & Abrahamsson, P. (2019). Implementing Ethics in AI: Initial Results of an Industrial Multiple Case Study. *Lecture Notes in Computer Science (Including Subseries Lecture Notes in Artificial Intelligence and Lecture Notes in Bioinformatics)*, 11915 LNCS, 331–338. https://doi.org/10.1007/978-3-030-35333-9_24

Vakkuri, V., Kemell, K. K., Kultanen, J., & Abrahamsson, P. (2020). The Current State of Industrial Practice in Artificial Intelligence Ethics. *IEEE Software*, 37(4), 50–57. https://doi.org/10.1109/MS.2020.2985621

Walz, A., & Firth-Butterfield, K. (2019). Implementing Ethics Into Artificial Intelligence: a Contribution, From a Legal Perspective, To the Development of an Ai Governance Regime. *Duke Law and Technology Review, 18*(1), 176.

Xie, X., Ho, J. W. K., Murphy, C., Kaiser, G., Xu, B., & Chen, T. Y. (2011). Testing and validating machine learning classifiers by metamorphic testing. *Journal of Systems and Software, 84*(4), 544–558. https://doi.org/10.1016/j.jss.2010.11.920

Chapter 8

Study and Analysis of Testing Effort Functions for Software Reliability Modeling

Javaid Iqbal, Nyla Manzoor, and Refath Farooq

Department of Computer Science, University of Kashmir, Srinagar, India

Acronyms with Definitions

SRGM	software reliability growth models
SE	software engineering
SRE	software reliability engineering
SD	software development
CTE	cumulative testing effort
EW	exponentiated Weibull
NHPP	non-homogenous Poisson process
SPSS	Statistical Package for the Social Sciences
TEF	testing effort functions
R^2	coefficient of multiple determination
SSE	sum of squared error
MSE	mean squared error
AIC	Akaike information criterion
BIC	Bayesian information criterion

DOI: 10.1201/9781032624983-8

NOTATIONS	
$W(t)$	cumulative testing-effort consumption at time t
$W^*(t)$	$W(t) - W(0)$
W_C	cumulative testing-effort consumption at time t for constant TEF
W_W	cumulative testing-effort consumption at time t for Weibull TEF
W_E	cumulative testing-effort consumption at time t for exponential TEF
W_R	cumulative testing-effort consumption at time t for Rayleigh TEF
$W_{EW}(t)$	cumulative testing-effort consumption at time t for exponentiated Weibull TEF
$W_{BX}(t)$	cumulative testing-effort consumption at time t for Burr type X TEF
$W_{BXII}(t)$	cumulative testing-effort consumption at time t for Burr type XII TEF
$W_L(t)$	cumulative testing-effort consumption at time t for logistic TEF
$W_k(t)$	cumulative testing-effort consumption at time t for generalized logistic TEF
$W_{GE}(t)$	cumulative testing-effort consumption at time t for generalized exponential TEF
$W_{LL}(t)$	cumulative testing-effort consumption at time t for log logistic TEF
$W_{LE}(t)$	cumulative testing-effort consumption at time t for logistic exponential TEF
$w(t)$	current testing effort expenditure
$w_C(t)$	current testing effort expenditure for Constant TEF
$w_W(t)$	current testing effort expenditure for Weibull TEF
$w_E(t)$	current testing effort expenditure for exponential TEF
$w_R(t)$	current testing effort expenditure for Rayleigh TEF
$w_{EW}(t)$	current testing effort expenditure for exponentiated Weibull TEF

NOTATIONS	
$w_{BX}(t)$	current testing effort expenditure Burr type X TEF
$w_{BXII}(t)$	current testing effort expenditure Burr type XII TEF
$w_L(t)$	current testing effort expenditure logistic TEF
$w_k(t)$	current testing effort expenditure for generalized logistic TEF
$w_{GE}(t)$	current testing effort expenditure generalized exponential TEF
$w_{LL}(t)$	current testing effort expenditure log logistic TEF
$w_{LE}(t)$	current testing effort expenditure for logistic exponential TEF
α	total testing effort expenditure
B	scale parameter
δ	shape parameter
θ	shape parameter
t	time
A	constant parameter in the logistic TEF
M	is a constant in generalized logistic TEF
N	total testing-effort eventually consumed
$b(t)$	Time-dependent fault detection rate function
K	structuring index having large value for modeling well structured SD efforts
y_i	actual values
$m(t_i)$	predicted values
z	total number of observations
u	number of parameters estimated by the model

8.1 Introduction

The development of extremely reliable computer software is one of the main challenges in SE. SD typically involves testing of implemented software systems to assess their quality and dependability. Software problems present in the system are found and fixed during the testing phase using a reasonable number of test resources, including CPU time, labor, test cases to be run, and money [1]. These test resource outlays are referred to as "test effort" in this respect. Software testing is believed to consume more than 50% of the time resource used for SD [2]. According to [2], *approximately 40–50% of the total SD resource outlay goes into software testing.* Furthermore, it is important to examine a software system within the allotted test time with an acceptable level of test effort. In order to understand how test effort behaves during its consumption process and what impact it has on software reliability, researchers are interested in defining or modeling the behavior of test effort. Using test data gathered during the software testing phase of SD, it is also crucial to assess and forecast software reliability. In the realm of SE, the reliability of software has received better attention. To represent a software error detection phenomenon or a software failure occurrence phenomenon in software testing, numerous SRGMs have been created in this field [3–17]. A software error that is still present in the system results in software failure, which is an unacceptable deviation from the expected program operation. An SRGM describes the link between the length of software testing and the total number of defects discovered over time or the time gap between software failures [1, 18]. An SRGM can be used to obtain software reliability metrics such as expected current error content, mean time between failures, software reliability, etc. Determining the amount of test effort required to meet the deadline for software release and to achieve the specified level of software reliability is a paramount SD concern. Although continuous test effort is preferred in terms of software testing control, this might occasionally be challenging in practice. A TEF explains how testing resources (such as CPU time, people, etc.) are distributed or consumed during the testing period [19]. Tracking the reliability growth in relation to testing effort expenditure is crucial for management to take informed decisions. Testing effort is highly relevant to the testing process. For example, more testing effort can make the testing phase more rigorous at any point in time. Most of the testing work is used up throughout the testing procedure. The amount of testing time used reveals how effectively faults are found in software and are modellable [20, 21]. To estimate the SD effort, TEFs are defined by researchers. A TEF explains the connection between the time spent on testing software (e.g., Line of Code) and the effort put forth (which can take many forms and can be expressed as total effort). The majority of studies make the assumption that the exponential, Rayleigh, Weibull, logistic, log-logistic, or generalized logistic curves represent the time-dependent behavior of TEF expenditure. However, as actual testing scenarios exhibit a variety of expenditure patterns, it can occasionally be challenging to represent the TEF expenditure just by these curves in many software testing scenarios [19]. Exponential and Rayleigh curve behaviors can be derived as special cases of Weibull curve behavior.

The rest of this chapter is organized as follows. Section 8.2 discusses the summary of 12 famous TEFs used in literature; Section 8.3 presents the brief summary of the analysis carried out in this study, employing six comparison criteria; and Section 8.4 presents the conclusion of this study, followed by the References section.

8.2 Summary of Some Famous TEFs Used in the Literature

The majority of studies have employed exponential, Rayleigh, Weibull, logistic, log-logistic, or generalized logistic curves to capture the time-dependent behavior of TEF expenditure. Exponential and Rayleigh curves are special cases of Weibull behavior. In this section, we explore 11 types of TEFs used in literature.

1. **Constant TEF**: As discussed in [22], under the assumption that $w(t)$ is a constant, expressible as:

$$w_C(t) = w \qquad (8.1)$$

the CTE, $W(t)$ can be obtained as

$$W_c(t) = wt \qquad (8.2)$$

Evidently, as t tends to infinity, CTE consumed also goes to positive infinity. This is not reasonable, as resources available cannot be infinite. If TEF is not taken into account, it might be interpreted as taking $w(t) = 1$.

Though a constant amount of test effort is preferred during testing phase, sometimes it is just not practicable. This is because the testing environment is itself dynamic subject to many non-controllables.

2. **Weibull TEF**: As discussed in [20–23], a reasonable assumption is that there is a cap on the resources available to test the software. Instantaneous testing effort realistically has to diminish as testing goes on, thus fulfilling the practical finite limit on CTE spent on testing. The rationality of this statement stems from the practical viewpoint that no software company will spend infinite resources on software testing. Researchers in [1, 20–21] assert that the instantaneous testing effort decreased during the testing life cycle and employed Weibull-type distribution to describe the TEF. Weibull TEF, being flexible, can fit most data used in the study of SRGMs. The Weibull distribution can feature distinct curves for distinct values of its shape parameter,

thereby rendering it generously flexible and suitable to capture processes with inconsistent rates [24]. The CTE consumed in time $(0,t]$ according to Weibull curve is

$$W_W(t) = \alpha\left(1 - e^{-\beta t^\delta}\right) \tag{8.3}$$

It should also be noted that the CTE consumed is finite and tends to α when t approaches positive infinity.

3. **Exponential TEF** [21,23]: The CTE consumed in time $(0,t]$ according to the exponential curve, is

$$W_E(t) = \alpha\left(1 - e^{-\beta t}\right) \tag{8.4}$$

The exponential curve is suitable to describe the testing environment, which has a monotonically declining testing effort rate.

4. **Rayleigh testing effort function** [21,23]: The CTE consumed in time $(0,t]$ according to the Rayleigh curve is

$$W_R(t) = \alpha\left(1 - e^{-\beta t^2}\right) \tag{8.5}$$

The Rayleigh testing effort rate first increases to its peak, then decreases with a decelerating speed to zero asymptotically without reaching zero.

The exponential and Rayleigh curves, respectively, are described by the Weibull curve when $\delta = 1$ or 2, making them special examples of the Weibull-type curve. In practice, if $\delta > 3$, many test effort datasets are not suited for these testing effort curves because they exhibit unrealistically apparent peak phenomenon (a non-smoothly ascending and dropping consumption curve) [23]. Although a Weibull-type curve fits the majority of the existing datasets well, it is not always advisable to adopt one because of the peak phenomenon for $\delta > 3$.

5. **Exponentiated Weibull TEF** [25]: During the SD process, the EW curve is a more adaptable and generic TEF that doesn't experience a peak phenomenon [25]. The CTE expenditure consumed in time $(0, t]$ [20–21, 23, 25–26] sired--

$$W_{EW}(t) = \alpha\left(1 - e^{-\beta t^\delta}\right)^\theta, \alpha > 0, \beta > 0, \delta > 0, \theta > 0 \tag{8.6}$$

The current testing effort expenditure at testing t is:

$$w_{EW}(t) = W_{EW}(t)' = \alpha \cdot \beta \cdot \delta \cdot \theta \cdot t^{\delta-1} \cdot e^{-\beta t^\delta} \left(1 - e^{-\beta t^\delta}\right)^{\theta-1} \tag{8.7}$$

When $\theta > 1$, the EW TEF $w(t)$ reaches its maximum value at the time:

$$t_{max} = \left[\frac{2(\delta\theta-1)}{\beta\delta(\theta+1)}\right]^{1/\delta} \tag{8.8}$$

6. **Burr-type X TEF** [19]: In real software projects, the Burr-type X distribution has a variable curve with a large range of potential spending patterns. A generalized Rayleigh curve is referred to as a "Burr-type X TEF." When $\delta = 2$, we obtain Burr-type X TEF from the EW TEF in Eq. (8.6). The CTE expenditure of Burr-type X TEF over time period $(0,t]$ is given by:

$$W_{BX}(t) = \alpha\left(1 - e^{-\beta t^2}\right)^\theta, \alpha > 0, \beta > 0, \theta > 0 \tag{8.9}$$

The current testing effort expenditure at testing t is:

$$w_{EW}(t) = W_{EW}(t)' = 2\alpha \cdot \beta \cdot \theta \cdot t \cdot e^{-\beta t^2} \left(1 - e^{-\beta t^2}\right)^{\theta-1} \tag{8.10}$$

When $\theta > 1/2$, the Burr-type X TEF $w(t)$ reaches its max value at the time [19]

$$t_{max} = \left[\frac{(2\theta-1)}{\beta(\theta+1)}\right]^{1/2} \tag{8.11}$$

7. **Burr-type XII TEF** [27–28]: The versatile Burr-type XII curve [27–28] allows for a wide range of potential spending patterns in actual software projects. Weibull, exponential, and log-logistic are examples of special cases in this family [28]. Burr XII's reliability and hazard rate functions have straightforward algebraic representations, which is another benefit. As a result, Burr-type XII offers a wide range of density shapes in addition to being functionally straightforward [28].

The CTE expenditure consumed in time $(0,t]$, according to Burr-type XII is

$$W_{BXII}(t) = \alpha\left(1 - \left(1 + (\beta t)^\delta\right)^{-\theta}\right), \alpha > 0, \beta > 0, \delta > 0, \theta > 0, t > 0 \tag{8.12}$$

The current testing effort consumption curve at testing time is given as

$$w_{BXII}(t) = \frac{\alpha\beta\theta\delta(\beta \cdot t)^{\delta-1}}{\left[1 + (\beta \cdot t)^{\delta}\right]^{\theta+1}} \tag{8.13}$$

the Burr-type XII TEF $w(t)$ reaches its max value at the time

$$t_{max} = \frac{1}{\beta}\left[\frac{\delta-1}{\delta\theta+1}\right]^{\frac{1}{\delta}} \tag{8.14}$$

8. **Logistic TEF** [29]: This is also known as the Parr model, first proposed by Parr [30] to characterize the utilization of resources used by software testing projects and as an alternative to the Rayleigh curve. Moreover, the peak phenomenon for $\delta > 3$ in the case of the Weibull-type curve, makes such curves unrealistic to use on many occasions [23]. As a result, [23] presented an SRGM employing Pharr's logistic TEF. With the exception of the project's initial stage, the logistic TEF exhibits behavior akin to that of the Rayleigh curve. The logistic TEF over time period (0,t] can be expressed as:

$$W_L(t) = \frac{\alpha}{1 + Ae^{-Nt}}, \alpha > 0, N > 0, A > 0 \tag{8.15}$$

Using the preceding TEF, the current testing effort consumption is given as

$$w_L(t) = W_L(t)' = \frac{\alpha \cdot A \cdot N \cdot \exp(-N \cdot t)}{\left[1 + A \cdot \exp(-N \cdot t)\right]^2}$$

$$= \frac{-\cdot A \cdot N}{\left[\exp\left(\frac{N \cdot t}{2}\right) + A \cdot \exp\left(\frac{-N \cdot t}{2}\right)\right]^2} \tag{8.16}$$

A is a constant.

Therefore, $w(t)$ is a smooth bell-shaped function and reaches its maximum value at

$$t_{max} = \frac{1}{N} \cdot \log(A) \tag{8.17}$$

In contrast to the Weibull-type TEF for which $W(0) = 0$, the initial condition for the logistic TEF is $W(0) \neq 0$. The early phases of SD are where the inconsistencies between the Weibull-type curve and the logistic curve are most noticeable [23]. Many researchers have developed SRGM using logistic TEFs. Kuo et al. [31] proposed many SRGM with constant, non-decreasing, and non-increasing fault detection rates using the logistic TEF. Huang et al. [32] studied the influence of testing effort consumption in the famous Yamada delayed S-shaped model.

9. **Generalized logistic TEF** [33]: The logistic TEF was generalized by Huang et al. [33]. The benefit of the logistic TEF is that it more closely links a work profile to the SD's inherent structure [33]. As a result, it may be utilized to accurately represent the resource usage during the SD process and obtain a noticeably better model for the distribution of testing effort costs.

   Additionally, top-down design and stepwise refining are two potential enhancements to the SD approach that can be taken into account and evaluated using logistic TEF [33]. Interestingly, relaxing or tweaking with some assumptions used for derivations of the original Parr model and incorporating the structured SD effort, we obtain the generalization of logistic TEF[33]. The generalized logistic TEF is given as

$$W_k(t) = \alpha \left(\frac{(k+1)/A}{1 + Me^{-\delta kt}} \right)^{1/k} \tag{8.18}$$

If $k = 1$ and $A = 2$, then we obtain the CTE of a logistic TEF. On the other hand, if we set $A = k + 1$, a better generalized CTE is obtained:

$$W_k(t) = \frac{\alpha}{\sqrt[k]{1 + Me^{-\delta kt}}} \tag{8.19}$$

For this, the curve reaches its maximum value t_{max} when

$$t^k \max = \frac{\ln(M/k)}{\delta k} \tag{8.20}$$

10. **Generalized exponential TEF** [34]: NHPP, which assumes that the test effort expenditure has time-dependent behavior, will follow an exponential, Weibull, logistic, or modified logistic curve, provides the foundation for the majority of SRGM research. However, as actual software testing displays a wide range of spending patterns, it can occasionally be difficult to accurately describe the testing effort expenditure in software testing scenarios using just

these curves. Especially, the Weibull-type TEF may display an unrealistic apparent peak when the shape parameter = 3, 4, or 5. The generalized exponential TEF may accommodate a variety of possible spending patterns. The CTE expenditure consumed in time $(0,t]$ is:

$$W_{GE}(t) = \alpha\left(1 - e^{-\theta t}\right)^{\beta}, \alpha > 0, \beta > 0, \theta \geq 0 \tag{8.21}$$

And the current testing effort consumed at testing time t is:

$$w_{GE}(t) = W_{GE}(t)' = \alpha \cdot \theta \cdot \beta \cdot e^{-\theta t}\left(1 - e^{-\theta t}\right)^{\beta-1} \tag{8.22}$$

When $\beta > 1$, the generalized exponential TEF $w(t)$ reaches its maximum value at the time:

$$t_{max} = \left[\frac{2(\beta - 1)}{\theta(\beta + 1)}\right] \tag{8.23}$$

11. **Log Logistic TEF** [35]: The log-logistic TEF was used by Bokhari and Ahmad [35] to predict software failure behavior. They came to the conclusion that this curve is suitable for evaluating the reliability of software and is extremely flexible. The time-dependent usage of testing effort is described by log-logistic curves. It is a unique instance of the Burr-type XII TEF. It has only one shape parameter, δ. The CTE expenditure consumed in $(0,t]$ is depicted as follows [36]:

$$W_{LL}(t) = \alpha\left[1 - \left\{1 + (\beta t)^{\delta}\right\}^{-1}\right] \tag{8.24}$$

$$= \alpha\left[(\beta t)^{\delta} / \left(1 + (\beta t)^{\delta}\right)\right], \alpha > 0, \beta > 0, \delta > 0 \tag{8.25}$$

Therefore, the current testing effort expenditure at testing is given by

$$w_{LL}(t) = \left[\alpha\beta\delta(\beta t)^{\delta-1}\right] / \left[1 + (\beta t)^{\delta}\right]^{2} \tag{8.26}$$

$w(t)$ is a smooth bell-shaped function and reaches its maximum value at

$$t_{max} = \frac{1}{\beta}\left[\frac{\delta - 1}{\delta + 1}\right]^{1/\delta} \tag{8.27}$$

12. **Logistic exponential TEF** [37–39]: This may be applied to a wide range of situations for modeling software failure data and is very flexible in supporting any hazard rate function shapes. The logistic-exponential CTE expenditure over time period (0,t] can be expressed as [38, 39]

$$W_{LE}(t) = \frac{\alpha(e^{\beta t} - 1)^{\delta}}{1 + (e^{\beta t} - 1)^{\delta}}, \ t > 0 \tag{8.28}$$

And its current testing effort is

$$w_{LE}(t) = \frac{a\delta\beta e^{\beta t}(e^{\beta t} - 1)^{\delta-1}}{\left(1 + (e^{\beta t} - 1)^{\delta}\right)^2}, \ t > 0 \tag{8.29}$$

8.3 Numerical Analysis of 12 TEFs Employed in This Study

We evaluated the performance of the various TEFs on the failure dataset collected from the SD project and compared the results based on six comparison criteria. In this study we have used the following comparison criteria:

Coefficient of multiple determination (R^2) [8, 40]: This is used to examine the fitting power of SRGMs, which is expressed as:

$$R^2 = 1 - \frac{\sum_{i=1}^{n}(y_i - m(t_i))^2}{\sum_{i=1}^{n}(y_i - \bar{y})^2} \tag{8.30}$$

The best model is the one that provides the higher R^2, that is, closer to 1.

Adjusted R^2 [8]: This is mathematically defined as:

$$\overline{R^2} = 1 - (1 - R^2)\frac{z - 1}{z - u_1 - 1} \tag{8.31}$$

The best model is the one that provides the higher adjusted R^2, that is, closer to 1. Sometimes it is equal to R^2 and also can be less than R^2.

Sum of squared error (SSE) [8]: SSE is defined mathematically as

$$SSE = \sum_{i=1}^{n}(y_i - m(t_i))^2 \tag{8.32}$$

The smaller the value of SSE is, better is the performance.

Mean square error (MSE)[8]: This represents the calculation of how far the estimated values vary from the actual observation and is expressed as:

$$\text{MSE} = \frac{SSE}{z - u}$$

The smaller the value of MSE is, better is the performance. To minimize MSE, the model has to be more accurate, thereby being closer to actual data. An MSE of 0 means that the estimated values accurately match the actual data. Though this sounds ideal, typically it is not possible.

MSE is also defined as the residual sum of squares (RSS) divided by the number of degrees of freedom (*df*): $df = z - u - 1$.

AIC (Akaike's information criterion) [8, 41, 42]: This is mathematically defined as

$$\text{AIC} = 2 * u + z * \ln(SSE) \tag{8.33}$$

A smaller AIC represents better performance.

Bayesian information criterion (BIC) [41, 42]: Mathematically, BIC is defined as:

$$\text{BIC} = z * ln\left(\frac{SSE}{z}\right) + u * ln(z) \tag{8.34}$$

The smaller the value of BIC is, better the performance will be.

When choosing a model from a limited number of options, statisticians use the BIC, also known as the Schwarz information criterion (SIC). Models with a lower BIC are typically chosen. It is strongly related to the AIC and partly based on the likelihood function [41, 42]. It is feasible to enhance the likelihood when fitting models by adding parameters, but doing so runs the risk of overfitting. By inserting a penalty term for the number of parameters in the model, BIC and AIC both seek to tackle this problem; the penalty term is stronger in BIC than in AIC [41, 42]. They penalize free parameters ($2*u$ in AIC; $ln(z)*u$ in BIC). The BIC penalty term is larger than that of AIC because, for the AIC, the penalty is $2*u$, whereas for BIC, it is $u*log(z)$ and $log(z) > 2$ in most cases. In the case of BIC, the penalty term is $u*log(z)$, which can be interpreted as the penalty derived from prior information (hence the name Bayesian information criterion). Thus BIC favors more parsimonious models than AIC.

8.4 Numerical Analysis

A programming language/I (PL/I, pronounced "P-L one") dataset is available in [43]. This is a small dataset with time unit of weeks, 381 cumulative faults were observed within 19 weeks, and the total amount of consumed testing effort was 47.65 CPU hours. All data points were used to fit the model and to estimate the model's parameters. We have used the least square estimation technique for which we used python coding for parameter estimation. Find more on regression methods at [44]. The resultant value of all the testing effort functions has been provided in Table 8.1. The 12 graphs in Figure 8.1 display the curves describing the actual data against the estimated testing effort using various testing effort functions. Figure 8.2 displays the comparison of all the goodness-of-fit curves for all the testing effort functions against the actual data described in this chapter. The criteria values for all the TEFs can be summarized as:

- **R^2**: The largest value of R^2 is 0.995, which is same for Weibull, exponential Weibull, Burr=-type X, Burr-type XII, generalized logistic, log logistic and logistic exponential TEFs; for constant, exponential and logistic, and generalized exponential, it is 0.991 . The value of R^2 for Rayleigh TEF is the smallest one, 0.974.
- **Adjusted_R^2**: The largest value of adjusted_R^2 is 0.994, which is same for Weibull, exponential Weibull, Burr-type X, Burr-type XII, log logistic, and logistic exponential TEF's; for constant TEF, it is 0.991. The smallest value of adjusted R^2 is shown by Rayleigh TEF, 0.971
- **MSE**: The smallest value of MSE is 1.026, shown by logistic exponential, and 1.027, shown by Weibull, log logistic TEF. Smaller values of MSE are also shown by Burr type XII. The largest value of MSE is shown by Rayleigh TEF, 5.753
- **SSE**: The smallest value of SSE is 16.357, shown by exponential Weibull TEF. Other TEF's also show smaller values of SSE. The largest value of SSE is shown by Rayleigh TEF, 97.806. TEFs like constant, exponential, logistic and generalized exponential also show larger values of SSE, which are 30.545, 30.558, 30.916, 30.584.
- **AIC**: The smallest value of BIC is shown by Burr-type X, which is 59.120. Other TEFs show smaller values than this. The largest value of AIC is shown by Rayleigh TEF, 91.076. TEFs like logistic TEF and generalized exponential TEF also show larger values, 71.1946 and 70.9895, respectively.
- **•BIC**: The smallest value of BIC, 5.988, is shown log logistic TEF. The second smallest values are shown by Burr-type X, Weibull, logistic exponential TEF, which are 6.009, 6.087, 6.089, respectively. The largest value of BIC is shown by Rayleigh TEF, 37.021.

Table 8.1   Estimated Parameters and Comparison of Results for Different TEF

No	Testing Effort Function	Estimated Parameters	R^2	Adj-R^2	MSE	SSE	AIC	BIC
1	Constant TEF	$w=2.460$	0.991	0.991	1.696	30.545	66.965	11.965
2	Weibull TEF	$\alpha=799.108$ $\beta=0.002$ $\delta=1.114$	0.995	0.994	1.027	16.443	59.198	6.087
3	Exponential TEF	$\alpha=322886.47$ $\beta=0.000007619$	0.991	0.990	1.797	30.558	68.973	14.917
4	Rayleigh TEF	$\alpha=49.319$ $\beta=0.013$	0.974	0.971	5.75	97.806	91.067	37.021
5	Exponential Weibull TEF	$\alpha=163.701$ $\beta=0.0001$ $\delta=2.285$ $\theta=0.486$	0.995	0.994	1.090	16.357	61.099	8.932
6	Burr-type X TEF	$\alpha=184.754$ $\beta=0.0002$ $\theta=0.557$	0.995	0.994	1.909	16.375	59.120	6.009
7	Burr-type XII TEF	$\alpha=958.965$ $\beta=0.0008$ $c=1.114$ $m=5.174$	0.995	0.994	1.096	16.444	61.199	9.032
8	Logistic TEF	$\alpha=54.836$ $A=13.033$ $N=0.226$	0.991	0.990	1.932	30.916	71.1946	18.083
9	Generalized logistic TEF	$\alpha=70.540$ $M=0.001$ $\delta=270.871$ $k=0.0004$	0.995	0.993	1.250	18.750	63.693	11.526
10	Generalized exponential TEF	$\alpha=105108.260$ $\beta=0.003$ $\theta=0.006$	0.991	0.990	1.911	30.584	70.9895	17.878
11	Log logistic TEF	$\alpha\ 1622.982$ $\beta=0.002$ $\delta=1.114$	0.995	0.994	1.027	16.445	59.200	5.988
12	Logistic exponential TEF	$\alpha=538.206$ $\beta=0.006$ $\delta=1.115$	0.995	0.994	1.026	16.427	59.179	6.089

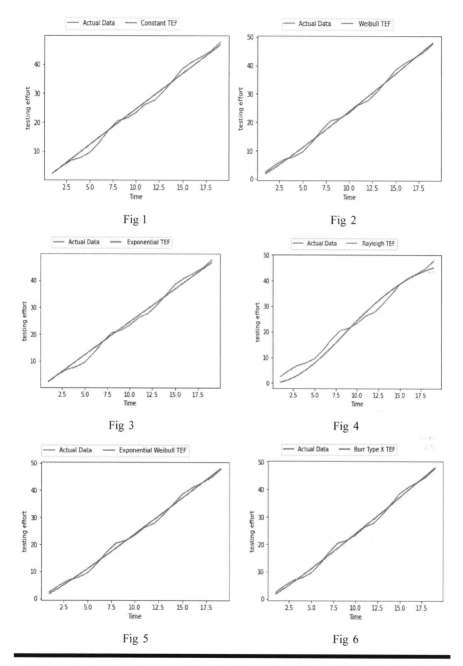

Figure 8.1 **(1–12) Actual effort and estimated testing effort vs. time for the 12 TEFs used in this study.**

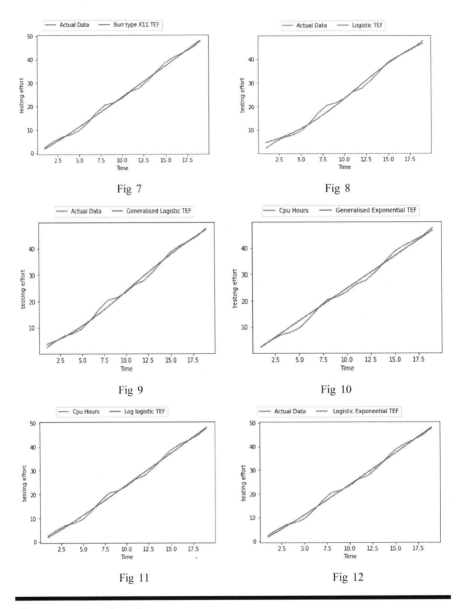

Fig 7

Fig 8

Fig 9

Fig 10

Fig 11

Fig 12

Figure 8.1   (Continued)

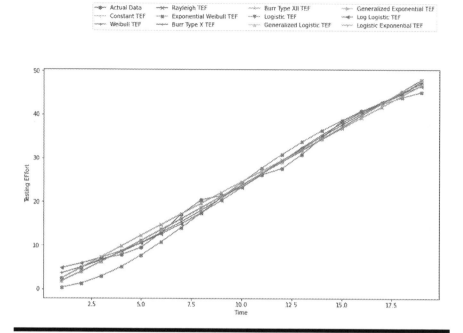

Figure 8.2   Fitting results of TEFs compared with actual effort data.

8.5 Conclusion

During the software testing phase, testing resources are typically not continuously allocated, which has a significant impact on the rate of fault detection and the turn-around time for fixing reported defects. For instance, the debugger might go a week without performing any testing work before working incredibly hard the next several days. Debuggers frequently make mistakes and introduce new defects while being tested. If more testing effort is expended because the code has undergone more changes, the debuggers tend to introduce more problems. An explanation of the distribution or use of testing resources during the testing period is provided by a TEF. It's important to monitor reliability growth in relation to testing effort expenditures. The testing process places a high value on testing effort. TEFs were developed in order to evaluate the SD effort. TEF explains the relationship between the effort made and the amount of time spent on testing software. This chapter summarizes 12 TEFs found in literature. It is not possible to cover all the TEFs available; those discussed are the very widely used ones. The parameter estimation was done using the least squares estimation method via python programming. Only one dataset was used in this research, so we couldn't conclude which is the best TEF, but for this chapter and dataset, almost all the TEFs performed well. The best performance was shown by the Weibull, Burr-type X, log logistic, and logistic exponential TEF's.

However, the actual potency of the TEFs can be demonstrated when each of them is integrated into any specific SRGM. This part of research work has not been carried out in this chapter. This chapter is about the individual and collective comparisons of TEFs against the actual CPU hours (effort) of the PL one failure dataset with the effort based on a timeline and their graphical modeling.

Acknowledgment

Javaid Iqbal (author) acknowledges JKST&IC, DST Srinagar, India, for providing the necessary support and facilities for this research work.

References

[1] Yamada, S., Hishitani, J., & Osaki, S. "Test-effort dependent software reliability measurement," *International Journal of Systems Science*, *22*(1), 73–83, 1991, doi: 10.1080/00207729108910590

[2] https://users.ece.cmu.edu/~koopman/des_s99/sw_testing/ [accessed on 01-12-2022]

[3] Iqbal, J., Quadri, S. M. K., & Ahmad, N. (2014, March). An imperfect-debugging model with learning-factor based fault-detection rate. In 2014 International Conference on Computing for Sustainable Global Development (INDIACom) (pp. 383–387). IEEE.

[4] Iqbal, J., Ahmad, N., & Quadri, S. M. K. (2013, December). A software reliability growth model with two types of learning. In 2013 International Conference on Machine Intelligence and Research Advancement (pp. 498–503). IEEE.

[5] Iqbal, J., Ahmad, N., & Quadri, S. M. K. (2013, December). A software reliability growth model with two types of learning and a negligence factor. In 2013 IEEE Second International Conference on Image Information Processing (ICIIP-2013) (pp. 678–683). IEEE.

[6] Iqbal, J. (2017). Software reliability growth models: A comparison of linear and exponential fault content functions for study of imperfect debugging situations. *Cogent Engineering*, *4*(1), 1286739.

[7] Khurshid, S., Shrivastava, A. K., & Iqbal, J. (2018). Fault prediction modelling in open source software under imperfect debugging and change-point. *International Journal of Open Source Software and Processes (IJOSSP)*, *9*(2), 1–17.

[8] Saraf, I., & Iqbal, J. (2019). Generalized multi-release modelling of software reliability growth models from the perspective of two types of imperfect debugging and change point. *Quality and Reliability Engineering International*, *35*(7), 2358–2370.

[9] Saraf, I., & Iqbal, J. (2019). Generalized software fault detection and correction modeling framework through imperfect debugging, error generation and change point. *International Journal of Information Technology*, *11*(4), 751–757.

[10] Khurshid, S., Shrivastava, A. K., & Iqbal, J. (2019). Generalized multi-release framework for fault prediction in open source software. *International Journal of Software Innovation (IJSI)*, *7*(4), 86–107.

[11] Saraf, I., Shrivastava, A. K., & Iqbal, J. (2020). Generalised fault detection and correction modelling framework for multi-release of software. *International Journal of Industrial and Systems Engineering*, *34*(4), 464–493.

[12] Khurshid, S., Shrivastava, A. K., & Iqbal, J. (2021). Effort based software reliability model with fault reduction factor, change point and imperfect debugging. *International Journal of Information Technology*, *13*(1), 331–340.

[13] Saraf, I., Iqbal, J., Shrivastava, A. K., & Khurshid, S. (2022). Modelling reliability growth for multi-version open source software considering varied testing and debugging factors. *Quality and Reliability Engineering International*, *38*(4), 1814–1825.

[14] Saraf, I., Shrivastava, A. K., & Iqbal, J. (2021). Effort-based fault detection and correction modelling for multi release of software. *International Journal of Information and Computer Security*, *14*(3–4), 354–379.

[15] Khurshid, S., Shrivastava, A. K., & Iqbal, J. (2022). Generalised multi release framework for fault determination with fault reduction factor. *International Journal of Information and Computer Security*, *17*(1–2), 164–178.

[16] Khurshid, S., Iqbal, J., Malik, I. A., & Yousuf, B. (2022). Modelling of NHPP Based Software Reliability Growth Model from the Perspective of Testing Coverage, Error Propagation and Fault Withdrawal Efficiency. *International Journal of Reliability, Quality and Safety Engineering*, 2250013.

[17] Iqbal, J., Firdous, T., Shrivastava, A. K., & Saraf, I. (2022). Modelling and predicting software vulnerabilities using a sigmoid function. *International Journal of Information Technology*, *14*(2), 649–655.

[18] Ramamoorthy C. V. & Bastani, F. B. (1982). Software Reliability Status and Perspectives, *IEEE Transactions on Software Engineering*, SE-8(4), 354–371, Jul. doi: 10.1109/TSE.1982.235728

[19] Ahmad, N., Khan, M. G. M., Quadri, S. M. K., and Kumar, M. (2009). Modelling and analysis of software reliability with Burr type X testing-effort and release-time determination. *Journal of Modelling in Management*, *4*(1), 28–54, doi: 10.1108/17465660910943748

[20] Yamada, S., Hishitani, J., and Osaki, S. (1993). Software-Reliability Growth with a Weibull Test-Effort: A Model & Application. *IEEE Transactions on Reliability*, *42*(1), 100–106, doi: 10.1109/24.210278

[21] Yamada, S., Ohtera, H., & Narihisa, H. (1986). Software Reliability Growth Models with Testing-Effort. *IEEE Transactions on Reliability*, *35*(1), 19–23, doi: 10.1109/ TR.1986.4335332

[22] Peng, R., Li, Y. F., Zhang, W. J., and Hu, Q. P. (Jun. 2014). Testing effort dependent software reliability model for imperfect debugging process considering both detection and correction. *Reliability Engineering & System Safety*, *126*, 37–43, doi: 10.1016/J.RESS.2014.01.004

[23] Huang, C. Y. & Kuo, S. Y. (Sep. 2002). Analysis of incorporating logistic testing-effort function into software reliability modeling. *IEEE Transactions on Reliability*, 51(3), 261–270, doi: 10.1109/TR.2002.801847

[24] Kapur, P. K., Singh, O., Shrivastava, A. K., & Singh, J. N. (2015, February). A software up-gradation model with testing effort and two types of imperfect debugging. In 2015 International Conference on Futuristic Trends on Computational Analysis and Knowledge Management (ABLAZE) (pp. 613–618). IEEE.

[25] Bokhari, M. U. & Ahmad, N. (2007). Software reliability growth modeling for exponentiated Weibull function with actual software failures data. Advances in Computer Science and Eng.: Reports and Monographs–Innovative Applications of Information Technology for the Developing World–Proc. of the 3rd Asian Applied Comput. Conf., AACC 2005, vol. 2, pp. 390–395, doi: 10.1142/9781860948534_0062

[26] Yamada, S. & Osaki, S. (1985). Software Reliability Growth Modeling: Models and Applications, *IEEE Transactions on Software Engineering*, SE-11(12), 1431–1437, doi: 10.1109/TSE.1985.232179

[27] Bokhari, M. U., Ahmad, M. I., & Ahmad, N. (2007). "Software Reliability Growth Modeling for Burr Type XII Function: Performance Analysis," International Conference on Modeling and Optimization of Structures, Processes and System (ICMOSPS' 07),Jan, 22–24, Durban, South Africa.

[28] Bokhari, M. U., & Ahmad, N. (2014). Incorporating Burr Type XII Testing-efforts into Software Reliability Growth Modeling and Actual Data Analysis with Applications. *Journal of Software*, 9(6), 1389–1400.

[29] Huang, C. Y., Kuo, S. Y., & Chen, I. Y. (1997). Analysis of Software Reliability Growth Model with Logistic Testing-Effort Function. Proceeding of the 8th International Symposium on Software Reliability Engineering (ISSR'97). Albuquerque, New Mexico, pp. 378–388.

[30] Parr, F. N. (1980). An alternative to the Rayleigh curve model for software development effort, *IEEE Transactions on Software Engineering*, vol. SE-6, no. 3, pp. 291–296, doi: 10.1109/TSE.1980.230475

[31] Kuo, S. Y., Huang, C. Y., and Lyu, M. R. (Sep. 2001). "Framework for modeling software reliability, using various testing-efforts and fault-detection rates," *IEEE Transactions on Reliability*, vol. 50, no. 3, pp. 310–320, doi: 10.1109/24.974129

[32] Huang, C., Kuo, S., & Lyu, M. (2007). An Assessment of Testing-Effort Dependent Software Reliability Growth Models, *IEEE Transactions on Reliability*, 56(2).

[33] Huang, C. Y., Lo, J. H., Kuo, S. Y., & Lyu, M. R. (1999). "Software reliability modeling and cost estimation incorporating testing-effort and efficiency," in Proceedings of the International Symposium on Software Reliability Engineering, ISSRE, pp. 62–72. doi: 10.1109/issre.1999.809311

[34] Quadri, S. M. K., Ahmad, N., Peer, M. A., & Kumar, M. (2006). Non homogeneous Poisson process software reliability growth model with generalized exponential testing effort function. *RAU Journal of Research*, 16, 159–163.

[35] Bokhari M. U. and Ahmad N., "Analysis of a software reliability growth models: the case of log-logistic test-effort function," Proceedings of the 17th IASTED international conference on modeling and simulation (MS'2006), Montreal, Canada, pp. 540–545, 2006.

[36] Ahmad, N., & Imam, M. Z. (2013). Software reliability growth models with Log-logistic testing-effort function: A comparative study. *International Journal of Computer Applications*, 75(12).

[37] Rafi, S. M. & Akthar, S. (2011). Software Reliability Growth Model with Logistic-Exponential Testing-Effort Function and Analysis of Software Release Policy. *ACEEE Int. J. on Network Security*, 2(2).

[38] Dhar, J., Ingle, S., & Sheshker, Y. (2014, May). Software reliability growth model with logistic-exponential TEF in imperfect debugging environment. In International Conference on Recent Advances and Innovations in Engineering (ICRAIE-2014) (pp. 1–4). IEEE.

[39] Lan, Y. & Leemis, L. M. (Apr. 2008). The logistic–exponential survival distribution. *Naval Research Logistics (NRL)*, vol. 55, no. 3, pp. 252–264, doi: 10.1002/NAV.20279

[40] Sharma, K., Garg, R., Nagpal, C. K., & Garg, R. K. (Jun. 2010). Selection of optimal software reliability growth models using a distance based approach. *IEEE Transactions on Reliability*, 59(2), 266–276, doi: 10.1109/TR.2010.2048657

[41] "Bayesian Information Criterion–an overview | ScienceDirect Topics." www.sciencedirect.com/topics/social-sciences/bayesian-information-criterion (accessed Jul. 01, 2022).

[42] Stoica P. & Selen, Y. (July 2004). Model-order selection: a review of information criterion rules, in *IEEE Signal Processing Magazine*, 21(4), 36–47, doi: 10.1109/MSP.2004.1311138

[43] Ohba, M. (1984). Software Reliability Analysis Models. *IBM Journal of Research and Development*, 28(4), 428–443, doi: 10.1147/rd.284.0428

[44] https://online.stat.psu.edu/stat462/node/204/(accessed December 12, 2022).

Chapter 9

Summary of NHPP-Based Software Reliability Modeling With Lindley-Type Distributions

Siqiao Li, Tadashi Dohi, and Hiroyuki Okamura

Graduate School of Advanced Science and Engineering,
Hiroshima University, Higashi-Hiroshima, Japan

9.1 Introduction

Over the past 40 years, a large number of software reliability models (SRMs) have been considered and studied in the literature [1, 2]. Among the existing SRMs, non-homogeneous Poisson process (NHPP)-based SRMs are very popular and can describe the stochastic behavior of the cumulative number of software detection faults during the testing phase. In modeling the software fault-detection time, Kuo and Yang [3] classified the existing NHPP-based SRMs into general order statistics SRMs and record value statistics SRMs. The same authors [3] referred to another classification by dividing NHPP-based SRMs into two types; finite-failure (finite) and infinite-failure (infinite) NHPP-based SRMs in terms of the mean value functions, which are defined as the expected cumulative number of software failures caused by software faults.

DOI: 10.1201/9781032624983-9

The representative existing NHPP-based SRMs are regarded as developed by basically two types of software fault-detection time distributions, the exponential distribution family and the extreme value distribution family [4]. More specifically, the fault-detection time distribution may follow exponential distribution [5], gamma distributions [6, 7], Pareto distribution [8], truncated normal distribution [9], log normal distribution [9, 10], truncated logistic distribution [11], log-logistic distribution [12], extreme-type distributions [13], and Weibull distribution [14]. Meanwhile, several infinite NHPP-based SRMs that were developed on the infinite-failure assumption have also been widely used for quantitative assessment of software reliability by introducing a series of lifetime CDFs in traditional reliability engineering for failure time modeling [15]. The power-law process models [16–18], the Cox Lewis model [19], and the logarithmic Poisson execution time model [1, 20] are recognized as this type of NHPP-based SRM.

On the one hand, the best SRM for fitting each software fault count data is considered to be nonexistent. Therefore, it is still critical to find a distribution that can describe fault-detection time more accurately. Hence, in the view of some authors [21, 22], it is a great option to integrate the existing NHPP-based SRMs or use some other more significant class of fault-detection time distribution. As an example, Okamura and Dohi [23–25] apply the phase-type and the hyper-Erlang distributions to an approximate arbitrary fault-detection time distribution. However, a serious model selection problem still exists; that is, even if the semi-parametric models are used, the structure of the underlying Markov chain is hard to determine. By way of explanation, in NHPP-based SRMs, unifying and generalizing the software fault-detection time distribution cannot always provide the model with improved goodness-of-fit and prediction performance. This fact provoked us to investigate other parametric classes of SRMs, which are superior to the existing NHPP-based SRMs [5–14].

Under fiducial and Bayesian statistics, a meaningful one-parameter continuous probability distribution called the *Lindley distribution* was proposed by Dennis Victor Lindley [26]. Recently, Lindley-type distributions have attracted extensive attention. In order to replace the common exponential distribution, Lindley-type distributions have been applied to the life data analysis of several products [27]. Subsequently, several authors expanded the basic Lindley distribution in a variety of ways. Mazucheli and Achcar [28] employed the Lindley distribution to analyze competing risks lifetime data. The power Lindley distribution was proposed by Ghitany et al. [29], applied to the analysis of tensile data in carbon fibers. Given that the relevant two random variables obey the Lindley distribution, Al-Mutairi et al. [30] considered an estimation of stress-strength parameters.

Nadarajah et al. [31] studied the exponentiated Lindley distribution, the gamma, log normal, and Weibull distributions comparison in terms of lifetime data analysis. After that, Ashour and Eltehiwy [32] developed the exponentiated power Lindley distribution, which can be regarded as the combination of the power

Lindley distribution [29] and the exponentiated Lindley distribution [31]. The gamma Lindley distribution was studied by Nedjar and Zeghdoudi [33], applied to the failure time data of electronic components and the number of cycles to failure for specimens of yarn. In order to analyze the failure time of electronic devices and the failure stresses of carbon fibers, Ghitany et al. [34] and Mazucheli et al. [35] also proposed the weighted Lindley distribution. Recently, the Gompertz Lindley distribution has also been carefully examined by Baqer [36], and several candidate distributions have been compared with it. We name these distributions developed from basic Lindley the *Lindley-type distributions*. In recent years, Xiao et al. [37] utilized seven Lindley-type distributions in finite NHPP-based software reliability modeling and investigated the goodness-of-fit and predictive performances using the fault count time interval data collected in the actual software development projects.

The main contribution of this chapter is to investigate the applicability of a comprehensive study of Lindley-type distributions to software systems. Most notably, we present seven infinite-failure (infinite) Lindley NHPP-based SRMs based on Lindley-type distributions consistent with the Lindley-type distributions considered in [37]. We investigate the goodness-of-fit and predictive performances of finite Lindley-type and infinite Lindley-type NHPP-based SRMs under two different types of software fault count data: software fault count time-domain data and software fault count time-interval data (group data). It is the most exhaustive investigation of Lindley-type distributions in software reliability modeling in the past four decades.

The organization of this chapter is as follows. Section 9.2 describes the definition of NHPP and existing finite and infinite SRMs under the finite-failure and infinite-failure assumptions of NHPP-based software reliability modeling. Section 9.3 presents the seven Lindley-type time distribution functions applied in this chapter. In Section 9.4, we describe how to obtain the model parameters by the well-known maximum likelihood estimation approach. Two different likelihood functions are provided for two types of software fault count data. Section 9.5 presents our numerical experiments. Eleven existing NHPP-based SRMs having the widely known fault-detection time distributions [5–14] are used to compare with our proposed Lindley-type NHPP-based SRMs in terms of goodness-of-fit and predictive performances. Throughout the numerical experiments with fault count time-domain data and time-interval (group) data collected in actual software development projects, the applicability of the Lindley-type SRMs is demonstrated. Section 0.6 contains some comments and conclusions of this chapter.

9.2 NHPP-Based Software Reliability Modeling

Assume that the software testing process starts from time $t = 0$. Let $\{N(t), t \geq 0\}$ be the cumulative number of software detection faults during the time period

$(0, t)$. In particular, the software fault counting process $N(t)$ can be considered as following a NHPP with the mean value function $\Lambda(t)$:

$$E\left[N(t)\right] = \Lambda(t) = \int_0^t \lambda(x)\,dx. \tag{9.1}$$

The probability mass function (p.m.f.) of NHPP is given by

$$\Pr\left\{N(t) = n\right\} = \frac{\Lambda(t)^n}{n!}\exp\left(-\Lambda(t)\right), n = 0,1,2,\cdots, \tag{9.2}$$

in which function $\lambda(t)$ in Equation 9.1 is called *the intensity function* of the corresponding NHPP and is an absolutely continuous (deterministic) function of only time t. Note that most textbooks [1, 2] point out that, when the mean value function is used to characterize the cumulative number of software faults by time t, there were two types of NHPP-based SRMs: finite-failure (finite) NHPP-based SRMs and infinite-failure (infinite) NHPP-based SRMs.

9.2.1 Finite-Failure (Finite) NHPP-Based SRMs

In NHPP-based software reliability modeling under the finite-failure assumption, the remaining number of software faults before testing, say, at time $t = 0$, is a Poisson distributed random variable with mean $\omega(>0)$. Each software fault is assumed to be detected at an independent and identically distributed random time and is fixed immediately just after it was detected. The time to each fault detection conforms to a non-decreasing cumulative distribution function (CDF), $F(t;\xi)$, with positive support $t \in (0,+\infty)$, where ξ indicates the free parameter vector in the CDF, $F(0;\xi) = 0$ and $F(\infty;\xi) = 1$. Then a binomial distributed random variable with probability $F(t;\xi)$ with a Poisson distributed population with parameter ω is employed to characterize the resultant software fault-detection process. From a simple algebraic manipulation, the cumulative number of software faults detected by the software testing up to time t can be derived as an NHPP with the mean value function:

$$\Lambda(t;\theta) = \omega F(t;\xi), \ \theta = \left(\omega, \xi\right) \tag{9.3}$$

where $\lim_{t \to \infty} \Lambda(t;\boldsymbol{\theta}) = \omega(>0)$. It is compatible with the assumption of finite NHPP-based software reliability modeling that the expected initial number of residual faults in the software is finite. Okamura and Dohi [4] implemented 11 representative existing NHPP-based SRMs with bounded mean function in the software reliability assessment tool on the spreadsheet (SRATS). The mean value function and c.d.f. of existing finite NHPP-based SRMs in SRATS are listed in Table 9.1.

Table 9.1   Representative Finite NHPP-Based SRMs in SRATS

SRMs	Mean Value Function and c.d.f.
Exponential dist. (exp) [5]	$\Lambda(t;\boldsymbol{\theta}) = \omega F(t;\boldsymbol{\xi})$, $F(t;\boldsymbol{\xi}) = 1 - e^{-bt}$
Gamma dist. (gamma) [6, 7]	$\Lambda(t;\boldsymbol{\theta}) = \omega F(t;\boldsymbol{\xi})$, $F(t;\boldsymbol{\xi}) = \int_0^t \dfrac{c^b s^{b-1} e^{-cs}}{\Gamma(b)} ds$
Pareto dist. (pareto) [8]	$\Lambda(t;\boldsymbol{\theta}) = \omega F(t;\boldsymbol{\xi})$, $F(t;\boldsymbol{\xi}) = 1 - (b/(b+t))^c$
Truncated normal dist. (tnorm) [9]	$\Lambda(t;\boldsymbol{\theta}) = \omega \dfrac{F(t;\boldsymbol{\xi}) - F(0)}{1 - F(0)}$, $F(t;\boldsymbol{\xi}) = \dfrac{1}{\sqrt{2\pi}b} \int_{-\infty}^t e^{-\frac{(s-c)^2}{2b^2}} ds$
Log-normal dist. (lnorm) [9, 10]	$\Lambda(t;\boldsymbol{\theta}) = \omega F(\ln t;\boldsymbol{\xi})$, $F(t;\boldsymbol{\xi}) = \dfrac{1}{\sqrt{2\pi}b} \int_{-\infty}^t e^{-\frac{(s-c)^2}{2b^2}} ds$
Truncated logistic dist. (tlogist) [11]	$\Lambda(t;\boldsymbol{\theta}) = \omega \dfrac{F(t;\boldsymbol{\xi}) - F(0)}{1 - F(0)}$, $F(t;\boldsymbol{\xi}) = \dfrac{1}{1 + e^{-\frac{t-c}{b}}}$

Table 9.1 (Continued)

SRMs	Mean Value Function and c.d.f.
Log-logistic dist. (llogist) [12]	$\Lambda(t;\theta)=\omega F(\ln t;\xi)$, $$F(t;\xi)=\frac{1}{1+e^{-\frac{t-c}{b}}}$$
Truncated extreme-value max dist. (txvmax) [13]	$\Lambda(t;\theta)=\omega\dfrac{F(t;\xi)-F(0)}{1-F(0)}$, $$F(t;\xi)=e^{-e^{-\frac{t-c}{b}}}$$
Log-extreme-value max dist. (lxvmax) [13]	$\Lambda(t;\theta)=\omega F(\ln t;\xi)$, $$F(t;\xi)=e^{-e^{-\frac{t-c}{b}}}$$
Truncated extreme-value min dist. (txvmin) [13]	$\Lambda(t;\theta)=\omega\dfrac{F(0)-F(-t)}{F(0)}$, $$F(t;\xi)=e^{-e^{\frac{t-c}{b}}}$$
Log-extreme-value min dist. (lxvmin) [14]	$\Lambda(t;\theta)=\omega(1-F(-\ln t))$, $$F(t;\xi)=e^{-e^{\frac{t-c}{b}}}$$

Source: [4].

Even though the finite NHPP-based SRMs are recognized as plausible models in terms of software reliability growth phenomena, it has to be acknowledged that reliability engineers sometimes feel discomfort when handling the finite-failure NHPPs, since the inter-failure time distributions in the finite NHPP-based SRMs are always *defective* [38]. Let us suppose that the random variables, $T_1, T_2, \cdots, T_n$, represent the first, second, $\cdots$, nth failure times since the software testing starts at $T_0 = 0$. Let the random variables, $X_1, X_2, \ldots, X_n$, denote the inter-failure times between two consecutive failures:

$$T_n = \sum_{j=1}^{n} X_j = T_{n-1} + X_n, \quad n=0,1,2,\ldots \tag{9.4}$$

From Equations 9.2 and 9.4, the CDF of T_n (probability that the nth failure occurs before time t) can be obtained as

$$G_n\left(t;\,\boldsymbol{\theta}\right)=P\{T_n\leq t\}$$

$$=1-\sum_{j=0}^{n-1}\frac{\left[\Lambda\left(t;\boldsymbol{\theta}\right)\right]^j}{j!}\exp\left(-\Lambda\left(t;\boldsymbol{\theta}\right)\right) \tag{9.5}$$

Then it is straightforward to see in the type-I NHPP-based SRMs that $\lim_{t\to\infty}G_n\left(t;\boldsymbol{\theta}\right)<1$ for an arbitrary n. In other words, even if the testing time tends to be infinite, there still exists a positive probability of the nth failure not occurring. It is obvious that the CDF of T_n is defective. Hence, for the finite NHPP-based SRMs, it is not meaningful to discuss some reliability metrics, such as mean time to failure (MTTF), because the finite moments of T_n always diverge. Similarly, for realizations of $T_i\,(i=1,2,\cdots,n)$, $t_1,\ t_2,\cdots,t_n$, we can obtain the CDF of the inter-failure time X_n in the time interval $\left[t_{n-1},\ t_{n-1}+x\right)$ as follows:

$$F_n\left(x;\,\boldsymbol{\theta}\right)=1-\exp\left(-\left(\Lambda\left(t_{n-1}+x;\,\boldsymbol{\theta}\right)-\Lambda\left(t_{n-1};\,\boldsymbol{\theta}\right)\right)\right), \tag{9.6}$$

where $\Pr\{N\left(t_{n-1}+x\right)-N\left(t_{n-1}\right)=0\,|\,N\left(t_{n-1}\right)=n-1\}$ denotes the probability that no failure occurs in the time interval $\left[t_{n-1},\ t_{n-1}+x\right)$. Since the mean value function is bounded, i.e., $\lim_{t\to\infty}\Lambda\left(t;\boldsymbol{\theta}\right)=\omega$, when x is infinite, Equation 9.6 can be reduced to $1-e^{-\left(\omega-\Lambda\left(t_{n-1};\boldsymbol{\theta}\right)\right)}<1$. This means that, regardless of the number of previous failures, the probability that the software fails over an infinite time horizon is always non-zero. Hence, the inter-failure time CDF of finite NHPP-based SRM is also defective.

9.2.2 *Infinite-Failure (Infinite) NHPP-Based SRMs*

In the finite NHPP-based SRMs, it is implicitly assumed that no new software fault is inserted at each software debugging. However, this assumption may be somewhat specific because the so-called *imperfect debugging* may occur in the actual software testing phases. In other words, any detected fault may not be corrected perfectly and the inherent number of faults before testing should not be considered as finite in such a situation. Hence, when the possibility of imperfect debugging is considered, the assumption of finiteness in the finite NHPP-based SRMs seems to be rather strong. Similar to the classical preventive maintenance modeling [15], if each software failure is *minimally* repaired through the debugging, the mean value function of the software fault-detection process is unbounded and is given by

$$\Lambda(t;\boldsymbol{\xi}) = -\ln\left(1 - F(t;\boldsymbol{\xi})\right) \tag{9.7}$$

where $\lim_{t\to\infty}\Lambda(t;\boldsymbol{\xi})\to\infty$. It is obvious that the CDF, $G_n(t;\boldsymbol{\theta})$ in Equation 9.5, is not defective, say, $\lim_{t\to\infty}G_n(t;\boldsymbol{\xi})=1$. Hence, it becomes significant to consider important metrics such as MTTF. In this modeling framework, investigating the residual number of software faults before testing has no significant meaning because it may increase by imperfect debugging through the software testing. As far as we know, the Cox–Lewis process [19] is one of the earliest type-II NHPPs. The unbounded mean value function of this model is given by $\Lambda(t;\boldsymbol{\xi}) = \dfrac{\left(\exp(b+ct) - \exp(b)\right)}{c}$ with the extreme-value distribution $F(t;\boldsymbol{\xi}) = 1 - \exp\left(\exp(b+ct) - \exp(b)\right)/c$, $\boldsymbol{\xi} \in (b,c)$. This distribution is also referred to as the truncated extreme-value minimum distribution in [4, 13]. The power-law process [16–18] is also recognized as another infinite NHPP-based SRM with the log-extreme-value minimum distribution; $F(t;\boldsymbol{\xi}) = 1 - \exp\left(-\exp\left(-\dfrac{c + \ln(t)}{b}\right)\right)$ in [4, 13], where the mean value function is given by $\Lambda(t;\boldsymbol{\xi}) = (c/b)t^{1/b}$. Besides the preceding two representative NHPPs, the well-known logarithmic Poisson execution time SRM [1, 20] belongs to the infinite category too. The mean value function of this model is given by $\Lambda(t;\boldsymbol{\xi}) = c\ln\left((1+t)/b\right)$ with the Pareto distribution $F(t;\boldsymbol{\xi}) = 1 - \left(b/(t+b)\right)^c$ in [8].

9.3 Lindley-Type Distribution

The original Lindley distribution specified by the c.d.f.

$$F(t) = 1 - \left(1 + \frac{\alpha t}{\alpha + 1}\right)\exp(-\alpha t), t > 0, \alpha > 0. \tag{9.8}$$

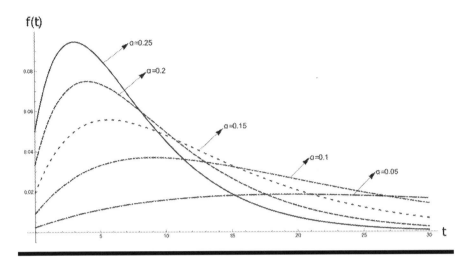

Figure 9.1 **Probability density function of Lindley distribution.**

It is consists of an exponential distribution with scale α and a gamma distribution having shape 2 and scale – with the mixing proportion is $\alpha/(\alpha+1)$ [26]. Hence, as a two-component mixture, the corresponding probability density function (p.d.f.), $f(t) = dF(t)/dt$ when $\alpha < 1$, is shown as

$$f(t) = \frac{\alpha^2}{\alpha+1}(1+t)\exp(-\alpha t). \qquad (9.9)$$

with $f(0) = \alpha^2/(\alpha+1)$ and $f(\infty) = 0$. This also shows that p.d.f. of Lindley distribution increases in $t\sqrt{b^2 - 4ac}$ or is unimodal in t. Figure 9.1 depicts the p.d.f. of Lindley distribution for different scale α values. Since the c.d.f. and p.d.f are given, an increasing failure rate (IFR) of Lindley distribution is shown as

$$h(t) = \frac{f(t)}{1-F(t)} = \frac{\alpha^2(1+t)}{\alpha+1+\alpha t} \qquad (9.10)$$

where $h(0) = \alpha^2/(\alpha+1)$ and $h(\infty) = 0$.

Next, to represent the fault-detection time distribution, we focus on several variations of the Lindley distribution. Set $\alpha(>0)$, $\beta(>0)$, and $\gamma(>0)$ to three arbitrary parameters; a total of six extensions of Lindley-type distribution are included in this chapter.

1. Gamma Lindley distribution [33] is a generalized Lindley distribution that is composed of the common Lindley distribution and a mixture of gamma $(2, \alpha)$:

$$F(t) = 1 - \frac{\{(\alpha\beta + \beta - \alpha)(\alpha t + 1) + \alpha\}\exp(-\alpha t)}{\beta(1 + \alpha)} \tag{9.11}$$

The p.d.f. of the gamma-Lindley distribution is given by

$$f(t) = \frac{\alpha^2 \{(\alpha\beta + \beta - \alpha)t + 1\}\exp(-\alpha t)}{\beta(1 + \alpha)} \tag{9.12}$$

2. Exponentiated Lindley distribution [31] is proposed because it is considered to have the closed form of the hazard rate as the Weibull and exponentiated exponential distributions. The c.d.f. and p.d.f. are shown as

$$F(t) = \left\{1 - \frac{1 + \alpha + \alpha t}{1 + \alpha}\exp(-\alpha t)\right\}^{\gamma} \tag{9.13}$$

$$f(t) = \frac{\gamma\alpha^2}{1 + \alpha}(1 + t)\left\{1 - \frac{1 + \alpha + \alpha t}{1 + \alpha}\exp(-\alpha t)\right\}^{\gamma - 1} \tag{9.14}$$

It is obvious that Equation 9.14 has two parameters, α and γ, shown as a mixture of Weibull, exponentiated exponential, and gamma distributions. Exponentiated Lindley distribution is reduced to the common Lindley distribution when $\gamma = 1$.

3. Power Lindley distribution [29] was considered a power transformation $t = x^{\frac{1}{\beta}}$ to Equation 9.9 as a new extension of the Lindley distribution, with c.d.f. and p.d.f. shown as

$$F(x) = 1 - \left(1 + \frac{\alpha x^\beta}{1 + \alpha}\right)\exp(-\alpha x^\beta) \tag{9.15}$$

$$f(x) = \frac{\beta\alpha^2}{1 + x^\beta}x^{\beta - 1}\exp(-\alpha x^\beta) \tag{9.16}$$

It is shown as a mixture of generalized gamma distribution with shape parameters 2 and Weibull distribution with scale α and shape β.

4. Exponentiated power Lindley distribution [32], a three-component mixture, involves the common Lindley distribution, exponentiated Lindley distribution, and power Lindley distribution. This distribution is considered to be more flexible than each component in describing different types of actual data.

$$F(t) = 1 - \left\{ 1 - \left(1 + \frac{\alpha t^\beta}{1+\alpha} \right) \exp\left(-\alpha t^\beta\right) \right\}^\gamma \qquad (9.17)$$

$$f(t) = \frac{\gamma \alpha^2 \beta t^{\beta-1}}{\alpha+1}\left(1+t^\beta\right)e^{-\alpha t^\beta}\left[1 - \left(1 + \frac{\alpha t^\beta}{\alpha+1}\right)e^{-\alpha t^\beta}\right]^{\gamma-1} \qquad (9.18)$$

5. Gompertz Lindley distribution [36]:

$$F(t) = 1 - \left(\frac{\alpha^2}{1+\alpha}\right)\frac{\alpha + \exp\left(\beta t\right)}{\left(\alpha - 1 + \exp\left(\beta t\right)\right)^2} \qquad (9.19)$$

6. Weighted Lindley Distribution [34, 35]:

$$F(t) = 1 - \frac{(\alpha+\beta)\Gamma_2(\beta,\alpha t) + (\alpha t)^\beta \exp(-\alpha t)}{(\alpha+\beta)\Gamma_1(\beta)} \qquad (9.20)$$

$$f(t) = \frac{\alpha^{\beta+1}t^{\beta-1}(1+t)\exp(-\alpha t)}{(\alpha+\beta)\Gamma_1(\beta)} \qquad (9.21)$$

where $\Gamma_1(\alpha) = \int_0^\infty x^{\alpha-1}e^{-xd}x$ and $\Gamma_2(\alpha,\beta) = \int_\beta^\infty x^{\alpha-1}e^{-x}dx$. Note that when $\beta=1$, the weighted Lindley distribution reduces to the Lindley distribution.

In Section 9.2, we have shown that it is possible to obtain two quite different NHPP-based SRMs, finite NHPP-based SRM and infinite NHPP-based SRM, by supposing one software fault-detection time distribution and importing it into finite and infinite failure NHPP software reliability modeling assumptions, respectively. Hence, we can obtain the corresponding finite and infinite Lindley-type NHPP-based SRMs, by importing seven Lindley-type time distributions c.d.f.s shown in Equations 9.8, 9.11, 9.13, 9.15, 9.17, 9.19, and 9.20 into the mean value function of finite and infinite NHPP (Equations 9.3 and 9.7). The mean value functions of finite and infinite Lindley-type NHPP-based SRMs are shown in Table 9.2 and Table 9.3.

Table 9.2 Finite Lindley-Type NHPP-Based SRMs

SRM	Mean Value Function
Finite Lindley	$\Lambda(t;\boldsymbol{\theta})=\omega\left(1-\left(1+\dfrac{\alpha t}{\alpha+1}\right)\exp(-\alpha t)\right)$
Finite gamma Lindley	$\Lambda(t;\boldsymbol{\theta})=\omega\left(1-\dfrac{\big((\alpha\beta+\beta-\alpha)(\alpha t+1)+\alpha\big)\exp(-\alpha t)}{\beta(1+\alpha)}\right)$
Finite exp Lindley	$\Lambda(t;\boldsymbol{\theta})=\omega\left(\left(1-\dfrac{1+\alpha+\alpha t}{1+\alpha}\exp(-\alpha t)\right)^{\gamma}\right)$
Finite power Lindley	$\Lambda(t;\boldsymbol{\theta})=\omega\left(1-\left(1+\dfrac{\alpha t^{\beta}}{1+\alpha}\right)\exp(-\alpha t^{\beta})\right)$
Finite exp power Lindley	$\Lambda(t;\boldsymbol{\theta})=\omega\left(1-\left(1-\left(1+\dfrac{\alpha t^{\beta}}{1+\alpha}\right)\exp(-\alpha t^{\beta})\right)^{\gamma}\right)$
Finite Gompertz Lindley	$\Lambda(t;\boldsymbol{\theta})=\omega\left(1-\left(\dfrac{\alpha^{2}}{1+\alpha}\right)\dfrac{\alpha+\exp(\beta t)}{\big(\alpha-1+\exp(\beta t)\big)^{2}}\right)$
Finite weighted Lindley	$\Lambda(t;\boldsymbol{\theta})=\omega\left(1-\dfrac{(\alpha+\beta)\Gamma_{2}(\beta,\alpha t)+(\alpha t)^{\beta}\exp(-\alpha t)}{(\alpha+\beta)\Gamma_{1}(\beta)}\right)$

Table 9.3 Infinite Lindley-Type NHPP-Based SRMs

SRM	Mean Value Function
Infinite Lindley	$\Lambda(t;\xi)=\alpha t-\ln(\alpha t+\alpha+1)+\ln(\alpha+1)$
Infinite gamma Lindley	$\Lambda(t;\xi)=-\ln\big((\alpha\beta-\alpha+\beta)(\alpha t+1)+\alpha\big)+\alpha t$ $+\ln(\alpha+1)+\ln(\beta)$
Infinite exp Lindley	$\Lambda(t;\xi)=-\ln\left(1-\left(1-\left(\dfrac{\alpha t}{\alpha+1}+1\right)e^{-\alpha t}\right)^{\gamma}\right)$

(Continued)

Table 9.3 (Continued)

SRM	Mean Value Function
Infinite power Lindley	$\Lambda(t;\xi) = -\ln(\alpha t^{\beta} + (\alpha+1)) + \alpha t + \ln(\alpha+1)$
Infinite exp power Lindley	$\Lambda(t;\xi) = -\ln\left(1 - \left(1 - \left(\dfrac{\alpha t^{\beta}}{\alpha+1} + 1\right)e^{-\alpha t^{\beta}}\right)^{\gamma}\right)$
Infinite Gompertz Lindley	$\Lambda(t;\xi) = 2\ln(\alpha + e^{\beta t} - 1) - \ln(\alpha + e^{\beta t}) - 2\ln(a) + \ln(\alpha+1)$
Infinite weighted Lindley	$\Lambda(t;\xi) = -\ln\left(e^{-\alpha}(\alpha t)^{b} + (\alpha+\beta)\Gamma(\beta,\alpha t)\right)$ $+\ln(\alpha+\beta) + \ln(\Gamma(\beta))$

9.4 Maximum Likelihood Estimation

Maximum likelihood (ML) estimation is a commonly utilized method for the parameter estimation of NHPP-based SRMs. In ML estimation, the estimates are given by the parameters maximizing the log-likelihood function. On the other hand, the maximum log-likelihood (MLL) function depends on the observed data as well as on the underlying NHPP-based SRMs.

Suppose that the fault count time-domain data $(t_1, t_2, \cdots, t_m)$ with censoring point t_m are available; then the likelihood function of the NHPP-based SRMs is given as

$$L(\boldsymbol{\theta} \text{ or } \boldsymbol{\xi}) = \exp\left[-\Lambda(t_m; \boldsymbol{\theta} \text{ or } \boldsymbol{\xi})\right] \prod_{i-=}^{m} \lambda(t_i; \boldsymbol{\theta} \text{ or } \boldsymbol{\xi}) \qquad (9.22)$$

Taking the logarithm, and we obtain the log likelihood function as follows.

$$\ln L(\boldsymbol{\theta} \text{ or } \boldsymbol{\xi}) = \sum_{i=1}^{m} \ln \lambda(t_i; \boldsymbol{\theta} \text{ or } \boldsymbol{\xi}) - \Lambda(t_m; \boldsymbol{\theta} \text{ or } \boldsymbol{\xi}) \qquad (9.23)$$

where $\boldsymbol{\theta}$ and $\boldsymbol{\xi}$ are the unknown parameter vectors of finite NHPP-based SRMs and infinite NHPP-based SRMs, respectively. Then suppose that the time-interval data (group data), which consists of the observation time (testing day) and the cumulative number of software faults, $(t_i, n_i)(i = 1, 2, \cdots, m)$, are available. m means the total number of testing data. The likelihood function for unknown parameter vector $\boldsymbol{\theta}$ or $\boldsymbol{\xi}$ is given by

$$L(\boldsymbol{\theta} \text{ or } \boldsymbol{\xi}) = \prod_{i=1}^{m} \frac{\left[\Lambda\left(t_i; \boldsymbol{\theta} \text{ or } \boldsymbol{\xi}\right) - \Lambda\left(t_{i-1}; \boldsymbol{\theta} \text{ or } \boldsymbol{\xi}\right)\right]^{\left(n_i - n_{i-1}\right)}}{\left(n_i - n_{i-1}\right)!}$$
$$e^{-\left[\Lambda\left(t_i; \boldsymbol{\theta} \text{ or } \boldsymbol{\xi}\right) - \Lambda\left(t_{i-1}; \boldsymbol{\theta} \text{ or } \boldsymbol{\xi}\right)\right]}$$

(9.24)

The log likelihood function is as follows:

$$\ln L(\boldsymbol{\theta} \text{ or } \boldsymbol{\xi})$$
$$= \sum_{i=1}^{m}\left\{\left(n_i - n_{i-1}\right)\ln\left[\Lambda\left(t_i; \boldsymbol{\theta} \text{ or } \boldsymbol{\xi}\right) - \Lambda\left(t_{i-1}; \boldsymbol{\theta} \text{ or } \boldsymbol{\xi}\right)\right] - \ln\left[\left(n_i - n_{i-1}\right)!\right]\right\}$$
$$- \Lambda\left(t_m; \boldsymbol{\theta} \text{ or } \boldsymbol{\xi}\right).$$

(9.25)

By maximizing Equations 9.23 and 9.25 with respect to $\boldsymbol{\theta}$ or $\boldsymbol{\xi}$, we obtain the maximum likelihood estimates $\hat{\boldsymbol{\theta}}$ or $\hat{\boldsymbol{\xi}}$, respectively.

Once the parameters of the SRM have been estimated, we employ Akaike information criterion (AIC) as the measure of goodness of fit for the past observation. In terms of goodness of fit with cumulative fault-detection count data, the smaller AIC result (close to 0) represents the better SRM, where

$$\text{AIC} = -2 \ln L\left(\hat{\boldsymbol{\theta}} \text{ or } \hat{\boldsymbol{\xi}}\right) + 2 \times \left(\text{number of parameters}\right)$$

(9.26)

We also think that it is of great significance to look at the vertical gap between the SRM under consideration and the underlying software fault count data. Hence, as an alternative goodness-of-fit measure, under the premise of using the maximum likelihood estimation, we also check the mean squared error (MSE),

$$\text{MSE} = \frac{\sqrt{\sum_{i=1}^{m}\{i - \Lambda\left(t_i; \hat{\boldsymbol{\theta}} \text{ or } \hat{\boldsymbol{\xi}}\right)\}^2}}{m}$$

(9.27)

and

$$\text{MSE} = \frac{\sqrt{\sum_{i=1}^{m}\{n_i - \Lambda\left(t_i; \hat{\boldsymbol{\theta}} \text{ or } \hat{\boldsymbol{\xi}}\right)\}^2}}{m}$$

(9.28)

in time-domain and group data, respectively. It is worth mentioning that the problem of overfitting often occurs in the minimization of MSE in statistical inference; so, in this chapter, MSE is only used to view the visual fitting of SRM to the underlying data.

To investigate the prediction performance, we apply the performance metrics; predictive mean squared error (PMSE). For time-domain data, suppose that the observed software fault time sequence consists of $(t_1, t_2, \ldots, t_m)$, and let $l (= 1, 2, \cdots)$ be the predictive time length, which is a positive integer. The PMSE is

$$\text{PMSE} = \frac{\sqrt{\sum_{i=m+1}^{m+l} \{i - \Lambda(t_i; \hat{\boldsymbol{\theta}} \text{ or } \hat{\boldsymbol{\xi}})\}^2}}{l} \tag{9.29}$$

Suppose that the group data are available and that the observed data consist of $(t_i, n_i)(i = 1, 2, \cdots, m)$. Meanwhile, the future fault count behaviors are given as $(t_{m+j}, n_{m+j})(j = 1, 2, \cdots, l)$. Then we have

$$\text{PMSE} = \frac{\sqrt{\sum_{i=m+1}^{m+l} \{n_i - \Lambda(i; \hat{\boldsymbol{\theta}} \text{ or } \hat{\boldsymbol{\xi}})\}^2}}{l} \tag{9.30}$$

where $\hat{\boldsymbol{\theta}}$ and $\hat{\boldsymbol{\xi}}$ are the estimated parameter vectors of finite and infinite NHPP-based SRMs before the observation point t_m in the software fault count data. In the sense of prediction performance, PMSE and MSE have the same evaluation scale; the smaller the result, the better the SRM.

9.5 Performance Illustration

9.5.1 Goodness-of-Fit Performance

In numerical experiments, we analyzed a total of eight time-domain data sets, labeled TDDS1–TDDS8, and eight group data sets, called TIDS1–TIDS8. The specific information and sources of the data sets are summarized in Table 9.4 and Table 9.5.

The plots for the best Lindley-type SRM and the best SRATS SRM with TDDS1 and TIDS1 are illustrated in Figures 9.2 and 9.3. At first glance, in TDDS1, it can be seen that the four SRMs are similar in Figure 9.2. It is difficult to identify a specific SRM with a better outperformance of the goodness-of-fit in this situation. But in contrast, in Figure 9.3, in TDDS1, we can obviously find two finite NHPP-based SRMs that show more accurate and complex software fault-detection behavior.

Table 9.4 Time-Domain Datasets

Data	No. Faults	Testing Length (CPU second)	Source
TDDS1	54	108708	SYS2 [39]
TDDS2	38	67362	SYS3 [39]
TDDS3	136	88682	SYS1 [39]
TDDS4	53	52422	SYS4 [39]
TDDS5	73	5090	Project J5 [2]
TDDS6	38	233700	S10 [39]
TDDS7	41	4312598	S27 [39]
TDDS8	101	19572126	S17 [39]

Table 9.5 Group Datasets

Data	No. Faults	Testing Length (week)	Source
TIDS1	54	17	SYS2 [39]
TIDS2	38	14	SYS3 [39]
TIDS3	120	19	Release 2 [40]
TIDS4	61	12	Release 3 [40]
TIDS5	9	14	NASA-supported project [41]
TIDS6	66	20	DS1 [42]
TIDS7	58	33	DS2 [42]
TIDS8	52	30	DS3 [42]

The main objectives of our numerical experiments are deriving the maximum likelihood estimates of the parameters of 11 existing finite NHPP-based SRMs, which were shown in Table 9.1; three existing finite NHPP-based SRMs (Musa–Okumoto SRM, Cox–Lewis SRM, and Duane SRM); and 14 finite and infinite Lindley-type NHPP-based SRMs that we consider in this chapter. Then we investigate and compare the goodness-of-fit and predictive performances of these NHPP-based SRMs by several criteria based on likelihood estimation in a total of 16 actual software fault count data sets.

In Table 9.6 and Table 9.7, we make a comparison of the best finite and infinite Lindley-type SRMs with the best existing finite and infinite NHPP-based SRMs in terms of AIC and MSE with time-domain data and group data, respectively. The best AIC/MSE in each data set is represented in bold font. From Table 9.6, it is obvious that the existing finite NHPP-based SRMs could outperform the finite and infinite Lindley-type SRMs in AIC and MSE in almost all cases. Only in TDDS2, TDDS3, and TDDS5 did the finite Lindley-type SRMs guarantee equal or better

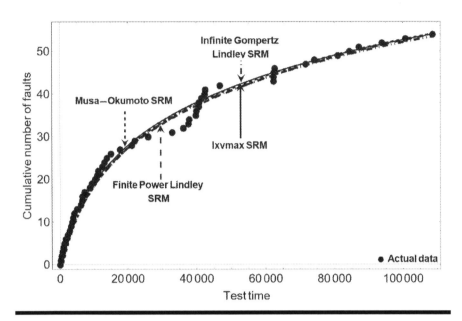

Figure 9.2 Cumulative number of software faults detected by finite and infinite Lindley-type and existing NHPP-based SRMs in TDDS1.

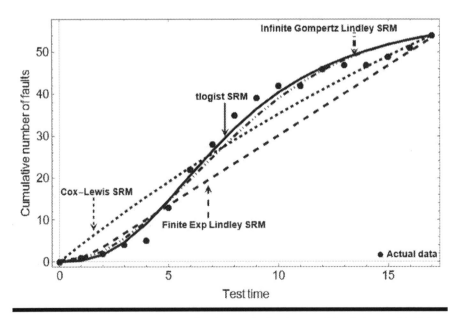

Figure 9.3 Cumulative number of software faults detected by finite and infinite Lindley-type and existing NHPP-based SRMs in TIDS1.

Table 9.6 Goodness-of-Fit Performances Based on AIC (Time-Domain Data)

			TDDS1	TDDS2	TDDS3	TDDS4	TDDS5	TDDS6	TDDS7	TDDS8
Existing NHPP-based SRMs	Infinite NHPP	MSE	0.21	0.22	0.24	0.67	0.51	0.47	0.41	0.79
		AIC	897.31 (Musa-Okumoto)	598.50 (Musa-Okumoto)	1941.60 (Musa-Okumoto)	769.06 (Musa-Okumoto)	757.03 (Duane)	731.02 (Musa-Okumoto)	1009.10 (Musa-Okumoto)	2505.37 (Musa-Okumoto)
	Finite NHPP	MSE	**0.19**	**0.21**	**0.22**	**0.27**	0.51	**0.20**	**0.38**	**0.69**
		AIC	**896.67 (lxvmax)**	**589.13 (lxvmax)**	**1938.20 (lxvmin)**	**759.75 (pareto)**	**757.87 (exp)**	**721.93 (lxvmax)**	**1008.22 (lxvmax)**	**2504.17 (pareto)**
Lindley-type NHPP-based SRMs	Infinite Lindley	MSE	1.63	1.64	2.68	2.37	1.07	1.44	1.50	3.09
		AIC	917.57 (Gompertz Lindley)	615.47 (Exp power Lindley)	2007.67 (Power Lindley)	819.03 (Gompertz Lindley)	764.60 (Gompertz Lindley)	742.73 (Gompertz Lindley)	1027.64 (Gompertz Lindley)	2623.60 (Gompertz Lindley)
	Finite Lindley	MSE	0.23	**0.21**	**0.21**	0.28	**0.48**	0.25	0.43	0.76
		AIC	898.04 (Power Lindley)	600.53 (Exp power Lindley)	1938.20 (Power Lindley)	759.95 (Gompertz Lindley)	758.53 (Exp Lindley)	724.45 (Power Lindley)	1009.40 (Power Lindley)	2511.64 (Exp Power Lindley)

Table 9.7 Goodness-of-Fit Performances Based on AIC (Group Data)

			TIDS1	TIDS2	TIDS3	TIDS4	TIDS5	TIDS6	TIDS7	TIDS8
Existing NHPP-based SRMs	Infinite NHPP	MSE	0.21	**0.47**	1.28	1.51	0.10	**1.00**	0.96	1.87
		AIC	86.94 (Cox-Lewis)	62.67 (Cox-Lewis)	91.92 (Cox-Lewis)	63.56 (Cox-Lewis)	29.91 (Cox-Lewis)	112.38 (Cox-Lewis)	141.13 (Duane)	174.17 (Duane)
	Finite NHPP	MSE	**0.49**	0.48	0.60	0.47	0.10	1.06	**0.25**	**0.53**
		AIC	**73.05 (tlogist)**	**61.69 (lxvmax)**	**87.29 (lxvmin)**	51.08 (tlogist)	29.90 (exp)	108.83 (lxvmax)	**123.27 (txvmin)**	**117.47 (llogist)**
Lindley-type NHPP-based SRMs	Infinite Lindley	MSE	1.69	1.52	3.26	2.18	0.14	1.07	0.87	3.79
		AIC	85.34 (Gompertz Lindley)	66.33 (Power Lindley)	107.87 (Weighted Lindley)	66.65 (Lindley)	**27.91 (Lindley)**	**104.28 (Lindley)**	138.03 (Gompertz Lindley)	150.38 (Power Lindley)
	Finite Lindley	MSE	0.57	0.51	**0.59**	**0.44**	**0.09**	1.03	0.34	0.59
		AIC	74.49 (Exp Lindley)	63.84 (Exp Power Lindley)	**87.27 (Gompertz Lindley)**	**51.05 (Gompertz Lindley)**	31.22 (Weighted Lindley)	111.36 (Exp Power Lindley)	126.93 (Gompertz Lindley)	120.63 (Gompertz Lindley)

AIC and MSE than the existing finite NHPP-based SRMs. Note that, although the results show that the infinite Gompertz Lindley SRM outperformed the seven infinite Lindley-type SRMs in almost all cases, it hardly guaranteed a better AIC or MSE in comparison with the other three types of NHPP-based SRMs.

In Table 9.7, our Lindley-type SRMs could provide the better AIC in half of the cases (TIDS3–TIDS6) and MSE in TIDS3, TIDS4, and TIDS5. In group data, the result suggests that the Gompertz Lindley distribution and Lindley distribution tend to be the best fault-detection time distribution in finite and infinite Lindley-type NHPP-based software reliability modeling. Hence, we are optimistic that Lindley-type SRMs still have a certain potential ability to describe software fault count data better. On one hand, we also believe that it is still of great significance to investigate the predictive performance of the Lindley-type SRMs because, as well as we know, the goodness-of-fit performance and the predictive performance do not have an inevitable connection.

9.5.2 Predictive Performance

In the second experiment, we focus on the predictive performance of Lindley-type SRMs. Figures 9.4, 9.5, and 9.6 depict the predicted number of detected faults after the 20% , 50%, and 80% observation points in TDDS1 by existing finite and infinite NHPP-based SRMs and by finite and infinite Lindley-type SRMs with minimum PMSE. In all three figures, the finite exp power Lindley-type SRM in Table 9.2, the log-extreme-value max distribution NHPP-based SRM [13], the pareto NHPP-based SRM [8] and Musa–Okumoto SRM [1, 20] provided the more accurate predictive performance at the 20% , 50%, and 80% points of TDDS1. On the one hand, we can observe that the infinite Gompertz Lindley-type SRM in Table 9.3 SRMs cannot accurately predict the future trend of software debugging. But we still need a more specific investigation to evaluate the predicted performance of our Lindley-type NHPP-based SRMs in both time-domain and group data.

The minimum PMSEs in existing NHPP-based SRMs and NHPP-based Lindley-type SRMs for time-domain data are shown in Tables 9.8, 9.9, and 9.10, where the best SRMs are chosen by the future data $\left(t_{m+j}, n_{m+j}\right)(j = 1,2,\cdots,l)$ obtained ex post facto. As demonstrated in Figures 9.4, 9.5, and 9.6, the predictive performance of our infinite Lindley-type NHPP-based SRM in TDDS1 is not as good as expected. In the early and middle prediction phases, respectively, only one case (TDDS6 at the 20% observation point and TDDS5 at the 50% observation point) shows that the Lindley-type SRM predicts the number of detected faults more accurately than the existing finite and infinite NHPP-based SRMs. However, as the testing time goes on, in almost all cases except for two (TDDS5 and TDDS6), the existing NHPP-based SRMs showed a smaller PMSE than Lindley-type SRMs. In the later prediction phase (at the 80% observation point), infinite the Lindley-type SRM is even less able to guarantee the smaller PMSE in all data sets. But on the other hand,

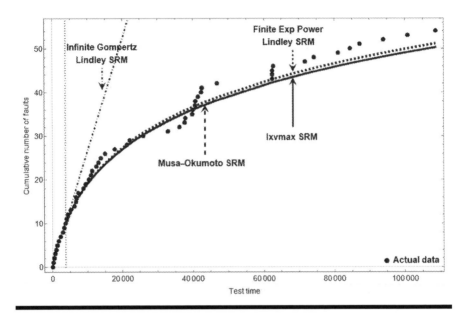

Figure 9.4   Predicted cumulative number of software faults in TDDS1 (at 20% observation point).

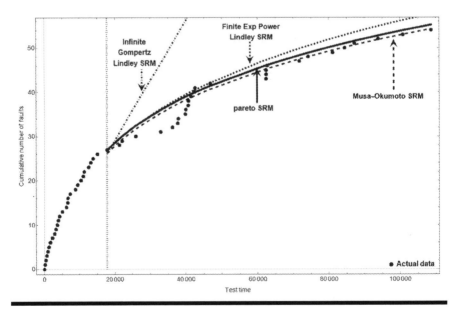

Figure 9.5   Predicted cumulative number of software faults in TDDS1 (at 50% observation point).

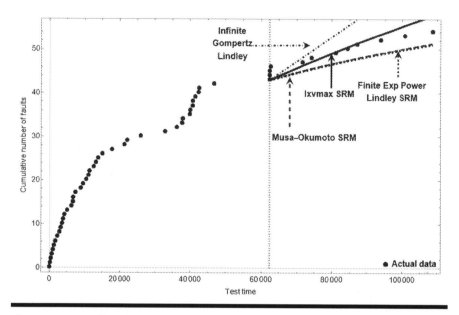

Figure 9.6 Predicted cumulative number of software faults in TDDS1 (at 80% observation point).

Table 9.8 Prediction Results in Time-Domain Data (20% Observation Point)

	Lindley-Type NHPP-Based SRMs		*Existing NHPP-Based SRMs*	
	Best finite SRM	*Best infinite SRM*	*Best finite SRM*	*Best infinite SRM*
TDDS1	**0.32** **(Exp power)**	13.58 (Gompertz)	0.33 (lxvmax)	1.58 (Musa–Okumoto)
TDDS2	3.02 (Exp power)	2.68 (Gompertz)	**1.13** **(tnorm)**	1.91 (Duane)
TDDS3	1.27 (Exp)	8.05 (Exp Power)	**0.54** **(lxvmax)**	6.97 (Duane)
TDDS4	1.77 (Exp power)	3.08 (Exp Power)	**1.21** **(lnorm)**	1.53 (Duane)
TDDS5	**1.89** **(Lindley)**	4.74 (Weighted)	12.62 (exp)	12.63 (Musa–Okumoto)
TDDS6	2.85 (Exp Lindley)	**1.59** **(Power Lindley)**	1.60 (exp)	1.60 (Musa–Okumoto)
TDDS7	1.45 (Exp power)	3.26 (Exp Power)	**0.96** **(lxvmax)**	4.78 (Musa–Okumoto)
TDDS8	**2.97** **(Lindley)**	34.66 (Gompertz)	4.72 (lxvmax)	18.15 (Duane)

Table 9.9 Prediction Results in Time-Domain Data (50% Observation Point)

	Lindley-Type NHPP-Based SRMs		Existing NHPP-Based SRMs	
	Best finite SRM	Best infinite SRM	Best finite SRM	Best infinite SRM
TDDS1	0.60 (Exp power)	8.17 (Gompertz)	**0.46 (pareto)**	0.47 (Musa–Okumoto)
TDDS2	**0.43 (Gompertz)**	0.81 (Exp)	0.84 (tlogist)	1.77 (Musa–Okumoto)
TDDS3	2.57 (Gamma)	11.56 (Gompertz)	0.41 (pareto)	**0.38 (Musa–Okumoto)**
TDDS4	**1.56 (Weighted)**	9.66 (Gompertz)	1.89 (tlogist)	2.66 (Musa–Okumoto)
TDDS5	1.41 (Gamma)	**1.04 (Lindley)**	2.23 (llogist)	1.43 (Cox–Lewis)
TDDS6	0.97 (Lindley)	3.68 (Gamma)	**0.71 (lxvmax)**	1.92 (Musa–Okumoto)
TDDS7	**3.83 (Gompertz)**	14.39 (Gompertz)	13.94 (exp)	14.26 (Musa–Okumoto)
TDDS8	**1.68 (Lindley)**	66.93 (Power)	24.71 (lxvmax)	1.93 (Duane)

Table 9.10 Prediction Results in Time-Domain Data (80% Observation Point)

	Lindley-Type NHPP-Based SRMs		Existing NHPP-Based SRMs	
	Best finite SRM	Best infinite SRM	Best finite SRM	Best infinite SRM
TDDS1	0.68 (Exp power)	1.49 (Gompertz)	0.67 (lxvmax)	**0.51 (Musa–Okumoto)**
TDDS2	0.25 (Exp power)	1.41 (Lindley)	**0.24 (lxvmax)**	0.28 (Musa–Okumoto)
TDDS3	1.08 (Power)	3.24 (Gompertz)	**0.56 (lxvmax)**	0.82 (Duane)
TDDS4	**0.57 (Gamma)**	11.76 (Gompertz)	**0.57 (txvmin)**	2.54 (Musa–Okumoto)
TDDS5	**0.56 (Lindley)**	2.52 (Gompertz)	1.12 (lxvmax)	1.74 (Duane)
TDDS6	**0.42 (Exp power)**	3.63 (Power)	0.45 (lxvmax)	1.50 (Musa–Okumoto)
TDDS7	1.16 (Exp power)	1.23 (Gompertz)	0.97 (lxvmax)	**0.62 (Duane)**
TDDS8	2.23 (Exp power)	1.64 (Gompertz)	1.59 (lxvmax)	0.63 (Duane)

we observed that the finite Lindley-type SRMs could provide the smaller PMSE in three cases (TDDS1, TDDS5 and TDDS8) at the 20% observation point, in four cases (TDDS2, TDDS4, TDDS7 and TDDS8) at the 50% observation point, and in three cases (TDDS4, TDDS5 and TDDS6) at the 80% observation point.

In Tables 9.11, 9.12 and 9.13, the PMSEs of finite and infinite Lindley-type SRMs and existing NHPP-based SRMs are also compared when the group data are available. We can observe that our infinite Lindley-type SRMs could provide the lower PMSE in some cases; i.e., half of the data sets at the 20% observation point, three out of eight data sets at the 50% observation point, and one case at the 80% observation point. On the other hand, finite Lindley-type SRMs outperformed the existing NHPP-based SRMs in two data sets at the 20% observation point, three out of eight data sets at the 50% observation point, and three out of eight data sets at the 80% observation point.

Hence, we can summarize that our infinite Lindley-type SRMs have better prediction accuracy at early software fault prediction but that prediction accuracy continuously diminishes as the testing process proceeds. The infinite Lindley-type SRMs, on the other hand, perform more smoothly. Therefore, overall, our Lindley-type NHPP-based SRMs have better predictive performance than the existing NHPP-based SRMs in the group data because Lindley-type NHPP-based SRMs

Table 9.11   Prediction Results in Group Data (20% Observation Point)

	Lindley-Type NHPP-Based SRMs		Existing NHPP-Based SRMs	
	Best finite SRM	Best infinite SRM	Best finite SRM	Best infinite SRM
TIDS1	**2.49** **(Lindley)**	5.12 (Weighted)	3.71 (gamma)	3.82 (Duane)
TIDS2	1.67 (Exp power)	7.52 (Power)	**1.44** **(lxvmax)**	8.72 (Musa–Okumoto)
TIDS3	3.64 (Weighted)	**2.69** **(Gompertz)**	**2.69** **(gamma)**	6.97 (Duane)
TIDS4	3.10 (Gompertz)	**2.46** **(Power)**	3.44 (exp)	3.60 (Cox–Lewis)
TIDS5	0.43 (Gamma)	**0.16** **(Lindley)**	0.43 (pareto)	0.45 (Musa–Okumoto)
TIDS6	2.63 (Lindley)	9.06 (Gompertz)	**2.34** **(tlogist)**	7.06 (Musa–Okumoto)
TIDS7	5.54 (Lindley)	**1.38** **(Weighted)**	3.65 (exp)	3.65 (Musa–Okumoto)
TIDS8	**3.53** **(Gamma)**	6.33 (Gamma)	4.03 (txvmin)	7.34 (Musa–Okumoto)

Table 9.12   Prediction Results in Group Data (50% Observation Point)

	Lindley-Type NHPP-Based SRMs		Existing NHPP-Based SRMs	
	Best finite SRM	Best infinite SRM	Best finite SRM	Best infinite SRM
TIDS1	**1.44** **(Gompertz)**	3.83 (Lindley)	3.77 (tlogist)	4.18 (Musa–Okumoto)
TIDS2	1.67 (Exp power)	1.36 (Power)	1.84 (txvmin)	**0.68** **(Duane)**
TIDS3	**4.09** **(Lindley)**	8.49 (Weighted)	6.83 (lxvmax)	10.26 (Musa–Okumoto)
TIDS4	9.77 (Exp power)	**3.69** **(Gompertz)**	3.92 (exp)	3.80 (Musa–Okumoto)
TIDS5	0.19 (Gamma)	**0.13** **(Power)**	0.19 (exp)	0.21 (Musa–Okumoto)
TIDS6	5.68 (Exp power)	**1.37** **(Power)**	5.50 (pareto)	1.60 (Cox–Lewis)
TIDS7	**0.98** **(Weighted)**	1.17 (Weighted)	1.10 (lxvmax)	1.89 (Duane)
TIDS8	2.80 (Gompertz)	4.33 (Lindley)	**1.31** **(txvmin)**	4.61 (Musa–Okumoto)

Table 9.13   Prediction Results in Group Data (80% Observation Point)

	Lindley-Type NHPP-Based SRMs		Existing NHPP-Based SRMs	
	Best finite SRM	Best infinite SRM	Best finite SRM	Best infinite SRM
TIDS1	0.80 (Gamma)	2.26 (Gompertz)	**0.53** **(lnorm)**	2.68 (Musa–Okumoto)
TIDS2	**0.30** **(Gamma)**	1.05 (Power)	**0.30** **(exp)**	0.43 (Musa–Okumoto)
TIDS3	0.29 (Gompertz)	5.46 (Weighted)	**0.23** **(tnorm)**	3.67 (Musa–Okumoto)
TIDS4	**0.32** **(Exp power)**	4.63 (Power)	**0.59** **(tnorm)**	5.30 (Musa–Okumoto)
TIDS5	0.15 (Exp)	**0.14** **(Gompertz)**	0.21 (tnorm)	0.30 (Duane)
TIDS6	**0.47** **(Lindley)**	2.74 (Power)	0.74 (txvmax)	1.34 (Musa–Okumoto)
TIDS7	1.94 (Gompertz)	2.23 (Gamma)	**0.82** **(txvmin)**	2.52 (Musa–Okumoto)
TIDS8	0.58 (Exp)	1.71 (Gamma)	**0.33** **(lxvmax)**	2.10 (Musa–Okumoto)

could guarantee smaller PMSEs in more than half of the data sets regardless of the phase of software fault-detection prediction. Since generally PMSE is recognized as the most plausible prediction metric, we believe that for software fault prediction, Lindley-type SRMs are as attractive as existing NHPP-based SRMs.

9.5.3 Software Reliability Assessment

Through the experiments of goodness-of-fit and predictive performances, we are not asserting that our Lindley-type SRMs could outperform the existing NHPP-based SRMs, but it should be stressed that, in the NHPP-based software reliability model, except for the existing SRMs [4], Lindley-type SRMs could also be good candidates. In describing the software fault-detection time distribution, Lindley-type distributions should be good choices.

Hence, in the end, we also concerned with quantifying the software reliability of our Lindley-type SRMs. We define $R(x)$ as the probability that software detects no faults during a time interval $(t, t + x]$, when the software test is stopped now at time t. For the NHPP-based SRM, $R(x)$ is

$$R(x) = \Pr\big(N(t+x) - N(t) = 0 N(t) = m\big)$$
$$= \exp\big(-\big[\Lambda(t+x) - \Lambda(t)\big]\big) \tag{9.31}$$

where m is the cumulative number of detected software faults at time t, and x is the assumed software operation time. We set 1 as the time of each testing length in CPU time for the time-domain data or calendar time (week) for the group data. Tables 9.14 and 9.15 present the quantitative software reliability calculated with time-domain data and group data, respectively, where the best goodness-of-fit model in each modeling category is assumed. From these results, our Lindley-type NHPP-based SRMs gave the smaller software reliability assessment than the existing ones; four out of eight datasets in time-domain data and five out of eight datasets in group data. From the fact that all the datasets are the software fault count data observed before releasing software products to the user/market in actual software development projects, it can be seen that the Lindley-type NHPP-based SRMs tended to provide more plausible reliability assessment.

9.6 Conclusion

In this chapter, based on the assumed seven alternative fault-detection time distributions developed through the original Lindley distribution, we have proposed seven novel infinite Lindley-type NHPP-based SRMs over the infinite-failure software reliability modeling assumption. We have investigated their goodness-of-fit

Table 9.14 Software Reliability by the Best AIC SRMs (Time-Domain Data)

	Lindley-Type NHPP-Based SRMs		Existing NHPP-Based SRMs	
	Best finite SRM	Best infinite SRM	Best finite SRM	Best infinite SRM
TDDS1	**8.49E-05** **(Power)**	2.35E-19 (Lindley)	2.67E-06 (lxvmax)	9.32E-06 (Musa–Okumoto)
TDDS2	**4.12E-03** **(Exp power)**	1.40E-09 (Exp Power)	3.75E-03 (lxvmax)	2.40E-03 (Musa–Okumoto)
TDDS3	6.95E-12 (Power)	8.63E-60 (Power)	2.52E-10 (lxvmin)	**2.64E-10** **(Musa–Okumoto)**
TDDS4	3.53E-01 (Gompertz)	2.64E-13 (Gompertz)	**1.00E+00** **(txvmin)**	**1.00E+00** **(Musa–Okumoto)**
TDDS5	8.36E-12 (Exp)	3.12E-75 (Gompertz)	**2.60E-08** **(exp)**	1.01E-19 (Duane)
TDDS6	**2.38E-01** **(Power)**	3.49E-06 (Gompertz)	4.69E-03 (lxvmax)	3.13E-17 (Musa–Okumoto)
TDDS7	9.42E-03 (Power)	**5.82E-05** **(Gompertz)**	2.40E-04 (lxvmax)	3.83E-15 (Musa–Okumoto)
TDDS8	**1.15E-05** **(Exp power)**	1.75E-07 (Gompertz)	7.74E-06 (pareto)	1.88E-32 (Musa–Okumoto)

Table 9.15 Software Reliability by the Best AIC SRMs (Group Data)

	Lindley-Type NHPP-Based SRMs		Existing NHPP-Based SRMs	
	Best finite SRM	Best infinite SRM	Best finite SRM	Best infinite SRM
TIDS1	**1.57E-04** **(Exp)**	2.21E-25 **(Gompertz)**	4.15E-03 (llogist)	3.57E-24 (Cox–Lewis)
TIDS2	**7.45E-05** **(Exp power)**	9.19E-17 (Power)	7.24E-05 (lxvmax)	3.17E-17 (Cox–Lewis)
TIDS3	2.59E-03 (Gompertz)	1.68E-49 (Weighted)	**3.87E-02** **(tnorm)**	6.59E-101 (Cox–Lewis)
TIDS4	**2.82E-01** **(Gompertz)**	4.61E-28 (Lindley)	2.81E-01 (tlogist)	9.99E-73 (Cox–Lewis)
TIDS5	**1.52E-02** **(Weighted)**	1.30E-28 (Lindley)	9.83E-04 (exp)	3.01E-05 (Cox–Lewis)
TIDS6	1.38E-07 (Exp power)	1.68E-33 (Lindley)	**1.94E-07** **(lxvmax)**	3.33E-77 (Cox–Lewis)
TIDS7	1.31E-01 (Gompertz)	1.26E-11 (Gompertz)	**9.63E-01** **(txvmin)**	5.47E-05 (Duane)
TIDS8	**9.66E-01** **(Gompertz)**	3.37E-17 (Power)	6.37E-01 (llogist)	3.32E-02 (Duane)

and predictive performances and made comparisons with the finite Lindley-type NHPP-based SRMs, 11 existing finite and three existing NHPP-based SRMs with representative 11 fault-detection time distributions. In most of the time-domain and group data sets, with Lindley-type NHPP-based SRMs it was difficult to provide a lower AIC when their parameters were obtained by maximum likelihood estimation. However, in the group data set, Lindley-type NHPP-based SRMs demonstrated predictive performance that did not lose out to the existing NHPP-based SRMs at any phase of software testing.

In the future, we will consider applying the proposed Lindley-type NHPP-based SRMs to a well-established software reliability assessment tool.

References

[1] J. D. Musa, A. Iannino, and K. Okumoto, *Software Reliability, Measurement, Prediction, Application*, McGraw-Hill, New York, 1987.

[2] M. R. Lyu (ed.), *Handbook of Software Reliability Engineering*, McGraw-Hill, New York, 1996.

[3] L. Kuo, and T. Y. Yang, "Bayesian computation for nonhomogeneous Poisson processes in software reliability," *Journal of the American Statistical Association*, vol. 91, no. 434, pp. 763--773, 1994.

[4] H. Okamura, and T. Dohi, "SRATS: software reliability assessment tool on spreadsheet," in *Proceedings of the 24th International Symposium on Software Reliability Engineering (ISSRE-2013)*, pp. 100--117, IEEE CPS, 2013.

[5] A.L. Goel, and K. Okumoto, "Time-dependent error-detection rate model for software reliability and other performance measures," *IEEE Transactions on Reliability*, vol. R-28, no. 3, pp. 206--211, 1979.

[6] S. Yamada, M. Ohba, and S. Osaki, ``S-shaped reliability growth modeling for software error detection," *IEEE Transactions on Reliability*, vol. R-32, no. 5, pp. 475--478, 1983.

[7] M. Zhao, and M. Xie, "On maximum likelihood estimation for a general nonhomogeneous Poisson process," *Scandinavian Journal of Statistics*, vol. 23, no. 4, pp. 597--607, 1996.

[8] A. A. Abdel-Ghaly, P. Y. Chan, and B. Littlewood, "Evaluation of competing software reliability predictions," *IEEE Transactions on Software Engineering*, vol. SE-12, no. 9, pp. 950--967, 1986.

[9] H. Okamura, T. Dohi, and S. Osaki, "Software reliability growth models with normal failure time distributions," *Reliability Engineering and System Safety*, vol. 116, pp. 135--141, 2013.

[10] J. A. Achcar, D. K. Dey, and M. Niverthi, "A Bayesian approach using nonhomogeneous Poisson processes for software reliability models," in *Frontiers in Reliability*, A. P. Basu, K. S. Basu, and S. Mukhopadhyay (eds.), pp. 1--18, World Scientific, Singapore, 1998.

[11] M. Ohba, "Inflection S-shaped software reliability growth model," in *Stochastic Models in Reliability Theory*, S. Osaki, and Y. Hatoyama (eds.), pp. 144--165, Springer-Verlag, Berlin, 1984.

[12] S. S. Gokhale, and K. S. Trivedi, "Log-logistic software reliability growth model," in *Proceedings of the 3rd IEEE International Symposium on High-Assurance Systems Engineering (HASE-1998)*, pp. 34--41, IEEE CPS, 1998.

[13] K. Ohishi, H. Okamura, and T. Dohi, "Gompertz software reliability model: estimation algorithm and empirical validation," *Journal of Systems and Software*, vol. 82, no. 3, pp. 535--543, 2009.

[14] A. L. Goel, "Software reliability models: assumptions, limitations and applicability," *IEEE Transactions on Software Engineering*, vol. SE-11, no. 12, pp. 1411--1423, 1985.

[15] R. E. Barlow, and F. Proschan, *Mathematical Theory of Reliability*, Wiley, New York, 1965.

[16] J. T. Duane, "Learning curve approach to reliability monitoring," *IEEE Transactions on Aerospace*, vol. 2, no. 2, pp. 563--566, 1964.

[17] E. Cretois, and O. Gaudoin, "New results on goodness-of-fit tests for the power-law process and application to software reliability," *International Journal of Reliability, Quality and Safety Engineering*, vol. 5, no. 3, pp. 249--267, 1998.

[18] B. Littlewood, "Rationale for a modified Duane model," *IEEE Transactions on Reliability*, vol. R-33, no. 2, pp. 157--159, 1984.

[19] D. Cox, and P. Lewis, *The Statistical Analysis of Series of Events*, Springer, Dordrecht, 1966.

[20] J. D. Musa, and K. Okumoto, "A logarithmic Poisson execution time model for software reliability measurement," in *Proceedings of the 7th International Conference on Software Engineering*, pp. 230--238, ACM, 1984.

[21] C. Y. Huang, M. R. Lyu, and S.-Y. Kuo, "A unified scheme of some nonhomogeneous Poisson process models for software reliability estimation," *IEEE Transactions on Software Engineering*, vol. 29, pp. 261--269, 2003.

[22] N. Langberg, and N. D. Singpurwalla, "Unification of some software reliability models," *SIAM Journal on Scientific Computing*, vol. 6, no. 3, pp. 781--790, 1985.

[23] H. Okamura, and T. Dohi, "Building phase-type software reliability models," in *Proceedings of the 17th International Symposium on Software Reliability Engineering (ISSRE-2006)*, pp. 289--298, IEEE CPS, 2006.

[24] H. Okamura, and T. Dohi, "Hyper-Erlang software reliability model," in *Proceedings of the 14th Pacific Rim International Symposium on Dependable Computing (PRDC-2008)*, pp. 232--239, IEEE CPS, 2008.

[25] H. Okamura, and T. Dohi, "Phase-type software reliability model: parameter estimation algorithms with grouped data," *Annals of Operations Research*, vol. 244, no. 1, pp. 177--208, 2016.

[26] D. V. Lindley, "Fiducial distributions and Bayes' theorem," *Journal of the Royal Statistical Society B*, vol. 20, no. 1, pp. 102--107, 1958.

[27] M. E. Ghitany, B. Atieh, and S. Nadarajah, "Lindley distribution and its application," *Mathematics and Computers in Simulation*, vol. 78, no. 4, pp. 493--506, 2008.

[28] J. Mazucheli, and J. A. Achcar, "The Lindley distribution applied to competing risks lifetime data," *Computer Methods and Programs in Biomedicine*, vol. 104, vol. 2, pp. 189--192, 2011.

[29] M. E. Ghitany, D. K. Al-Mutairi, N. Balakrishnan, and L. J. Al-Enezi, "Power Lindley distribution and associated inference," *Computational Statistics and Data Analysis*, vol. 64, no. 1, pp. 20--33, 2013.

[30] D. K. Al-Mutairi, M. E. Ghitany, and D. Kundu, "Inference on stress-strength reliability from Lindley distributions," *Communications in Statistics—Theory and Methods*, vol. 42, no. 8, pp. 1443--1463, 2013.

[31] S. Nadarajah, H. S. Bakouch, and R. Tahmasbi, "A generalized Lindley distribution," *Sankhya*, vol. 73, no. 2. pp. 331--359, 2011.

[32] S. K. Ashour, and M. A. Eltehiwy, "Exponentiated power Lindley distribution," *Journal of Advanced Research*, vol. 6, no. 6, pp. 895--905, 2015.

[33] S. Nedjar and H. Zeghdoudi, "On gamma Lindley distribution: properties and simulations," *Journal of Computational and Applied Mathematics*, vol. 298, no. 1, pp. 167--174, 2016.

[34] M. E. Ghitany, F. Alqallaf, D. K. Al-Mutairi, and H. A. Husain, "A two-parameter weighted Lindley distribution and its applications to survival data," *Mathematics and Computers in Simulation*, vol. 81, no. 6, pp. 1190--1201, 2011.

[35] J. Mazucheli, F. Louzada, and M. E. Ghitany, "Comparison of estimation methods for the parameters of the weighted Lindley distribution," *Applied Mathematics and Computation*, vol. 220, no. 1, pp. 463--471, 2013.

[36] A. A. Baqer, "Gompertz-Lindley distribution and its applications," *Master Thesis in the College of Graduate Studies, Kuwait University*, 2019.

[37] Q. Xiao, T. Dohi and H. Okamura, "Lindley type distributions and software reliability assessment," in *Proceedings of the 8th Asia-Pacific International Symposium on Advanced Reliability and Maintenance Modeling (APARM 2020)*, 6 pages, IEEE CPS, 2020.

[38] J. Hishitani, S. Yamada, and S. Osaki, "Reliability assessment measures based on software reliability growth model with normalized method," *Journal of Information Processing*, vol. 14, no. 2, pp. 178--183, 1991.

[39] J. D. Musa, "Software Reliability Data," *Technical Report in Rome Air Development Center*, 1979

[40] A. Wood, "Predicting software reliability," *IEEE Computer*, vol. 20, no. 11, pp. 69--77, 1996.

[41] M. A. Vouk, "Using reliability models during testing with non-operational profile," in *Proceedings of the 2nd Bell-core/Purdue Workshop on Issues in Software Reliability Estimation*, pp. 254--266, 1992.

[42] H. Okamura, Y. Etani, and T. Dohi, ``Quantifying the effectiveness of testing efforts on software fault detection with a logit software reliability growth model," in *Proceedings of 2011 Joint Conference of the 21st International Workshop on Software Measurement (IWSM 2011) and the 6th International Conference on Software Process and Product Measurement (MENSURA-2011)*, pp. 62--68, IEEE CPS, 2011.

Chapter 10

Artificial Intelligence and Machine Learning Problems and Challenges in Software Testing

Imtiaz Ahmed and Pramod Kumar Yadav

National Institute of Technology, Srinagar, India

10.1 Introduction

10.1.1 Overview of Machine Learning and Artificial Intelligence

An intelligent system that demonstrates human-like intelligence is referred to as artificial intelligence (AI), a generally accepted subfield of computer science. AI enables machines to mimic intelligent human behavior by learning to mimic human perception, logical and rational cognition, and decision-making ability. AI, which is increasingly popular in the use of computers to solve problems that would otherwise be insoluble and outperform the efficiency of current computer systems, has considerably improved efficiency in several fields in recent years [1]. The relationship between artificial intelligence (AI) and software engineering is illustrated by Derek Partridge in several broad categories (SE). The usage of industry-standard software in AI systems, software support environments, and AI tools and methodologies

DOI: 10.1201/9781032624983-10

are some of these areas of communication. In Mark Kandel and H. Bunke made an effort to relate AI with software engineering on a certain level. They discussed whether AI can be used to solve SE problems directly and whether SE processes can benefit from AI techniques.

10.1.2 Impact of AI on Software Testing

Software testing uses up company resources and doesn't improve the functionality of the program, based on studies. When regression testing identifies a new error brought on by a revision code, a new regression cycle begins. Engineers are frequently required by software applications to be equally skilled as those who created the original app in order to write testing scripts. The rising overhead costs associated with the quality assurance process are proportional to the growing complexity of software products. AI capability, performance, and speed must be a constant priority for automated testing developers [2]. AI would logically become more and more necessary to certify intelligence-containing systems. Currently, monotonous data is mostly utilized to train models for various methods for classification and grouping using AI.

10.1.3 Role of AI in Software Testing

A developing area of research that has been well documented in a number of finished publications is artificial intelligence applications approaches and techniques to software engineering and testing. Numerous AI tools are utilized for test data generation, data appropriateness research, coverage analysis, optimization, and test management. Genetic algorithm (GA) and its two modified iterations, annealing genetic algorithm (AGA) and restricted genetic algorithm (RGA) have been tested in [3]. ACO may be used to create model-based test data, and ant colonies can efficiently explore a graph and produce the best test data possible to meet the test coverage requirement. State-based software testing has made use of test sequence generation [4]. A number of other AI-based techniques and approaches have been used for requirements-based testing based on particle swarm optimization (PSO), partition testing also based on PSO, test case minimization using an artificial neural network (ANN), test case minimization using a data mining info-fuzzy network, building a Bayesian network (BN) model to predict software fault content and fault proneness, and use of artificial neural networks. All of these techniques and approaches are discussed.

10.2 Issues and Challenges of AI

Artificial intelligence (AI) is omnipresent in many sectors, from consumer apps to business intelligence, and will soon be one of the major forces driving productivity, development, and innovation. The field of artificial intelligence has gone a long way in the past 60 years, but there are still numerous challenges, some of which need to be addressed if AI is to reach its full potential. Testing AI software faces several challenges due to a lack of technical expertise and research findings [5].

10.2.1 Recognizing Test Data

The strategy and training of the AI model, as well as the availability of training data sets, are crucial for the precision of functional predictions made by AI software testing. How can we utilize a structured approach to create high-quality test datasets that concentrate on coverage and training datasets for learning-based AI functional features. Text, image, audio, and video inputs can be used to create a variety of rich media inputs that numerous AI functions can process to provide a variety of rich media outputs and events/actions. Different training and test data sets for the same AI model may produce different results and have varying accuracy.

10.2.2 Algorithmic Uncertainty

Any type of software testing faces difficulties due to uncertainty. Incomplete specifications or poorly understood requirements lead to uncertainty. Algorithmic instability is particularly important in AI applications [6]. This is because the algorithms used to create AI are inherently unpredictable. There is no coding in an AI application in accordance with a predetermined algorithm. Instead, the creator strives to train a model using a set of test data. For neurons and weights in that model, there must be a starting point. There is no secret method to find the ideal starting point; the initial weights and number of neurons are chosen by the developer.

10.2.3 Measures of Effectiveness That Are Not Accurate

Black-box testing assesses an application's functionality without knowing the implementation's organizational structure. The necessary specifications are used to create test suites for black-box testing. Applying black box testing to AI models includes putting the model through its paces without knowing its defining traits or the algorithm that created it. The challenging element of this is locating the test oracle that might compare the test result to the predicted values beforehand [7]. There are no predefined predicted values in the case of AI models. It might be tough to assess or validate the forecast vs. expected value due to the prediction form of the models. Data scientists evaluate the model performance during the model creation phase by contrasting the expected values with the actual values. (See Figure 10.1)

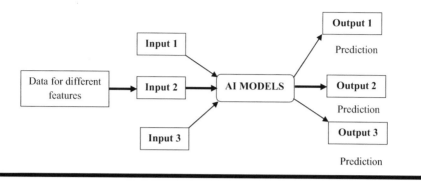

Figure 10.1 Challenges to effective output prediction.

10.2.4 Data Splitting Into Training and Testing Sets

An automated system for dividing the available data into distinct training and testing datasets is typically used by data scientists. SciKit-Learn is a well liked tool for this, allowing programmers to divide the needed size of the dataset by random selection. It's vital to override the random seed that was utilized to divide the data when evaluating or retraining several models. If this is not done carefully, the findings will not be consistent, comparable, or reproducible. The knowledge is often employed for model training to the tune of 70– 80%, with the remaining 20% being set aside for model evaluation. To ensure that testing and training data are properly separated in a representative manner, several specific approaches are available [8].

An important consideration is the planning of regression testing efforts. Functional regression is typically not significant unless fairly significant changes are made, which is not a problem in traditional software development. When it comes to AI, there is a very significant danger of regression for previously verified functionality, and nearly any modification to the model's parameters, the algorithm, or the training data often requires starting the model again from scratch. This is because, depending on the necessary adjustments, it's possible that the entire model could change rather than just a small piece [9].

10.3 Related Work

Software testing for AI has not received significant research. The key difficulty in defining quality assurance standard systems and creating an acceptable quality test coverage, as well as using systematic methods to create quality test models, is connecting quality assurance needs and testing coverage criteria for AI systems based on big data. It also presents some new challenges that AI systems must overcome to predict system behavior, such as determining the precise requirements and inputs needed to produce a quality test model [10].

Goals and output optimizations may not be apparent, and parameters may be complicated. The difficulties the model faces in modifying itself to more properly identify gender images have been thoroughly described, which arise from the difficulties with testing AI technologies for facial recognition. Because predictive analysis is used in AI approaches, data privacy is a significant additional concern. The transparency of personal data is an issue for organizations. Due to the discrepancy between the selection of training data and test data, overfitting is another issue that AI models are now confronting. During the integration testing of an AI system, various challenges can arise when dealing with data transformation, cleansing, extraction, and normalization. These challenges can impact the overall performance and reliability of the AI system.

10.3.1 Artificial Intelligence Overview

John McCarthy first used the term "artificial intelligence" in 1955 at a symposium that the Dartmouth Conference sponsored. This phrase was used to describe all "programming methods in which the machine is simulating some intelligent human behaviour." According to John McCarthy, it is "the science and engineering of developing intelligent devices, notably clever computer programmes" [11]. Here, we go over the key branches of artificial intelligence that have been utilized the most in software testing. (See Figure 10.2.)

10.3.2 Artificial Neural Network

An artificial neural network (ANN) is created by modeling artificial intelligence after a biological neural network. The ANN is a network of connected nodes, much like the neurons in a biological neural network. Node characteristics, network design, and learning principles are the three essential elements of every neural network. How a node processes signals depends on its character. Nodes are grouped and connected

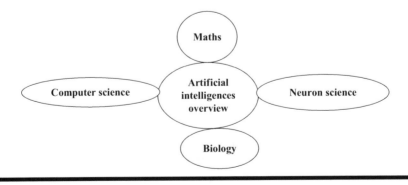

Figure 10.2   AI overview.

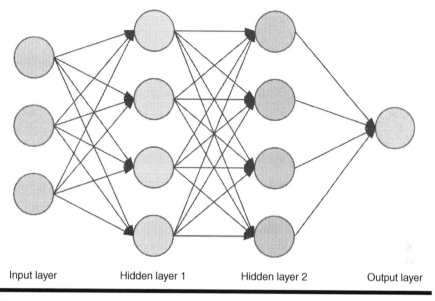

Figure 10.3   Artificial neural network.

according to network topology. Weight adjustment schemes are used to initialize and adjust the weights according to learning rules. This kind of network transforms into a computational tool that can learn with practice, hence enhancing its performance [12].

The image in Figure 10.3 appears if we zoom in on one of the hidden or output nodes.

10.3.3 AI Planning

The logic theorist program, created by Newell and Simon in the 1960s, contains research on AI planning [13]. AI planning aims to find a set of efficient actions in a specific planning domain that can efficiently move the planning problem's initial state to its final state after the actions are taken.

10.3.4 Machine Learning

Machine learning, in its broadest sense, can be characterized as computer techniques that draw on experience to enhance performance or to produce reliable predictions. Experience in this context refers to the previous knowledge that the learner has access to, which frequently takes the form of electronically gathered data that is presented for analysis [14]. This information could be gained via digitalized training sets with human labels or from other sources by interacting with the environment. (See Figure 10.4.)

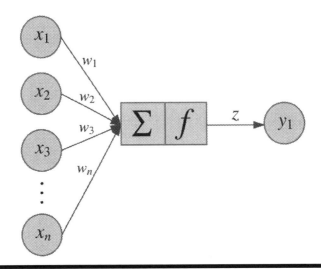

Figure 10.4 **Weight of artificial neural network.**

10.3.5 Natural Language Processing (NLP)

The process of using a natural language, such as English, to communicate with an intelligent system is known as natural language processing (NLP) [15]. When we need an intelligent system to follow our directions, or when we need a clinical expert system that engages in dialogue to give us advice etc., we need to process natural language. (See Figure 10.5.)

10.3.6 Fuzzy Logic

Fuzzy logic (FL) is a way of thinking that simulates human reasoning. By taking into account all compromises between the digital values Yes and No, the FL approach simulates how humans make judgments. The foundation of FL is the notion that there is no clear demarcation between the two extremes. A number of rules are integrated to obtain a conclusion using the FL way of reasoning, which is used to arrive at decisions [16]. The rules are fuzzy sets that serve as the foundation for making decisions.

10.4 Artificial Intelligence in Agriculture

Due to its rapid scientific advancement and broad range of applications, artificial intelligence (AI) is one of the main research areas in software engineering. Adaptability, rapid performance, precision, and financial viability are the fundamental

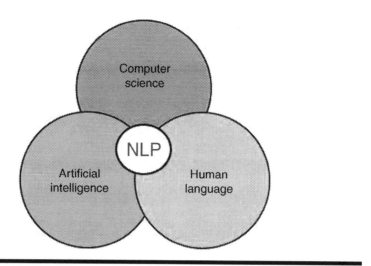

Figure 10.5   Natural language processing.

AI principles in agricultural [17]. In addition to assisting farmers in using their natural farming abilities, artificial intelligence in agriculture also encourages direct farming, which delivers larger yields and better quality while using fewer resources [18]. Several industries, including the agricultural one, use AI-based technology to manage challenges like crop harvesting, irrigation, soil content sensitivity, crop monitoring, weed, harvest, and establishment, which also contributes to greater efficiency in all industries

10.4.1 Software Testing in the Area of Artificial Intelligence for Agriculture

Artificial intelligence is starting to revolutionize the agricultural industry. Real-time crop monitoring, harvesting, processing, and marketing have all improved artificial intelligence, which, in turn, has increased crop yield [19].

10.4.2 Development Spurred by the Internet of Things (IoT)

The Internet of Things (IoT) will have an impact on a wide range of industries and businesses, including manufacturing, health, communications, energy, and agriculture. In order to provide farmers with the decision-making instruments and automation technologies that seamlessly integrate goods, information, and services for increased productivity, quality, and profitability, the Internet of Things (IoT) is being used in agriculture [20].

10.5 Software Testing Overview

According to the ANSI/IEEE 1059 standard, testing is the process of examining a software item to find discrepancies between existing and necessary conditions (i.e., faults, bugs, errors), as well as to evaluate the software item's features. Program testing is the process and approach used to check that the software is error-free and that its actual findings match those anticipated by the criteria and guidelines. Finding faults, failures, gaps, and missing information features in compliance with specifications and standards is the goal of software testing [21]. (See Figure 10.6.)

There are two types of software testing:

- Manual testing: Software is tested manually, without using any scripts or automated tools.
- Automated testing: The tester uses another piece of software and writes scripts to test the software; this process is also referred to as "test automation."

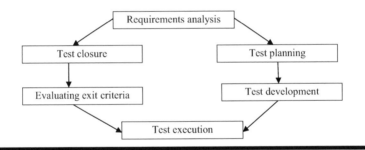

Figure 10.6 Phases of the software testing life cycle.

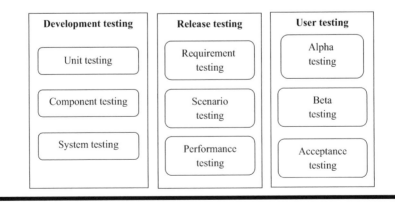

Figure 10.7 Testing level.

The software development life cycle (SDLC) has stages for testing software. It typically consists of the following discrete processes, as depicted in Figure 10.7: analysis of the test requirements, development of the test, execution of the test, evaluation of the exit criteria, and test closure [22].

10.6 Tools

Several of the most widely used AI-based test automation solutions.

10.6.1 Testim.io

This tool uses machine learning to create, run, and maintain automated tests. It places a focus on user interface, functional, and end-to-end testing. With repeated usage, the tool improves test suite stability and becomes more intelligent. To write complicated programming logic, testers can utilize JavaScript and HTML.

testim

10.6.2 Appvance

Utilizing artificial intelligence, Appvance creates test cases based on user behavior. The test portfolio thoroughly simulates end user behavior on live systems. As a result, it is entirely user-centric [23].

10.6.3 Test.ai

Regression testing is carried out using AI by Test.ai, a mobile test automation platform. It is helpful for obtaining performance information for it is more of a monitoring tool than a functional testing tool for your application.

△ **test.ai**

10.6.4 Functioned

Functional testing is done using machine learning. The capabilities of Functioned are equivalent to those of other products available on the market [24], including the ability to quickly build tests (without scripts), execute several tests in a short period of time, and do in-depth analysis.

10.7 Conclusion

Researchers' interest has been drawn to the convergence of machine learning and two software testing significant active research areas. Our methodical mapping surveyed research projects that supported software testing by employing ML algorithms. We think that mapping research offers a fair summary of scholars and practitioners attempting to comprehend this research. The Application of cutting-edge ML to software testing is a beneficial field with the intention of exploiting it or making a contribution to it. The majority of ML-based approaches presented in the primary research are anticipated to scale quite well, which is their principal advantage. As a result, we think they may be utilized to support ever more complicated testing activities. Another benefit is that few methods necessitate much human involvement. Upon reviewing our findings, we discovered that one need of ML algorithms is that testers must confirm that relevant data is accessible. Additionally, the data must be in a format that makes it easier for ML algorithms to learn from it. As a result, one drawback of several ML algorithms is that they require preprocessing of all the accessible data.

10.8 Future Work

Undoubtedly, AI will play a part in software usability testing in the future. Machine learning is about to revolutionize the way human usability testers conduct their work, and this period is just beginning. While self-learning software will not likely take on the role of people but will eliminate the necessity for many of the tiresome chores they currently perform at the moment, as long as people can grow to have faith that it is not trying to rule the globe. Future research can examine further software and AI fields. One potential field of AI is deep learning, which produces superior outcomes compared to conventional AI systems, that is, to determine the role that it can play in software testing.

References

1. Okereafor, K., & Adebola, O. (2020). Tackling the cybersecurity impacts of the coronavirus outbreak as a challenge to internet safety. *International Journal in IT & Engineering*, *8*(2).
2. Mohanty, S. P., Hughes, D. P., & Salathé, M. (2016). Using deep learning for image-based plant disease detection. *Frontiers in Plant Science*, *7*, 1419.
3. Prasanna Mohanty, S., Hughes, D., & Salathe, M. (2016). Using Deep Learning for Image-Based Plant Disease Detection. *arXiv e-prints*, arXiv-1604.
4. Khaliq, Z., Farooq, S. U., & Khan, D. A. (2022). Artificial Intelligence in Software Testing: Impact, Problems, Challenges and Prospect. *arXiv preprint arXiv:2201.05371*.
5. Sugali, K. (2021). Software Testing: Issues and Challenges of Artificial Intelligence & Machine Learning.
6. Berendt, B. (2019). AI for the Common Good?! Pitfalls, challenges, and ethics pen-testing. *Paladyn, Journal of Behavioral Robotics*, *10*(1), 44–65.
7. Felderer, M., & Ramler, R. (2021, January). Quality Assurance for AI-Based Systems: Overview and Challenges (Introduction to Interactive Session). In *International Conference on Software Quality* (pp. 33–42). Springer, Cham.
8. Sarathy, V., & Scheutz, M. (2018). MacGyver problems: Ai challenges for testing resourcefulness and creativity. *Advances in Cognitive Systems*, *6*, 31–44.
9. Azar, K. Z., Hossain, M. M., Vafaei, A., Al Shaikh, H., Mondol, N. N., Rahman, F., ... & Farahmandi, F. (2022). Fuzz, Penetration, and AI Testing for SoC Security Verification: Challenges and Solutions. *Cryptology ePrint Archive*.
10. Raghothaman, B. (2021). Training, Testing and Validation Challenges for Next Generation AI/ML-Based Intelligent Wireless Networks. *IEEE Wireless Communications*, *28*(6), 5–6.
11. Xu, J., Yang, P., Xue, S., Sharma, B., Sanchez-Martin, M., Wang, F., ... & Parikh, B. (2019). Translating cancer genomics into precision medicine with artificial intelligence: applications, challenges and future perspectives. *Human Genetics*, *138*(2), 109–124.
12. Stahlke, S. N., & Mirza-Babaei, P. (2018). User testing without the user: Opportunities and challenges of an AI-driven approach in games user research. *Computers in Entertainment (CIE)*, *16*(2), 1–18.
13. Lehmann, L. S. (2021). Ethical Challenges of Integrating AI into Healthcare. In *Artificial Intelligence in Medicine* (pp. 1–6). Cham: Springer International Publishing.
14. Cabot, J., Burgueno, L., Clarisó, R., Daniel, G., Perianez-Pascual, J., & Rodriguez-Echeverria, R. (2021, June). Testing challenges for NLP-intensive bots. In *2021 IEEE/ACM Third International Workshop on Bots in Software Engineering (BotSE)* (pp. 31–34). IEEE.
15. Khorram, F., Mottu, J. M., & Sunyé, G. (2020, October). Challenges & opportunities in low-code testing. In *Proceedings of the 23rd ACM/IEEE International Conference on Model Driven Engineering Languages and Systems: Companion Proceedings* (pp. 1–10).
16. Zöldy, M., Szalay, Z., & Tihanyi, V. (2020). Challenges in homologation process of vehicles with artificial intelligence. *Transport*, *35*(4), 447–453.
17. Kurshan, E., Shen, H., & Chen, J. (2020, October). Towards self-regulating AI: challenges and opportunities of AI model governance in financial services. In *Proceedings of the First ACM International Conference on AI in Finance* (pp. 1–8).

18. Raz, A. K., Guariniello, C., Blasch, E., & Mian, Z. (2021). *An Overview of Systems Engineering Challenges for AI-Enabled Aerospace Systems*. AIAA SciTech.

19. Ajayi, A. I., Awopegba, O., Owolabi, E. O., & Ajala, A. (2021). Coverage of HIV testing among pregnant women in Nigeria: progress, challenges and opportunities. *Journal of Public Health*, *43*(1), e77-e84.

20. Shevadronov, A. S. (2020). Development of Methods for Integrating Expert Systems into Local Onboard Aircraft Network Computing Systems to Response the Challenges of AI Integration. In *Наука, технологии и бизнес* (pp. 91–94).

21. Knauss, A., Schroder, J., Berger, C., & Eriksson, H. (2017, May). Software-related challenges of testing automated vehicles. In *2017 IEEE/ACM 39th International Conference on Software Engineering Companion (ICSE-C)* (pp. 328–330). IEEE.

22. Stoica, I., Song, D., Popa, R. A., Patterson, D., Mahoney, M. W., Katz, R., ... & Abbeel, P. (2017). A Berkeley view of systems challenges for ai. *arXiv preprint arXiv:1712.05855*.

23. Liu, T. (2021). Grand Challenges in AI in Radiology. *Frontiers in Radiology*, *1*, 629992.

24. Asatiani, A., Malo, P., Nagbøl, P. R., Penttinen, E., Rinta-Kahila, T., & Salovaara, A. (2020). Challenges of explaining the behavior of black-box AI systems. *MIS Quarterly Executive*, *19*(4), 259–278.

Chapter 11

Software Quality Prediction by CatBoost
Feed-Forward Neural Network in Software Engineering

Sudharson D.,[1] Kailas P. S.,[2] K. Vignesh,[3]
Senthilnathan T.,[4] Poornima V.,[2] and Shreya Vijay[2]

[1]Assistant Professor, Department of AI&DS, Kumaraguru College of Technology, Coimbatore, Tamil Nadu, India

[2]Department of AI&DS, Kumaraguru College of Technology, Coimbatore, Tamil Nadu, India

[3]Thiagarajar School of Management, Madurai, Tamil Nadu, India

[4]CHRIST (Deemed to be University), Bangalore, India

11.1 Introduction

One of the crucial factors to address in real-time software development is software quality improvement. All the steps involved in software quality improvement are related to software engineering (SE). The software development life cycle (SDLC) [1, 2] ensures that the complexity of the software is reduced, and that the software product is timely delivered within the defined budget. Multiple quality parameters can be streamlined through software engineering (SE) by implementing systematic and measurable procedures. These will also ensure that multiple tasks are completed

DOI: 10.1201/9781032624983-11

on time with better quality. Sectors such as networking, software maintenance, graphical user interface, include many software applications. These need to be designed efficiently to ensure software quality.

Nowadays, many quality ensuring aspects in SE are still unable to achieve better efficiency, which results in the failure to meet industry demands. Multiple factors influence this software's quality such as mode of development, software environment, software process, and software plan [3, 4]. The efficiency and quality aspects of software will be different with respect to geographical locations and tools used for development. Even more, there are multiple requirements to analyze the efficiency of the software before their deployment in the client's server or workstations. One of the best ways is to assess the software's efficiency during their implementation and testing phase. However, this research specializes in predicting software efficiency [4] using CatBoost and feed-forward neural network [5] on a machine learning framework.

The motto of this research is to implement enhanced feed-forward neural network to predict software performance with the support of CatBoost. This is achieved as follows:

- To develop a predictive and efficient machine learning framework, this chapter used the data PROMISE Software Engineering Repository [6]. This real dataset is trained and implemented using machine learning for devising an effective prediction model.
- To analyze the various features in software quality such as design complexity, time to develop the software, mean time between failure (MTBF), software recovery time, lines of code, and quality (success or failure) [3, 7–10], this proposed method used CatBoost, a type of ensemble algorithm that reduces the time spent on tuning the parameter since CatBoost yields high precision with default parameters in association with a feed-forward neural network.

This chapter is curated in such a way that the literature review is presented in Section 11.2, which contains the research carried out in terms of existing work. Section 11.3 narrates the method of implementation. The results are derived in Section 11.4. Finally, Section 11.5 depicts the conclusion with respect to the results.

11.2 Literature Review

This section narrates about the parameters of software quality and its influence on software efficiency in software engineering [11]. The impact of machine learning in the streams of software efficiency and quality is also depicted in the survey.

11.2.1 Parameters That Influence Software Quality

Multiple parameters influence the quality of the software. The primary factor affecting software quality is software efficiency. The history of errors that software has resulted in is a prerequisite knowledge that needs to be analyzed before designing any software. The second aspect is related to the mode of development of the software. This is important as every software mode may involve multiple software tools or programming languages. All frameworks have their own characteristics and features that cannot be compared on a linear scale. The other important aspect is the developer or development team that leads the entire plan. These are some of the important parameters that decide the software quality directly or indirectly.

11.2.1.1 Software Efficiency

Software efficiency is another key factor that critically decides the quality of the software. Software is said to be reliable if it is free from errors. When software produces undesired result, even with minimum time delay, then it cannot be called reliable. Due to undefined or irrelevant inputs, the software may crash at times, taking a longer time to recover. The time taken by the software to recover from a software crash is called the mean time to recover (MTTR) [12]. Mean time between failures (MTBF) should be reduced to ensure maximum software quality.

11.2.1.2 Mode of Software Development

To develop any software successfully, the mode that is used needs to be well equipped. The development could be implemented using common off the shelf (COTS) or rapid application development (RAD) or by prototyping a design through any programming language. In major cases, prototyping models are implemented with limited features initially. Software development done with the concept of prototyping may involve any of the programming languages as they are developed from scratch. Documentation in any of these models may be of higher complexity and remain generic. RAD and COTS are implemented when the final software product is well-defined in the documentation. If the incremental framework is correct, then it will ensure the exact objectives are met as requested by the client. The software needs to be developed such in a way that it ensures maximum efficiency to achieve quality.

11.2.1.3 Developer or Developer Team

The developer's interest is the key factor in developing the software. Otherwise, it will be difficult to ensure the quality of the software. Subject matter experts (SMEs) should ensure that all the functionalities are met in the software product. Functional testing is done to ensure that all the features are executed in the developed software product. Furthermore, developers have different exposures and abilities. Developing methods and coding skills are different for each developer. Few developers are flexible enough to collaborate in a team, while others prefer other ways. Nonfunctional testing is performed in accordance with the development team to ensure the efficiency of the software.

11.2.2 *Machine Learning Framework*

Machine learning is one of the most intelligent technologies that supports the ability of a program to learn from past experiences and that helps in solving many real-time problems. Machine learning (ML) aims to produce results with high accuracy. Machine learning has been implemented in several areas and domains for quality improvements. Software quality prediction with support of machine learning framework is successful in terms of high precision and accuracy. Hence this proposed research is concentrated on the prediction of software quality using the enhanced feed-forward neural network machine learning framework with support of CatBoost. Boosting is a strategy to enhance the algorithms used in machine learning to achieve maximum accuracy. CatBoost is predominantly a categorical boosting framework. This was introduced by Yandex in 2017. CatBoost has resolved many real-time issues that were not completely addressed by other boosting algorithms.

Meanwhile, this study used feed-forward neural network (FFNN) in prediction, which is one of most powerful algorithms in the artificial neural network (ANN) stream [13]. This has yielded prominent results in software quality research areas. FFNN is a nature-inspired neural network curated from the concept of a neuron of the brain. It consists of a pack of outputs from a defined set of inputs in multiple layers. Hence this proposed research involves the combined model of FFNN and CatBoost to improve the accuracy of the software quality prediction of software developed using programming languages, common off the shelf (COTS), and rapid application development (RAD).

If each neuron is assigned a weight, then it can be mathematically represented in a matrix. The weighted matrix of a neural network is given by

$$
W = \begin{bmatrix} w(1,1) & w(1,2) & . & . & . & w(1,n-1) & w(1,n) \\ w(2,1) & w(2,2) & . & . & . & w(2,n-1) & w(2,n) \\ . & . & . & . & . & . & . \\ . & . & . & . & . & . & . \\ w(n,1) & w(n,2) & . & . & . & w(n,n-1) & w(n,n) \end{bmatrix} \qquad X = \begin{bmatrix} x(1) \\ x(2) \\ . \\ . \\ x(n) \end{bmatrix}
$$

W represents weights assigned to each neuron, and X represents the inputs to the network.

$$a1 = w(1,1) * x(1) + w(1,2) * x(2) + \ldots\ldots + w(1,n-1) * x(n-1) + w(1,n) * x(n)$$

$$a2 = w(2,1) * x(1) + w(2,2) * x(2) + \ldots\ldots + w(2,n-1) * x(n-1)$$
$$+ w(2,n) * x(n)$$

$$a(n) = w(n,1) * x(1) + w(n,2) * x(2) + \ldots\ldots + w(n,n-1) * x(n-1)$$
$$+ w(n,n) * x(n)$$

The overall pre-activation of a layer is given here, where b is the bias, and W is the weights assigned.

$$a = W * x + b$$

Conceptually, a perceptron in a feed-forward network (FFN) is illustrated as shown in Figure 11.1.

Overall loss is denoted by $L = L\left(\hat{y}_n, F\right)$.

The $\hat{y}_n$ is the ith output, from function F that computes the matrix multiplication, summation, and overall activation.

The goal is to reduce the overall loss to improve prediction, i.e., $\arg\min(L)$.

CatBoost, or Categorical Boosting, is an open-source framework designed and developed by Yandex. Mainly used in regression and classification, this framework is widely adopted in recommended systems, in forecasting, and, in some cases, even in personal assistants. Mathematically, the target estimates of the ith categorical variable of the kth element of I, where I denotes the data or document in general, can be represented as

$$\hat{y}^i = \frac{\sum_{x_i \in} I_k \ x_k^i = x_k^j \ y_i + ap}{\sum_{x_i \in} I_k \ x_k^i = x_k^j \ + a}; \ if \ I_k = \{x_j : \sigma(j) < \sigma(i)\}$$

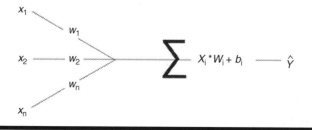

Figure 11.1   Forward pass in a FFNN.

The output denoted by $\hat{y}_i$, in a general use case, is the predicted target class after boosting is applied and overall loss L is reduced. The algorithm is found to be effective with default parameters, thereby reducing the need for further optimization through hyperparameter turning.

11.2.3 *Analysis With Respect to Existing Work*

This module analyzes and compares both the proposed and existing frameworks of software quality in software engineering. Table 11.1 summarizes the articles that was executed for software performance evaluation. Two experiments used a statistical framework to evaluate the software's performance for software developed using linear programming. Deep learning source code modeling is also deployed to evaluate the software quality where this model is not applicable for rapid application development (RAD). Another method used decision tree without CatBoost; this proposed framework is deployed with CatBoost with a feed-forward neural network, resulting in curating the enhanced FFNN. In addition, the proposed work used datasets from PROMISE Software Engineering Repository. The dataset includes parameters such as lines of code, cyclomatic complexity, essential complexity, design complexity,

Table 11.1 Comparative Study With Earlier and Proposed Work

Titles	Frameworks	Methods
JAGS module for applications. involving the piecewise exponential distribution	Errors were made to fit a Bayesian model and piecewise exponential (PE) distribution	Statistical framework
Deep learning for source code modelling and generation: models, applications, and challenges	Lines of source code are analyzed using deep learning modules	Deep learning source code model.
Decision tree model for software development teams	Lines of source code are analyzed using deep learning modules	Decision tree without CatBoost
CatBoost-feed-forward neural network for predicting quality in software engineering	Detect software quality in software engineering	Used nature-inspired machine learning (CatBoost-FFNN) to detect software quality

Halstead and McCabe metrics, time estimator, unique software ID, time to deployment, test plan time, cohesion rate, coupling rate, and so on.

11.3 Methodology or Framework

Figure 11.2 depict the framework in this research work. Primarily, we used the dataset from PROMISE Software Engineering Repository. All the filtering and implementations are done using KNIME analytics.

11.3.1 Exploratory Analysis

Prior to creating a predictive model, one should understand the dataset by exploratory analysis. In this exploratory analysis, it is intended to find answers to some questions:

- What are the factors that decide whether the software will be a quality one?
- How to predict that software will be efficient and error free in future?

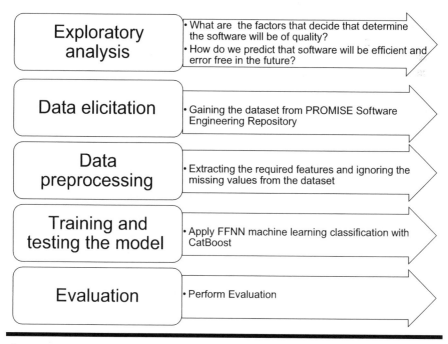

Figure 11.2 Framework for implementation.

Some other important aspects to be noted during data elicitation includes the aspects of missing values, certain features with irrelevant values or outliers, response feature and its balance, and finally the distribution of the data points with respect to the quality aspects.

11.3.2 Data Preprocessing

The missing values in numerical and categorical features must be changed accordingly. In the case of the categorical features, the NAs (not applicable) confronted were swapped with the mode of that aspect. In the case of categorical features that were one-hot encoded, each of the distinct categories in a particular feature was converted to a numerical field. For numerical features, the NAs were replaced on a case-by-case basis. Features like "functional units, number of versions" were replaced with the median as it handles the presence of outliers, unlike mean imputation. The test set used has 127,886 attributes for each of the models.

11.3.3 Feature Engineering

In feature engineering, the motto is to clean and organize the data since it is still unprocessed. The process involves removing the data that will be unclear, missing, incomplete, and irrelevant. Data such as the software that it belongs to, time of development, and developer information will not be included in analyzing software quality. Hence, these data can be ignored, and the extracted features can be processed for prediction of software quality (success or failure). When a software product is in the highest band, then it can be understood that the software is of higher quality.

Figure 11.3 depicts the relationship between software quality (success or failure) and the PROMISE software result. Software quality tests are done with respect

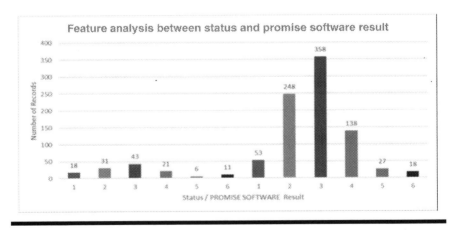

Figure 11.3 **Feature analysis between status and PROMISE software result.**

Table 11.2   PROMISE Software Quality Band With Levels

Band	1	2	3	4	5	6
Software efficiency	Poor	Low	Moderate	Convincing	Proficient	Excellent
Status	Failure	Failure	Failure	Failure	Success	Success

to the conditions given by the Software Process Improvement and Capability Determination Standards Council to ensure the quality of the software. Table 11.2 depicts the bands with their quality level. Band 1 includes software whose efficiency is poor. Band 2 includes software that is low in response time and classified as low. Band 3 includes software whose response time is satisfactory but does not produce accurate results; hence it is classified as moderate. Band 4 includes software whose response time is effective and achieves results. Band 5 includes software that is proficient such that its efficiency and results are proficient. Band 6 includes software whose efficiency and result are more precise and faster.

The combination of features among status (success or failure) for software development mode with respect to rapid application development, common off the shelf, and software developed using programming languages in the case of a prototyping model is shown in Figure 11.4. In total, 452 software applications were analyzed for this process. Figure 11.4 shows that 132 pieces of software were developed using rapid application development, 176 software applications were developed using common off the shelf, and 144 software applications were developed using programming languages either as prototypes or as minimum usable prototypes (MUP). It shows that almost 68.14% were developed using rapid application development and common off the shelf. But less than 32% is spread across software built using programming languages either as a prototype or as MUP.

Software applications were developed using rapid application development (RAD) and common off the shelf (COTS), which are classified as non-prototype units. These non-prototype units are built in a shorter time, and they have a higher coupling rate. The software applications curated from scratch are termed "programming language models"; hence they include a higher cohesion rate and lower coupling rate.

11.3.4 Training and Testing the Model

Training of the dataset is done well in advance to ensure the predictions. The predictive algorithm is given with a training dataset for iterations. Cross-validation testing is implemented as it excludes the complication of overfitting. Reducing overfitting makes the predictions general and precise. Data that need to be tested is different from the training dataset.

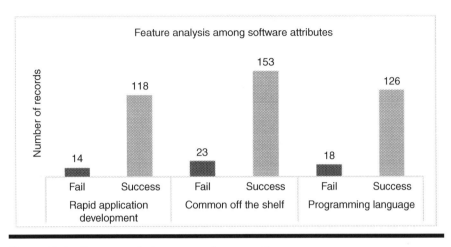

Figure 11.4 **Feature analysis among software attributes.**

CatBoost is used on the dataset to boost FFNN algorithm (CatBoost-FFNN) to determine the accuracy of the predictive model. The training dataset for the predictive process is generalized to ensure that it becomes a general classifier with default parameters. *Kfold* cross-validation is applied in this proposed work to avoid the problem of overfitting. Here, tenfold cross-validation is deployed that divides data into ten subsets. For precise accuracy *K*-10 folds are re-deployed in training. In the case of testing, onefold is employed.

11.3.5 Evaluation

This proposed work evaluates the CatBoost-FFNN performance in prediction. The accuracy of the software quality is the benchmark. This shows the accuracy in classifying the software quality as either success or failure.

11.4 Results

This section portrays the results from CatBoost-FFNN prediction in software quality as either successful or failure. The prediction accuracy is 93.62% in classifying the efficiency as either successful or failure. By implementing the CatBoost-FFNN model, this research work can estimate and predict software quality before the entire phase of testing is implemented. If the software quality is predicted to be a failure, then the design phase needs to be analyzed and changed accordingly to improve the software quality.

11.5 Conclusion

The objective of this proposed research work was achieved, and it was able to predict the software quality before it was deployed. Feed-forward neural network along with CatBoost has achieved 93.62% accuracy in predicting software quality as a success or failure. This prediction helps the developers to understand and change the framework in the design or implementation phase. If a software's quality is predicted as a failure in advance, it helps the entire team in deciding on a better plan to develop the software on time with successful quality.

References

1. S. Aleem, L. F. Capretz, and F. Ahmed, "Game development software engineering process life cycle: a systematic review," *J. Softw. Eng. Res. Dev.*, vol. 4, no. 1, p. 6, Dec. 2016, doi: 10.1186/s40411-016-0032-7

2. M. Barenkamp, J. Rebstadt, and O. Thomas, "Applications of AI in classical software engineering," *AI Perspect.*, vol. 2, no. 1, pp. 1–15, 2020, doi: 10.1186/s42467-020-00005-4

3. X. Liu, Y. Zhang, X. Yu, and Z. Liu, "A software quality quantifying method based on preference and benchmark data," Proc.–2018 IEEE/ACIS 19th Int. Conf. Softw. Eng. Artif. Intell. Netw. Parallel/Distributed Comput. SNPD 2018, pp. 375–379, 2018, doi: 10.1109/SNPD.2018.8441145

4. A. Yamashita, "Experiences from performing software quality evaluations via combining benchmark-based metrics analysis, software visualization, and expert assessment," in 2015 IEEE International Conference on Software Maintenance and Evolution (ICSME), Sep. 2015, pp. 421–428, doi: 10.1109/ICSM.2015.7332493

5. R. Kiran and D. L. Naik, "Novel sensitivity method for evaluating the first derivative of the feed-forward neural network outputs," *J. Big Data*, vol. 8, no. 1, p. 88, Dec. 2021, doi: 10.1186/s40537-021-00480-4

6. M. Autili, I. Malavolta, A. Perucci, G. L. Scoccia, and R. Verdecchia, "Software engineering techniques for statically analyzing mobile apps: research trends, characteristics, and potential for industrial adoption," *J. Internet Serv. Appl.*, vol. 12, no. 1, p. 3, Dec. 2021, doi: 10.1186/s13174-021-00134-x

7. G. Huang et al., "Evaluation of CatBoost method for prediction of reference evapotranspiration in humid regions," *J. Hydrol.*, vol. 574, pp. 1029–1041, 2019, doi: 10.1016/j.jhydrol.2019.04.085

8. A. Samat, E. Li, P. Du, S. Liu, Z. Miao, and W. Zhang, "CatBoost for RS Image Classification With Pseudo Label Support From Neighbor Patches-Based Clustering," *IEEE Geosci. Remote Sens. Lett.*, vol. 19, pp. 1–5, 2022, doi: 10.1109/LGRS.2020.3038771

9. S. Lessmann, B. Baesens, C. Mues, and S. Pietsch, "Benchmarking Classification Models for Software Defect Prediction: A Proposed Framework and Novel Findings," *IEEE Trans. Softw. Eng.*, vol. 34, no. 4, pp. 485–496, Jul. 2008, doi: 10.1109/TSE.2008.35

10. J. P. Correia and J. Visser, "Benchmarking Technical Quality of Software Products," in 2008 15th Working Conference on Reverse Engineering, Oct. 2008, pp. 297–300, doi: 10.1109/WCRE.2008.16

11. H. Sun et al., "Domain-Specific Software Benchmarking Methodology Based on Fuzzy Set Theory and AHP," in 2010 International Conference on Computational Intelligence and Software Engineering, Dec. 2010, pp. 1–4, doi: 10.1109/CISE.2010.5676892

12. M. Engelhardt and L. J. Bain, "On the Mean Time between Failures for Repairable Systems," *IEEE Trans. Reliab.*, vol. 35, no. 4, pp. 419–422, 1986, doi: 10.1109/TR.1986.4335491

13. A. Khraisat and A. Alazab, "A critical review of intrusion detection systems in the internet of things: techniques, deployment strategy, validation strategy, attacks, public datasets and challenges," *Cybersecurity*, vol. 4, no. 1, 2021, doi: 10.1186/s42400-021-00077-7

Chapter 12

Software Security

Tawseef Ahmed Teli,[1] Alwi M. Bamhdi,[2]
Faheem Syeed Masoodi,[3] and Vahida Akhter[1]

[1]Department of Higher Education, J&K, India

[2]College of Computing in Al-Qunfudah, Umm Al-Qura University, Kingdom of Saudi Arabia

[3]Department of Computer Science, University of Kashmir, Srinagar, India

12.1 Introduction

In the modern world, as technologies advanced in the development of software, software threats have also increased manifold. Every software is vulnerable to several software threats. These threats may lead to software failure, malfunctioning of software, and even erroneous results. To protect software from these attacks, the concept of software security was introduced.

Software security is a branch of software engineering that refers to the design and development of software in such a way that it may function correctly despite various kinds of malicious attacks [1]. The computer security problem is closely connected to the software security problem. Software security aims to secure the software without the need for any extra security layer and to train the users of the software to use it in a secure way to avoid being attacked by malicious users [2] and infected software. Once the software is infected, its integrity, reliability, authentication, and availability is compromised, thus making the software inappropriate for use. A better way to counter software attacks is to take a proactive approach. The most common threat to software is from internet-based software applications.

DOI: 10.1201/9781032624983-12

12.1.1 Software Security Process

To inculcate security in software, it is important to consider security during the SDLC. The researchers in [3] studied various approaches for the software security process. One method is to consider seven operations that include security requirements, penetration testing, etc., for the design and development of secure software. Another approach is to create a team software process to develop robust and secure software. It emphasizes creating highly professional teams for the design of robust secure software for the best results. One more approach to the software security process is appropriate and effective guidance for information security (AEGIS), starting with an evaluation of hardware assets and interdependencies and followed by risk analysis that explores associated weaknesses, threats, and risks.

Software security in the work done by authors in [4] used a technique known as software security vulnerabilities, commonly known as software patching. It is a difficult task to use patching in complex software. The researchers in [4] identified various challenges in software security patching and proposed various solutions. The authors provided an all-inclusive insight into the gap between the solutions and challenges in the software security process. Software security is a diverse mechanism that involves the identification, obtaining, testing, installation, and verification of security patches for software systems.

12.2 Challenges and Requirements

Some researchers have emphasized clearly defining and modeling security requirements [5]. The issues with implementing these techniques are the complexity of and the gap between the current deployment methods and the trivial process [6].

12.2.1 Security Requirements Modeling

Almost all present-day applications face serious threats in terms of security due to the availability of technologies [7]. In previous times, security issues were only found in network-based applications in the network infrastructure layer. However, due to the increasing use of networks and internet-based applications like cloud computing, software as a service, etc., significant vulnerabilities are being found by attackers in the application layer itself. As a result of this, consideration of the application security layer emerged as an important and foremost task in the software development process.

There are many techniques for security requirements, as shown in Figure 12.1. Modeling is one of the most important processes for specifying and analyzing security requirements. A well developed model is one that helps to inculcate security in the software during the software development life cycle. The model can further analyze the correctness of the implemented system by verifying the conformity of the

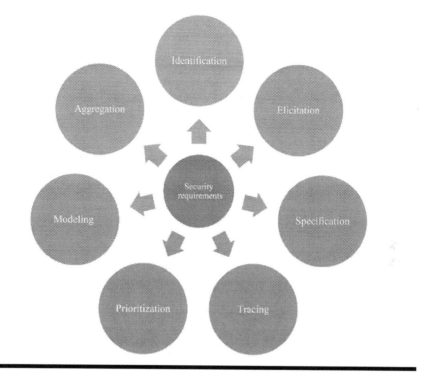

Figure 12.1 Security requirements techniques.

system to its requirement specifications. There are several modeling languages and formalisms. The most widely used is unified modelling language (UML). A useful models is Goal-Oriented Requirement Language (GRL), which is used to deal with non-functional requirements of the system like security and performance [7]. Another model is SecureUML, an extension of UML that is used to specify role-based access control to the software system and is used to implement authorization requirements in software systems.

12.2.2 Validation Requirements Modeling

Software faults or security-related issues are very crucial as they may have serious impacts like loss of property or life. Therefore, the development and testing of safety-critical software technologies are very important. Validation of software security is an important task to make the software more reliable and robust. Researchers in [8] focused on testing safety for software systems using AADL. This defines various components of software like data, subprograms, etc. and components of platforms like memory and finally hybrid components like systems. To map security and safety with software, the authors in [8] focused on adding properties and design of the system as per appropriate modeling patterns. To model the system with security and safety, one must model partitioned architecture followed by the specification of security levels for each software partition, followed further by the specification of a security classification for each partition and finally defining faults and fault handling and fault propagation.

12.3 Software Security Vulnerabilities

In the modern technologically advanced world, software like machine learning libraries is widely used for finding hidden patterns from data in several domains like image classification, pattern recognition, speech recognition, and many more [9, 10]. These machine-learning libraries are vulnerable to various types of security problems and may cause catastrophic results. It has been found in recent years that the number of errors, bugs, and failures found in different software systems is related to the application programming interface usage of machine learning libraries. To deal with such problems, one must answer some basic questions:

- What are the various kinds of security vulnerabilities that can be present in machine learning libraries?
- What are the sources of various security susceptibilities found in machine learning libraries?
- What symptoms are associated with the security vulnerabilities of machine learning libraries?
- Is there any solution to the security vulnerabilities associated with machine learning libraries?
- What efforts are needed to address these machine learning security vulnerabilities?

Figure 12.2 gives a description of vulnerability detection techniques.

12.3.1 Security Automation in Software-Defined Networks

To automate the security process for networks such as cloud computing, IoT, etc., one of the promising solutions is software-defined networking [11]. Basically, the SDN was introduced to manage complex networks with less human intervention so that the number of errors could be minimized. Later, the researchers found the application of SDN in providing automation of security for complex software systems. The automation of security is measured using various qualitative parameters like auto-healing, auto-adaptation, auto-configuration, and auto-optimization. SDN is the latest networking representation in which furthering hardware is detached from switch decisions.

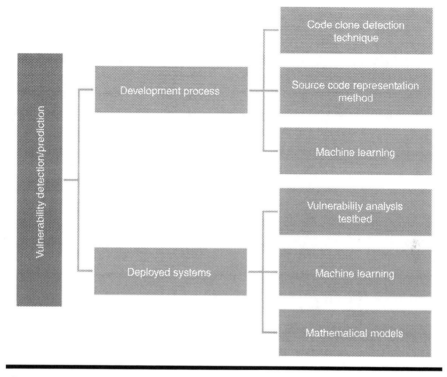

Figure 12.2 **Vulnerability detection.**

12.3.2 Security Threat-Oriented Requirements Engineering Methodology

Researchers in [12] provided a ten-step sequential step procedure that gives an efficient, reliable, and methodical technique for engineering and reporting safety requirements for any standalone or web-based software application and is applicable from the initial stages of software development. They provide steps for consideration of security concerns of various users of the software system, along with identification of threats and risks associated with various threats, and thus help in effective and efficient requirement engineering for system security. Security requirement engineering calls for a number of steps:

Step 1. Identification of goals for system security
Step 2. Various users of the system as per the priority
Step 3. Goals to be accepted as final goals
Step 4. Identification of assets associated with the system
Step 5. Analysis of security attacks

■ Attacking point
■ Belief point
■ Conjecture point
■ Dependency point

Step 6. Identify various threats to the system and categorize these threats into various classes
Step 7. Analyze various risks associated with threats as per priority
Step 8. Security requirement engineering and validation
Step 9. SRSD

12.4 Environment and System Security

Software security is accomplished by considering several measures during the SDLC and in software testing processes. Some of the measures are:

■ Defining security requirements for the system,
■ Using coding practices that are secure,
■ Analysis of static code blocks,
■ Testing the software for penetration attacks,
■ Access control limitation.

Information security includes a variety of measures in SDLC:

■ Requirements definition
■ Secure coding practices
■ Static code analysis
■ Penetration testing
■ Limiting access control

System security is a combative and continuous technique that begins with a review and changes slowly into security maintenance.

12.4.1 Levels of Security

Software threats are evolving day by day in terms of complexity and volume. It is important to evolve the protection across all-web-based applications including servers, databases, platforms, services, etc. However, the software security measures to be applied depend on the scope of the software company offering the software as a service as well as on its financial capabilities. As per the scope and financial capabilities, different levels of software security are available.

12.4.2 Level I—Minimal Protection

This level of security is applicable to companies that offer small software services to their clients. The security measures usually include configured firewall protection along with antivirus software.

12.4.3 Level II—Advanced Protection

This level of security is suitable for corporate networks to provide security against non-targeted attacks like malware, spoofing, spamming, etc. Midsized software service providers fall victim to such attacks and need protection that includes:

- Email security: This filters all the incoming email messages for malware, spam etc., so that the services offered by the company remain secure.
- Network segmentation: Various divisions of the company are separated and then connected using firewalls so that the malicious code does not travel from one segment to another.
- Intrusion detection/intrusion prevention system: The aim of this kind of security is to log information about every activity to look for possible security attacks, block them, and stop them from spreading.

12.4.4 Level III—Maximal Protection

This level of protection is suitable for large corporate networks to ensure protection against targeted attacks like phishing, advanced malware, spear, etc. The security requirements to protect against such attacks are:

- Endpoint security: Limiting access to products by various devices like laptops, desktops, smartphones etc. This kind of protection is ensured by installing security software on the server within the corporate network along with the installation of security software on each client device.
- Data loss prevention: This kind of security prevents the loss or exposure of sensitive, confidential, and personal data like passwords, PINs, card numbers, etc. to unknown persons.
- Security information and event management: This kind of security keeps a log of every activity that takes place in the corporate network and then reports the log to the security administrator so that any malicious activity may be tracked and blocked.

12.5 Cloud Security

We see that cloud computing is becoming increasingly popular with each passing day. Cloud computing provides several services like PaaS, SaaS, and IaaS. Various

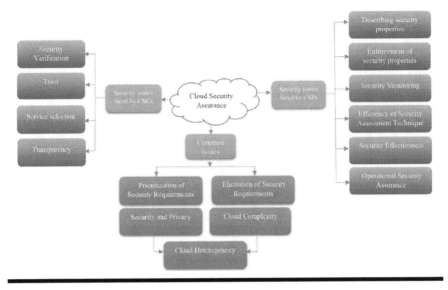

Figure 12.3   Cloud security issues.

companies offering cloud services should give proper attention to protecting cloud assets. Nowadays most cloud users store their confidential data on cloud storage. Safeguarding the data of millions of users is a big challenge for security providers. To provide cloud security, different strategies are used depending on the model of the cloud (Figure 12.3).

12.5.1 Infrastructure-as-a-Service (IaaS) and Platform-as-a-Service (PaaS)

To provide IaaS and PaaS security, the best option is to select a trustworthy service provider, get the services offered by them, and then use an adequate level of control for virtual machines offered by them and monitor all traffic for malicious activities.

12.5.2 Software-as-a-Service (SaaS)

In this service, the vendors are responsible for building, hosting, and finally providing security for the software. The company's responsibility is only to focus on controlling access to applications through proper user access control.

12.5.3 Software Testing Metrics

The most important task of any software service provider is to measure how secure their software is. Software with less security is of no use no matter how useful its features are. The five metrics that every software company should track for appropriate security are:

- Apps covered by security,
- The time needed to resolve vulnerabilities,
- Flaw creation rate,
- Number of automated tests and tooling,
- Application block rate.

Apart from applications in varied fields of cryptographic networks [13–16], navigation [17], and, most importantly, deep learning techniques with applications in secure healthcare [18–22], many ML techniques could be used in every facet of secure software processes from threat detection, penetration detection, threat avoidance, etc.

12.6 Conclusion

Software is the single most impactful and significant tool out there in the age of information. No conglomerate, business, or industry can work without software. It is present everywhere, making it vulnerable to threats and attacks. In order to cope with these security issues, software must follow and meet security requirements. Several traditional tools and techniques are available to provide various phases to design and test different facets of the software security process. However, many tools focus on a single component. There are many modeling techniques to come up with security requirements, but current methods are limited in the sense of correctness, validation, effectiveness, evaluation, etc.

References

[1] G. Mcgraw, "Building Security In," 2004. [Online]. Available: www.computer.org/security/

[2] A. Shukla, B. Katt, L. O. Nweke, P. K. Yeng, and G. K. Weldehawaryat, "System security assurance: A systematic literature review," *Computer Science Review*, vol. 45. Elsevier Ireland Ltd, Aug. 01, 2022. doi: 10.1016/j.cosrev.2022.100496.

[3] R. A. Khan, S. U. Khan, M. Alzahrani, and M. Ilyas, "Security Assurance Model of Software Development for Global Software Development Vendors," *IEEE Access*, vol. 10, pp. 58458–58487, 2022, doi: 10.1109/ACCESS.2022.3178301

[4] N. Dissanayake, A. Jayatilaka, M. Zahedi, and M. A. Babar, "Software Security Patch Management —A Systematic Literature Review of Challenges, Approaches, Tools and Practices," Dec. 2020, [Online]. Available: http://arxiv.org/abs/2012.00544

[5]   M. Ouedraogo, H. Mouratidis, D. Khadraoui, E. Dubois, An agent-based system to support assurance of security requirements, in 2010 Fourth International Conference on Secure Software Integration and Reliability Improvement, IEEE, 2010, pp. 78–87.

[6]   K. Taguchi, N. Yoshioka, T. Tobita, H. Kaneko, Aligning security requirements and security assurance using the common criteria, in: 2010 Fourth International Conference on Secure Software Integration and Reliability Improvement, IEEE, 2010, pp. 69–77.

[7]   A. H. Seh et al., "Hybrid computational modeling for web application security assessment," *Computers, Materials and Continua*, vol. 70, no. 1, pp. 469–489, 2021, doi: 10.32604/cmc.2022.019593

[8]   J. Delange, L. Pautet, and P. Feiler, Validating safety and security requirements for partitioned architectures, in: Reliable Software Technologies–Ada-Europe 2009: 14th Ada-Europe International Conference, Brest, France, June 8–12, 2009. Proceedings 14 (pp. 30–43). Springer Berlin Heidelberg.

[9]   N. S. Harzevili, J. Shin, J. Wang, and S. Wang, "Characterizing and Understanding Software Security Vulnerabilities in Machine Learning Libraries," Mar. 2022, [Online]. Available: http://arxiv.org/abs/2203.06502

[10] N. S. Harzevili, J. Shin, J. Wang, and S. Wang, "Characterizing and Understanding Software Security Vulnerabilities in Machine Learning Libraries," Mar. 2022, [Online]. Available: http://arxiv.org/abs/2203.06502

[11] N. M. Yungaicela-Naula, C. Vargas-Rosales, J. A. Pérez-Díaz, and M. Zareei, "Towards security automation in Software Defined Networks," Computer Communications, vol. 183. Elsevier B.V., pp. 64–82, Feb. 01, 2022. doi: 10.1016/j.comcom.2021.11.014.

[12] M. T. J. Ansari, D. Pandey, and M. Alenezi, "STORE: Security Threat Oriented Requirements Engineering Methodology," *Journal of King Saud University– Computer and Information Sciences*, vol. 34, no. 2, pp. 191–203, Feb. 2022, doi: 10.1016/j.jksuci.2018.12.005.

[13] T. A. Teli, R. Yousuf, and D. A. Khan, "MANET Routing Protocols Attacks and Mitigation Techniques: A Review." *International Journal of Mechanical Engineering*, vol. 7, no. 2, pp. 1468–1478, 2022.

[14] T. A. Teli, F. Masoodi, and R. Yousuf, "Security Concerns and Privacy Preservation in Blockchain based IoT Systems: Opportunities and Challenges," 2020. [Online]. Available: https://ssrn.com/abstract=3769572

[15] F. Masoodi, A. M. Bamhdi, and T. A. Teli, "Machine Learning for Classification analysis of Intrusion Detection on NSL-KDD Dataset," 2021.

[16] T. A. Teli, F. S. Masoodi, and A. M. Bahmdi, HIBE: Hierarchical Identity-Based Encryption. 2021. doi: 10.1007/978-3-030-60890-3_11

[17] T. A. Teli and M. A. Wani, "A fuzzy based local minima avoidance path planning in autonomous robots," *International Journal of Information Technology (Singapore)*, vol. 13, no. 1, pp. 33–40, Feb. 2021, doi: 10.1007/s41870-020-00547-0

[18] O. Shafi, S. J. Sidiq, T. A. Teli, and M. Zaman, "A Comparative Study on Various Data Mining Techniques for Early Prediction of Diabetes Mellitus," in Global Emerging Innovation Summit (GEIS-2021), O. Shafi, S. J. Sidiq, T. A. Teli, and

M. Zaman, Eds. Bentham Science Publishers, 2021, pp. 51–61. doi: 10.2174/9781681089010121010009

[19] S. Mushtaq, A. Roy, and T. A. Teli, "A Comparative Study on Various Machine Learning Techniques for Brain Tumor Detection Using MRI," in Global Emerging Innovation Summit (GEIS-2021), S. Mushtaq, A. Roy, and T. A. Teli, Eds. Bentham Science Publishers, 2021, pp. 125–137. doi: 10.2174/9781681089010121010016.

[20] T. Ahmed Teli and F. Masoodi, "Blockchain in Healthcare: Challenges and Opportunities," *SSRN Electronic Journal*, 2021, doi: 10.2139/ssrn.3882744.

[21] O. Shafi, J. S. Sidiq, T. Ahmed Teli, and K.–, "Effect of Pre-Processing Techniques in Predicting Diabetes Mellitus With Focus on Artificial Neural Network," 2022.

[22] O. Shafi Zargar, A. Baghat, & T. A. Teli. (2022). A DNN Model for Diabetes Mellitus Prediction on PIMA Dataset. https://infocomp.dcc.ufla.br/index.php/infocomp/article/view/2476

Chapter 13

Definitive Guide to Software Security Metrics

Suhail Qadir,[1] Alwi M. Bamhdi,[2]
and Faheem Syeed Masoodi[3]

[1]Information Systems Department, King Khalid
University, Abha, Kingdom of Saudi Arabia

[2]College of Computing in Al-Qunfudah, Umm
Al-Qura University, Kingdom of Saudi Arabia

[3]Department of Computer Sciences, University of Kashmir, India

13.1 Introduction

In the last decade or so, software has evolved from being merely an information processing tool to being the main driver of critical infrastructure for nations all over the world. Given their paramount significance, software vulnerabilities pose a threat to system security, customer trust, and the ability to provide indispensable services and products. Moreover, a wide variety of the nation's critical infrastructure, including e-governance, industrial and other control systems, financial institutions, and other essential public and private applications, rely on safe, reliable, and consistent software [1]. Traditionally, when looking to incorporate software security and quality, the software industry has recently shifted its attention to enhancing the quality of its source code by decreasing the number of coding and design mistakes in the program. Vulnerabilities are errors that can be abused by

DOI: 10.1201/9781032624983-13

an attacker, and errors cause software to behave inconsistently with the expected behavior defined by the software's specification. In theory, all flaws in software can be found and fixed with regard to a given specification using formal correctness proof techniques, making the software completely secure. However, in practice, it remains difficult to construct large-scale and complex software free of errors and, by extension, security holes.

As the number of security incidents in networks, systems, and applications has increased in the past two decades, security metrics have drawn a lot of interest in the realm of information protection. Measuring security is the process of quantifying the efficacy of an information system's security measures, and software security is an important aspect of the realm of IT security. For a long time, system security was addressed by bolting on protections to a system once it had already gone through all of its development phases [2]. Studies in computer and network security typically involve in-depth analysis of complicated protocols or processes, which is why flaws in these areas are often traced to design flaws in the underlying infrastructure. In addition, if we embrace the current way of handling the security of systems, we will still come across areas that have not been fully researched. That is, factors that influence attack–defense interactions include the severity of the threat (or attack), the system's level of vulnerability, the efficiency of its defensive mechanisms, and the context in which the system is placed. These are a few areas that are still not much talked about. The primary explanation could be that implementing security methods and principles after the system has been developed will always leave the system with some compromises at various stages of development, resulting in a system with a significant number of vulnerabilities. The security paradigm has changed somewhat in the past ten years, moving from research into intricate protocols to the point where connected, time-ordered evaluations of secure system designs are possible (individual assessments of quantifiable elements), as well as how to build systems gauged by security so that the system can still carry out its intended function even in the presence of an adversarial environment [3]. This method of assessing the security of measurable components at the system design level is centered on processes and components designed in such a way that makes security measurement possible [4]. Given the early adoption of safeguards, during development we assert the statement that "an early estimation (during the design phase) about the security of a system will definitely produce a better performing system with fewer compromises and vulnerabilities."

The development of a robust method for the composition of independently assessed modules of the system such that security is guaranteed, is still an open subject for the research community, and there is also no technique at the system design level (lower levels in software architecture) to measure security at such levels. Additionally, relatively few approaches accurately measure the security of a specific software system [5, 6], and even fewer researchers are discussing such quantification of security at the design level.

13.2 Related Work

Quantitative and qualitative security measurement has long eluded the research community, despite its relevance to the software industry [7]. Vaughn [8] categorized cyber security measurements into two categories: organization-based security measurement and TTOA metrics. Different groups like the Base metric group, the temporal metric group, and the environmental metric group were recommended by NIST [9]. *QoS*, security, and availability are the three categories proposed in [10]. An ontology based on process control systems was recommended by the I3P [11]. To assess the overall resistance of networked information systems to attacks, model-based network security metrics (NSMs) can be used. A few model-like quantifiable NSMs have been suggested over the past two decades, and the work in [12] presents a complete survey of the present scenario of these proposals. At the outset, a general introduction to security metrics and how they are classified is provided so that the metrics described in this survey can be distinguished from those of other forms. Also, the primary current model-based quantitative NSMs and their benefits and drawbacks are reviewed in depth. Management of information security, business administration, security of software, and network security technology are the four pillars of this discipline presented by [13]. The management of risks associated with electronic business, the management of information security, and technical security are the three categories of security [14]. The author of [15] discussed an approach that involves measurement of risk in the realm of information assurance and two risk-based perspectives: (1) an information security risk assessment model that takes into account both the threat system and the capabilities of the security system in place, and (2) an information security risk assessment model that incorporates the threat system, plus the capabilities of the security system in place, measuring information security using a model predicated on metrics established for evaluating the quality of an IT system. The paper also mentions that metrics, factors, quantitative methods, and the characteristics of a specific system all play a role in establishing an accurate assessment of the present state of the security of information. Four categories of security measurements can be utilized for the assessment of the security policies of an organization [16]. In [17], not just technical elements but also non-traditional variables such as organizational structure and social and behavioral factors were incorporated in the evaluation of system security. [18] divided security metrics into two groups, effectiveness and efficiency, based on their perceived value. A security metrics framework that pulls from both security and reliability to form its foundational attributes. These characteristics are organized in accordance with a preexisting conceptual system model, after which we will offer a metrication scheme. The paper proposes the introduction of metrics for both security and behavior and perhaps even for system correctness [19]. The work in [20] emphasized the importance of establishing operational standards for the security of a system. Examples of categorizing models, methods, or methodologies for gauging information security abound in the available literature, with the majority of these focusing on detecting threats and quantifying risks [21]. Aspects of ensuring the privacy, availability, verifiability, and integrity of information are quantified through information security measurements. Information systems ought to have certain qualities that ascertain attributes like functionality and security; this was adopted when developing the system model in order to evaluate the reliability of a particular information system. While measuring the safety of an information processing system, it is critical to consider the safety of independent information resources, the system's larger perspective, the nature of its operations (as a sub-system of the organization), and the close and distant environments in which it operates. It appears that research results can aid in resolving practical issues related to evaluating information security and keeping it at an acceptable level. The theoretically grounded proposed models are flexible enough to meet the requirements of a variety of different systems, including quality management (QM), safety management (SM), and integrated organization management (MIOR).

13.3 Software Security Measurement Primer

The classifications [8] in Figure 13.1 can be used to examine the attributes of software security metrics.

1. Software security measurements can yield either a quantitative (numerical) or a qualitative (behavioral) result. Because of the relative lack of precision in qualitative outcomes, quantitative ones are preferred. In addition, it is more difficult to produce robust quantitative metrics than qualitative ones.
2. When gauging security, the resulting measurement could be either objective or subjective. The most effective measurement is the one that can be independently verified, and objective security metrics do just that. It expresses a component's, information systems or a process's security level on a scale from very low to middle level to very good. The subjective counterpart of the metrics takes into account human behavior in security.

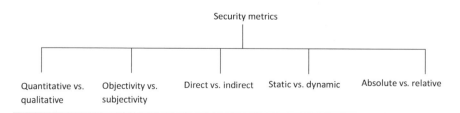

Figure 13.1 **Vaughn's classification of security metrics attributes.**
Source: [8].

3. In contrast to indirect metrics, which involve numerous attributes that are reliant on one another, a direct metric monitors one elemental property of the system in such a way that the property that is accountable for security does not rely on the other properties.
4. In contrast to static metrics, which don't factor time into their calculations, a dynamic metric changes as more data is collected and analyzed.
5. In contrast to relative metrics, which depend on the results of other metrics, absolute metrics are self-contained (atomic) units.

The primary goal of security measurements is to elucidate the state of security in a system, allowing for the identification of the most crucial security-related components. For the purposes of security evaluation, [22] identified three primary goals: security correctness, security effectiveness, and security efficiency.

■ Security correctness: This verifies that the system in question satisfies its security needs and has been properly implemented to enforce those needs.
■ Security effectiveness: This guarantees that the examined system behaves as expected and that all specified security needs have been met.
■ Security efficiency: This verifies that the system under scrutiny has attained a sufficient level of security.

13.4 Security Metrics Taxonomies

Several different security taxonomies out there seek to classify security metrics at different levels of abstraction; here are some of the metrics that talk about security measurement from a software vulnerability perspective.

Cyber security encompasses many functional areas and skills. Security is perceived differently by a database or system manager than it is by a network administrator or app developer within a company and even more so between enterprises. Therefore, to explain software security goals, one must understand their context. The United Kingdom's cyber security body, CyBoK, guides us through security issues in this endeavor [23]. The UK's National CyBoK project offers a cyber security ontology and a linkage to conventional references. (See Figure 13.2.)

When reporting the severity of security flaws in widely deployed software, governments and businesses alike turn to a scoring system CVSS (common vulnerability scoring system) [24], a dynamic framework developed to standardize reporting. The measurements vary from 0 to 10, with 10 indicating an extremely vulnerable system based on its exploitability and impact. A higher exploitability score indicates that the vulnerability can be compromised with less effort due to a lower access vector complexity and fewer authentication tries. To assign severity ratings, we must first understand the extent to which an exploit could compromise

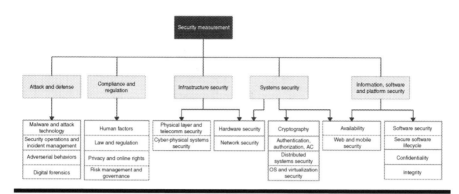

Figure 13.2   Cyber-security measurement key areas.
Source: [23].

Figure 13.3   Software vulnerability metrics.
Source: [26].

the privacy or security (confidentiality, integrity, and availability) of the system. Also, static analysis [25] is widely used to discover potential flaws in software that aren't covered by the CVSS set.

As a taxonomy for cyber security metrics, [26] discussed the classification of cyber security metrics into five primary areas: vulnerable components, defense mechanisms, risks, end users, and situational face-offs. In addition, each of these indicators is broken down further into sub-metrics. In the vulnerability portion, the author discussed software security metrics in the form of measuring the weaknesses in software. The paper classified this class of metrics into four categories: threat vectors, misconfigured SSL certificates, malware, and patching frequency. Such metrics can be very useful in determining the vulnerabilities that software is exposed to. Figure 13.3 illustrates the vulnerability portion of the metrics.

The study in [27] explored the topic of security measurement at the system level and presented a measurement framework with the following four individual measures: (1) metrics for measuring system weaknesses; (2) defense capability; (3) attack or threat severity or vulnerability; (4) situational metrics. In the vulnerability metrics section, user vulnerability, interface-induced vulnerability, and system software vulnerability are covered. Cognitive bias (or errors) and cognitive

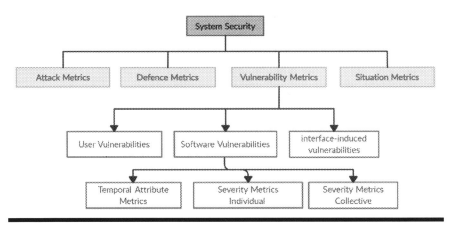

Figure 13.4 **Pendleton's software vulnerability taxonomy.**
Source: [27].

limitations are two forms of user vulnerabilities discussed. The metrics for software vulnerability are further classified as:

- Temporal attribute: This includes metrics about the evolution of vulnerabilities and metrics for vulnerability lifetime. The work in the paper further classifies these two attributes into their respective subcategories.
- Severity metrics individual software vulnerabilities: This metric focuses on the CVSS [28] and its metrics in three main categories: foundational (such as exploitability and effect), temporal, and environmental metrics.
- Severity metrics of collection of vulnerabilities: Real-world attacks sometimes involve numerous phases and aim to breach multiple vulnerabilities. The likes of attack graphs, attack trees, and all the others mentioned in [27] are looked at as the deterministic and probabilistic metrics used to assess the severity of a set of vulnerabilities, in particular those found in attack graphs. (See Figure 13.4.)

Pendleton does not explicitly state these important attributes for confirmation or go so far as to enumerate all of the common metric qualities in the conclusions, but he does allude to some characteristics that are acceptable in almost set of every security metrics.

Morrison [29] explained that the basic principle of security measurement for the SDLC is research into the correlation between source code characteristics and security vulnerabilities. Vulnerability count, the most discussed and implemented statistic, can be understood in a variety of ways. The author also stresses the need for double-checking vulnerability count definitions.

The majority of the software security measures found by Morrison are either expansions of previously established software metrics or normalized versions of such

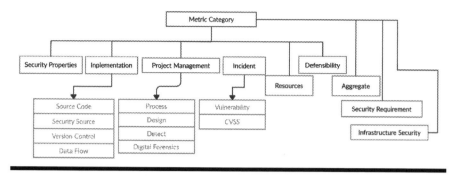

Figure 13.5 **Security metric taxonomy.**
Source: [29].

measurements. It appears that security attribute subdivisions are based on statistics of listed property; however, this could be a reflection of the source writers rather than an inability to automate collection. Since no evidence suggests that successful attacks are being analyzed, incident metrics more accurately map to the vulnerability categories used in earlier studies. Morison's article finds that 85% of the surveyed metrics comprise only the author's hypotheses and evaluations, highlighting the significance of validations in measurements. Some of the SDLC indicators are relevant for evaluating the design or testing phases because they are geared toward deployment in production. The vast bulk of the metrics are based purely on the opinions of users. Researchers in their work believe there is room for investigation into metrics for the specification, architecture, and testing stages of development in addition to the refinement of vulnerability measurement. From the research, the author infers that the area of software development security metrics has not yet settled on a common set of measures. (See Figure 13.5.)

The work in [3] proposed a metric intended for a system with an integrated component design. The metric relies on latency and interdependency analysis of the software's constituent parts. The author proposes a metric for measuring the availability of a software system. Availability is an important security attribute when we talk about the attributes of dependability, and it's worth mentioning here that in the case of validating software security, the classical benchmarks are the dependability attributes [30, 31].

The work in [3] asserts the fact that, if the security measurements are done beyond the application level (user interaction level) of a software system to the level where the different components interact directly or indirectly (component level), we can analyze the interconnections among the various connected software components to assess availability or risk analysis. The work in [32] introduces a novel component-level availability metric that offers a sense of measuring the security risk in the component composition design. The dependency metric among the components is time-based. The metric considers system component interactions and processing

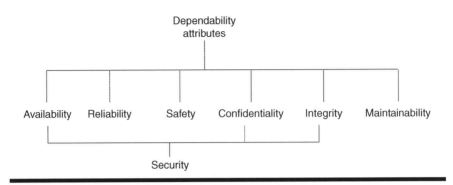

Figure 13.6 Attributes of dependability and security.

Source: [31].

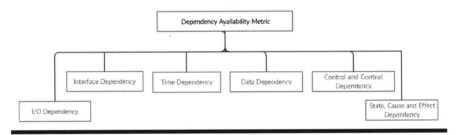

Figure 13.7 Component dependency availability metric.

Source: [30].

time, whether local or distant. The more dependencies a component has, the more complicated the architecture, which may lead to low performance and affect information system workability/availability. After analyzing each component's dependencies and processing durations, the availability metric gives a verdict about the overall system's availability. The values are divided into five zones (A1 to A5). A value of 0 indicates completely unavailable service, while a higher value nearing A5 indicates an adequate level of availability. The metric here is software-based, but it could be expanded to include hardware, users, and networks. Work on this project can be extended to distributed-OS environments having complicated hardware, software, and networking architectures. (See Figures 13.6 and 13.7.)

13.5 Conclusion

Moving forward in the secure system development lifecycle, security assessment and security metrics must be taken seriously and addressed the same way other things in the development of a system are. Because not much substantial research is done in the realm of software security metrics, the security analysis of a software product across different taxonomies is still a distant dream. As a result, practically speaking, relatively little is known about the available measuring techniques, whereas the discipline has largely concentrated on the definitional and theoretical aspects. The taxonomies discussed in this chapter present the findings of a comprehensive investigation of system security metrics, concentrating on the measurement of software security. Each of the studies discussed in this chapter provides its own categorization methodology that is suitable for the study and the respective metrics carried out; however, none of these ontologies is able to generalize a common security metric valid across all the attributes of the security paradigm. We also came across taxonomies talking about a common set of attributes while evaluating the security of a software system.

References

[1] Qadir, Suhail, and S. M. K. Quadri. "Information availability: An insight into the most important attribute of information security." *Journal of Information Security* 7.3 (2016): 185–194.

[2] Gilliam, David P., et al. "Software security checklist for the software life cycle." *WET ICE 2003. Proceedings. Twelfth IEEE International Workshops on Enabling Technologies: Infrastructure for Collaborative Enterprises, 2003*. IEEE, 2003.

[3] Mir, Suhail Qadir, and S. M. K. Quadri. "Metric for evaluating availability of an information system: a quantitative approach based on component dependency." *International Journal of Network Security & Its Applications* 9 (2017): 1–11.

[4] Jansen, W. "Directions in security metrics research." NIST Interagency/Internal Report (NISTIR), National Institute of Standards and Technology, Gaithersburg, MD, [online], https://doi.org/10.6028/NIST.IR.7564 (2009).

[5] Neto, Afonso Araújo, and Marco Vieira. "Untrustworthiness: A trust-based security metric." *2009 Fourth International Conference on Risks and Security of Internet and Systems (CRiSIS 2009)*. IEEE, 2009.

[6] Cheng, Y., Deng, J., Li, J., DeLoach, S. A., Singhal, A., & Ou, X. "Metrics of Security. In Cyber Defense and Situational Awareness" *Springer International Publishing* (2014) (pp. 263–295).

[7] Manadhata, Pratyusa K., and Jeannette M. Wing. "An attack surface metric." *IEEE Transactions on Software Engineering* 37.3 (2010): 371–386.

[8] Vaughn, Rayford B., Ronda Henning, and Ambareen Siraj. "Information assurance measures and metrics-state of practice and proposed taxonomy." *36th Annual Hawaii International Conference on System Sciences, 2003. Proceedings of the*. IEEE, 2003.

[9] Swanson, Marianne M., et al. Security Metrics Guide for Information Technology Systems, Special Publication (NIST SP), National Institute of Standards and Technology, Gaithersburg, MD (2003).

[10] Seddigh, N., Pieda, P., Matrawy, A., Nandy, B., Lambadaris, I., & Hatfield, A. (2004, October). Current Trends and Advances in Information Assurance Metrics. In *PST* (pp. 197–205).

[11] Cheng, Yi, and Julia Deng. "i3p: Institute for Information Infrastructure Protection."

[12] Ramos, A., Lazar, M., Holanda Filho, R., & Rodrigues, J. J. (2017). Model-based quantitative network security metrics: A survey. *IEEE Communications Surveys & Tutorials*, *19*(4), 2704–2734.

[13] Savola, Reijo M. "A security metrics development method for software intensive systems." *Advances in Information Security and Its Application: Third International Conference, ISA 2009, Seoul, Korea, June 25–27, 2009. Proceedings 3.* Springer Berlin Heidelberg, 2009.

[14] R. Geleta, P.K. Pattnaik, Cyber Safety Certainty Performance in Business: Degree Assessment with Analytic Hierarchy Process, *Journal of Advanced Research in Dynamical and Control Systems* (2018) 1085–1087.

[15] Hoffmann, Romuald, et al. "Measurement models of information security based on the principles and practices for risk-based approach." *Procedia Manufacturing* 44 (2020): 647–654.

[16] Bhol, Seema Gupta, J. R. Mohanty, and Prasant Kumar Pattnaik. "Cyber security metrics evaluation using multi-criteria decision-making approach." *Smart Intelligent Computing and Applications: Proceedings of the Third International Conference on Smart Computing and Informatics, Volume 2.* Springer Singapore, 2020.

[17] Tashi, Igli, and Solange Ghernaouti-Hélie. "Security metrics to improve information security management." *Proceedings of 6th Annual Security Conference.* 2007.

[18] Ahmed, Rana Khudhair Abbas. "Overview of security metrics." *Softw. Eng* 4.4 (2016): 59–64.

[19] Jonsson, Erland, and Laleh Pirzadeh. "A framework for security metrics based on operational system attributes." *2011 Third International Workshop on Security Measurements and Metrics.* IEEE, 2011.

[20] Littlewood, B., Brocklehurst, S., Fenton, N., Mellor, P., Page, S., Wright, D., ... & Gollmann, D. (1993). Towards operational measures of computer security. *Journal of Computer Security*, *2*(2–3), 211–229.

[21] Payne, S. C. (2006). A Guide to Security Metrics: SANS Security Essentials GSEC Practical Assignment Version 1.2 e (2007). SANS.

[22] Savola, Reijo M. "A security metrics taxonomization model for software-intensive systems." *Journal of Information Processing Systems* 5.4 (2009): 197–206.

[23] Burnap, P., Carolina, R., Rashid, A., Sasse, M. A., Troncoso, C., Lee, W., ... & Smart, N. (2019). The cyber security body of knowledge, version 1.0 . *KA. UK*, *12*, 2020.

[24] Mell, P., et al. The Common Vulnerability Scoring System (CVSS) and Its Applicability to Federal Agency Systems. 2007.

[25] Basili, V., Briand, L., and Melo, W. A validation of object-oriented design metrics as quality indicators. *IEEE Transactions on Software Engineering* 22, 10 (Oct. 1996), 751–761. issn: 00985589. doi: 10.1109/32.544352.

[26] S. Gupta Bhol, J. Mohanty and P. Kumar Pattnaik, Taxonomy of cyber security metrics to measure strength of cyber security, Materials Today: Proceedings, https://doi.org/10.1016/j.matpr.2021.06.228.

[27] Pendleton, M., Garcia-Lebron, R., Cho, J. H., & Xu, S. (2016). A survey on systems security metrics. *ACM Computing Surveys (CSUR)*, *49*(4), 1–35.

[28] Mell, P., Scarfone, K., & Romanosky, S. (2007, June). A complete guide to the common vulnerability scoring system version 2.0. In *Published by FIRST-forum of incident response and security teams* (Vol. 1, p. 23).

[29] Morrison, P., Moye, D., Pandita, R., & Williams, L. (2018). Mapping the field of software life cycle security metrics. *Information and Software Technology, 102,* 146–159.

[30] Mir, I. A., & Quadri, S. M. K. (2012). Analysis and evaluating security of component-based software development: A security metrics framework. *International Journal of Computer Network and Information Security,* 4(11), 21.

[31] Laprie, J. C. (1995, June). Dependable computing: Concepts, limits, challenges. In *Special Issue of the 25th International Symposium On Fault-Tolerant Computing* (pp. 42–54).

[32] Mir, S.Q., Quadri, S.M.K. Component based metric for evaluating availability of an information system: an empirical evaluation. *International Journal of Information Technology,* 11, 277–285 (2019). https://doi.org/10.1007/s41 870-018-0220-2

Chapter 14

Real-Time Supervisory Control and Data Acquisition (SCADA) Model for Resourceful Distribution and Use of Public Water

Binnaser Aziz Abdullah

*Department of Computer Science, Sir Sayyed College of
Arts, Commerce & Science, Aurangabad, India*

14.1 Introduction

Water resource management is a key area of concern for governments and nations. Today water is a commodity that must be utilized judiciously. The need is to explore the automation technology and its application in various areas of concern relating to water use and management. This chapter proposes the real-time SCADA model for appropriate distribution and use of public water in the field of water resource management. This is an important area where a system could be designed and developed for proper monitoring and control of water at various levels. Today information technology and processing of real-time data are becoming the specialized

DOI: 10.1201/9781032624983-14

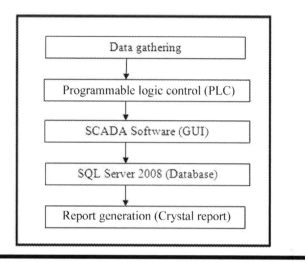

Figure 14.1   Real-time SCADA flow path.

tool for designing and developing intelligent systems in the different fields of real-life applications. Real-time applications have become significant in our daily lives and as used in different fields such as offices, industries, water, waste water applications, medical equipment, oil, gas, etc. [1]. Figure 14.1 shows the data collection method.

The system is implemented through the following four activities:

14.2 Stage 1 (Automatic Water Pumping)

Water pumping from a well is done through the setup of a water model in automatic mode. It is observed by PLC program and will show signal in the form of ON or OFF pumping motor. The pumping motor on position indicates the green signal and Pumping Motor off position indicates the red signal.

14.3 Stage 2 (Automatic Water Distribution in the City)

The automatic water distribution of different areas in a specific geographical location of a specific city is done by means of the SCADA system. It indicates the supply of water to a particular area by following the specification on the screen. Site color will have a green indication, showing that the water is in the process of distribution in that particular area of the city.

14.4 Stage 3 (Automatic Water Leakage Detection System)

Water leakage is found after by noting different readings by flowmeter and pressure meter at one point. The pressures and flows are compared at both ends; if a difference occurs, the existence of leakage in the pipe is confirmed.

14.5 Stage 4 (Pressure or Storage Tank)

Water pumping is done in an automatic mode by observing the water level of the pressure tank by the setup of SCADA monitoring devices as a float sensor switch.

14.6 System Simulation Environment

All the preceding four stages are programmed and implemented in the simulation environment, simulation software for PLC, and devices are used that provide simulation data through the ladder program made in the unity pro XL.

Figure 14.2 shows the block diagram of the simulation environment for the research model, which consists of PLC, instruments, and SCADA software.

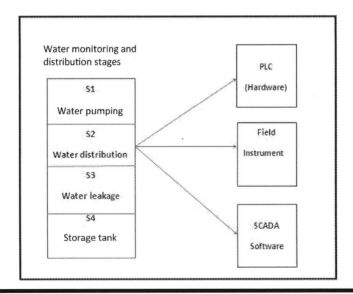

Figure 14.2   Block diagram of simulation environment.

14.7 Programmable Logic Controllers (PLCs)

PLCs are considered the "brain" of the SCADA system [2]. The real control program for this process or its control systems is performed within the PLC. A PLC can work with local physically connected inputs and outputs or with remote inputs and outputs given by a remote terminal Unit (RTU). PLCs can give two different types of control: discrete and continuous.

14.8 Field Instruments

Field instrumentation means that the sensors and actuators are directly interfaced to the plant or equipment. They produce the analog and digital signals that can be observed by the remote station. Signals are also conditioned in such a way that that they are compatible with the inputs/outputs of the RTU or PLC at the remote station [3].

Field instrumentation also involves devices that are connected to the equipment or machines and controlled and monitored by the SCADA. These are sensors for noting specific parameters and actuators for controlling particular modules of the system. These instruments convert physical parameters to electrical signals readable by the remote station equipment. Outputs can either be analog or in digital [4].

14.9 SCADA Software

SCADA software consists of two types: proprietary or open. Companies evolve proprietary software to communicate with their hardware. These systems are sold as turnkey solutions. The main problem with the system is the complete dependence on the system supplier. Open software systems became popular due to their interoperability within the system. Interoperability involves the mixing of different manufacturers' equipment within the same system. Citect and Wonderware InTouch are two open software packages available in the market for SCADA systems. Some packages includes asset management integrated within the SCADA system. Wonderware InTouch software is used for developing the SCADA model.

14.10 InTouch Application Manager

Wonderware InTouch creates human–machine interface (HMI) applications easily and fast for the Microsoft products. InTouch is a component of the Wonderware Factory Suite. InTouch is applied in food processing, semiconductors, oil and gas, automotive, chemical, pharmaceutical, pulp and paper, transportation, utilities. InTouch enables the creation of powerful, full-featured applications that utilize the key features of Microsoft Windows, including ActiveX controls, OLE, graphics, networking, etc. Extension such as custom ActiveX controls, wizards, generic objects, and InTouch Quick Script can be added to InTouch. InTouch contains three major programs: InTouch Application Manager, Window Maker, and Window Viewer [5].

14.11 Human–Machine Interface (HMI)

The HMI (human–machine interface) enables the user (operator) to interact with the SCADA system. HMI provides a precise and simple computer representation of what is being controlled or monitored by the SCADA. It provides for interaction, in the form of either a touch screen, a specialized keyboard, or both. Current-generation SCADA HMIs are not simply an alternative for push buttons and pilot lights of the past. They offer a simpler user interface for even the most complex SCADA systems. The "usability" of the HMI can be gauged from how effectively a user can interact with the SCADA. HMI implementations provide high levels of usability provide SCADA

14.12 Research Tools and Techniques

Software used for designing and developing the SCADA simulation model for research experiments is the PLC Software Unity Pro 5.0 & 6.0, SCADA Software Wonderware InTouch 10.1, the device integration software IO SERVER (MBENET), the database software MS SQL Server 2008 [6], and the business intelligence software Crystal Report 8.5 [7].

This software is used to design and develop the system with the help of SCADA. The basic objective is to access the monitoring data from various monitoring devices and to process it in PLC by programming various processes. The graphical user interface with simulated SCADA is used for better access and understanding. The device integration is done through the IO server with MS SQL 2008 as a database and Crystal Report 8.5 for report generation.

The SCADA models are made for a large range of applications. The model is developed for the resourceful distribution of water in a geographical location of a particular city. These simulation models are based on a real-life entity, which helps in understanding the real use of technology in the monitoring and distribution of water. Some models that are developed for research are:

A. Automatic pumping of water from well
B. Automatic water distribution system in the city
C. Automatic water leakage detection system
D. Pressure or storage tank pumping station with SCADA system

14.12.1 A. Automatic Pumping of Water From Well

In the real-time SCADA model, the motor automatically starts or stops according to a time parameter. The performance of the motor, such as the date, time, pressure, and volume of water, is recorded in a database system. The connectivity is provided between the Wonderware InTouch software (SCADA Software) with Unity Pro 5.0 software (simulator and the ladder programming software) and SQL Server 2008 with Crystal Report 8.5.

The model can perform in SCADA manual mode or SCADA auto mode. In the SCADA manual mode, the motor can be made to start or stop through buttons in the SCADA software. In auto mode, the time is specified and for that time the motor should remain ON and after that time, the motor should be stopped.

14.13 Automatic Water Pumping

Figure 14. 3 shows the block diagram of a model that consists of a pumping motor place in a well, valve, pressure meter, flowmeter, panel, and timer. The water flows are pumped by the motor to the frame when the motor is ON and the valve is ON. The panel is used to turn the pumping motor ON/OFF and to select the motor operation in auto or manual. In the timer, the time is specified, and for that time the motor runs and stops automatically.

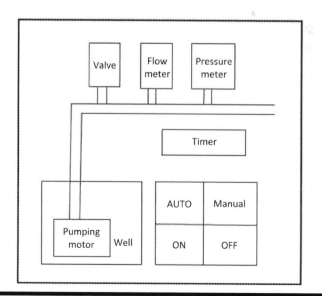

Figure 14.3   Block diagram of obtaining water from well and pumping in farm automatically.

14.13.1 B. Automatic Water Distribution System in the City

In this model, a real photo of the area is taken from Google map and different sites. To develop pressure, first the water comes into a ground tank and then moves into a tower tank, from where it is supplied through gravity to different sites. Multiple sites are made on the screens, which have valves that can be ON or OFF graphically. When the valve is ON, the sites change color, which indicates the flow of water and simulated values of flow and pressure. The water flow from each site is recorded in a database, and then the total daily flow of water from each site is recorded along with the daily hours of running the motor [8].

14.14 Automatic Water Distribution

Figure 14.4 shows the block diagram of automatic water distribution, which consists of ground tank, pressure tank, pumping motors, the number of sites, valve, pressure meter, and flowmeter. Figure 14.4 is the main diagram, and Figure 14.5 is the diagram of site.

The water flow from the ground tank to tower tank when the pumping motor is When ON occurs, the water flows to different sites by gravity. One site is placed at a higher height so that booster pumps are required to increase the pressure.

The block diagram of Figure 14.4 is for all the sites. When the valve is ON, the water flows to a house, which comes under that site, and stops flowing when the valve is OFF. The flowmeter and pressure meter are connected for recording the flow and pressure of each site.

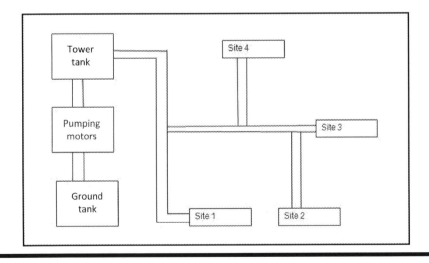

Figure 14.4   Block diagram of the automatic water distribution system in city.

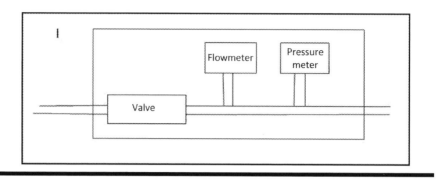

Figure 14.5   Block diagram of site.

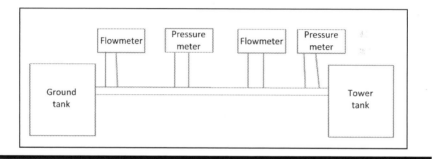

Figure 14.6   Block diagram of the water leakage detection system.

14.14.1 C. Automatic Water Leakage Detection System

This model is used to detect and calculate the water leakage between two tanks, i.e., the ground tank and tower tank. In this model, the pressure meter and flowmeter are connected to both the tanks. This model is very useful for solving the losses of water as water leakage can be prevented. This will be a computerized system model used for monitoring and controlling the water leakage. For long pipes, the pressure meter is mounted on the pipe after some distance to measure the pressure of water; a change in the pressure shows that leakage has occurred at that point.

14.15 Water Leakage System

Figure 14.6 shows the block diagram of a water leakage detection system, which consists of the ground tank, tower tank, pressure meter, and flowmeter. The flowmeter and pressure meter are connected to both ends. When the motor is ON, the water starts flowing from the ground tank to the tower tank. Readings are recorded at the ground tank (flow and pressure), and readings are also recorded at the tower tank and are compared. If the readings are equal, there is no leakage, but if the readings are different, there is leakage between the ground tank and the tower tank. If the distance is long, a multiple pressure meter is connected at some distance and pressure is recorded.

14.15.1 D. Automatic Water Pumping System Using SCADA

The automatic system is a simple model, which has a storage tank, pressure tank, a float switch sensor, and a pumping motor. The pumping motor will start automatically when the water level of the pressure tank goes low and will be OFF when the pressure is full. There is also pump protection float that will not start the pumping motor even if the water level in the storage tank goes low, thus protecting the motor against damage.

14.16 Automatic Water Pumping System

This is a main screen of model, which consists of two tank pressures and storage, pumping motor, float switch, and a manual operation panel at which the pumping motor can be controlled.

14.17 Storage Water Pumping

Figure 14.7 shows the block diagram of an automatic water pumping system, which consists of a storage tank (Tank 1), a pressure tank (Tank 2), a pumping motor, three float switches. Two float switches are connected to the pressure tank, and one float switch is connected to the storage tank. In the pressure tank, one float switch is connected at the bottom of the tank (to start the pumping motor), and the second

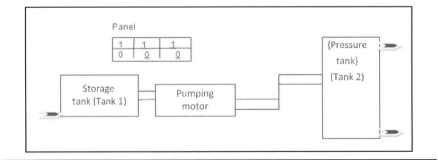

Figure 14.7 Block diagram of the automatic water pumping system.

float switch is connected to the upper part of the pressure tank. The function of the pumping station is to pump water from the storage tank to the pressure tank.

14.18 Conclusion

SCADA includes industrial control systems (ICS) computer systems, which monitor and control industrial, infrastructure, or facility-based processes. Real-time data, often referred to as RTD, is data that updates on its own schedule. The SCADA takes the real-time data from programmable logic controllers (PLCs) that monitor and control graphically and stores the data in an SQL Server. For generating different reports according to requirements, Crystal Reports are used. We have designed and developed different simulated SCADA models for various stages of the water distribution process. The simulation environment gives much space for experimentation as compared to the physical environment. The entire simulation project has been thoroughly tested with test data and has been connected to all the peripheral physical devices of the water distribution system.

References

1. D. Bailey and E. Wright (2003) Practical SCADA for Industry, Associates, Perth, Australia. ISBN 07506 58053, 2003.
2. Hugh Jack, Automating Manufacturing Systems with PLCs (Version 4.7, April 14, 2005).
3. Farkhod Alsiherov, Taihoon Kim, Research Trend on Secure SCADA Network Technology and Methods, WSEAS Transactions on Systems and Control, ISSN: 1991-8763 635 Issue 8, Volume 5, August 2010.
4. Terry Bartelt, Industrial Electronic. Circuit, Instruments, and control Techniques. DELMAR CENGAGE learning, ISBN -13:978-81-315-0879-4, 2009.
5. Wonderware® FactorySuite™ InTouch® Reference Guide September 2002 Invensys Systems, Inc. 33 Commercial Street Foxboro.
6. Ross Mistry & Stacia, Introducing Microsoft SQL Server 2008 R2 by Misner.
7. Crystal Reports™ 8.5 User's Guide by Seagate Software IMG Holdings
8. Michael Barnett1*, Tony Lee1, Larry Jentgen2, Steve Conrad2, Harold Kidder2, Real-time Automation of Water Supply and Distribution for the City of Jacksonville, Florida, USA.

Index

Printed in the United States
by Baker & Taylor Publisher Services